ENGLISH NATIONAL IDENTITY AND FOOTBALL FAN CULTURE

For Stacey, Georgia, Nathanael and bump

English National Identity and Football Fan Culture
Who Are Ya?

TOM GIBBONS
Teesside University, UK

LONDON AND NEW YORK

First published 2014 by Ashgate Publishing

2 Park Square, Milton Park, Abingdon, Oxfordshire OX14 4RN
52 Vanderbilt Avenue, New York, NY 10017

Routledge is an imprint of the Taylor & Francis Group, an informa business

First issued in paperback 2019

Copyright © 2014 Tom Gibbons

Tom Gibbons has asserted his right under the Copyright, Designs and Patents Act, 1988, to be identified as the author of this work.

All rights reserved. No part of this book may be reprinted or reproduced or utilised in any form or by any electronic, mechanical, or other means, now known or hereafter invented, including photocopying and recording, or in any information storage or retrieval system, without permission in writing from the publishers.

Notice:
Product or corporate names may be trademarks or registered trademarks, and are used only for identification and explanation without intent to infringe.

British Library Cataloguing in Publication Data
A catalogue record for this book is available from the British Library

The Library of Congress has cataloged the printed edition as follows:
Gibbons, Tom.
  English national identity and football fan culture : who are ya? / by Tom Gibbons.
     pages cm
  Includes bibliographical references and index.
  ISBN 978-1-4724-2328-3 (hardback : alk. paper)
1. Soccer—England—Psychological aspects. 2. Soccer fans—England—Psychology.
3. National characteristics, English. I. Title.
  GV944.G7G54 2014
  796.3340941—dc23
  [B]
                                                                                    2013034156

ISBN 978-1-4724-2328-3 (hbk)
ISBN 978-0-367-33291-4 (pbk)

Contents

Acknowledgements		*vii*
1	Introduction	1
2	Theoretical Approach for Understanding Contemporary English National Identity	19
3	The Unintended Consequences of Global and European Forces on English Football Fan Culture	51
4	Manifestations of Englishness in Pubs during World Cup 2006	71
5	Fan Debates on Team GB at the London 2012 Olympics and the Almunia Case	87
6	The Club versus Country Debate in English Football and the Diverse Use of the St George's Cross	123
7	Conclusion: Diminishing Contrasts, Increasing Varieties in English Football	147
Appendix: Research Strategy		161
Bibliography		*175*
Index		*195*

Acknowledgements

A large debt of gratitude is owed to the football fans that have provided the data for this book. I thank Dr Jim Golby, Mike McGuinness, Dr Dave Morland and Dr Martin Johnes for their expert guidance and feedback on the research that informs the book. Thanks are also due to my colleagues within the Sports Studies team at Teesside University, Dr Kevin Dixon and Stuart Braye, for their constructive criticism on my work, their honesty in informal discussions, for helping to keep me motivated and for providing much needed periods of respite and laughter along the way. I must also thank Ashgate publishers for commissioning the project and the academic reviewers for their supportive comments.

Finally, I thank God for providing me with such a wonderful family who remain my main source of support and inspiration in all that I do.

Chapter 1
Introduction

At the turn of the twenty-first century two of the most prominent exponents for the sociological significance of football,[1] Giulianotti (1999) and King (2002), suggested that much sociological research on football up to that point had lacked theoretical sophistication and empirical rigour. According to Giulianotti (1999: 170), 'social researchers on football leave themselves open to the accusation of "armchair theorizing"' by failing to engage in empirical research themselves. He went on to call for future generations of UK researchers 'to adopt a far more critical and theoretically sophisticated approach in studying football culture' (Giulianotti, 1999: 170).

According to King (2002: 210), sociologists of football have a responsibility to show how the game reflects, impacts and challenges societal issues 'which fill the public's imagination'. King suggested that the sociology of football fandom had been dominated by the study of football hooliganism. Yet, football hooliganism is 'only one of a number of important issues surrounding football' (King, 2002: 3). Other issues relating to football fan culture have either been completely ignored or somewhat under-researched. Whilst the concerns voiced by Giulianotti and King are now over a decade old, it seems that the relationship between English national identity and football fan culture is still in desperate need of theory-led empirical research.

In this book it is argued that football fan culture illustrates a number of broader debates relating to contemporary English national identity. It is maintained that many of what Elias (2000) would term 'unintended consequences' of broad societal processes such as globalisation, European integration and devolution can be observed in the ways English fans regularly display and articulate their identities around the men's national football team and the men's professional club game. This not only demonstrates the centrality of football fan culture to sociological understanding, particularly in relation to the fields of nationalism and globalisation, but it also contributes to understanding the fragility of English national identity in the first decade of the twenty-first century.

The distinctive contribution of this book is both theoretical and empirical in nature. The book aims to provide a sound justification for utilising the theoretical approach of Norbert Elias to suggest that the relationship between English national identity and football fan culture is more multi-faceted than previous research has contended. The book aims to provide entirely new empirical evidence from two

---

1 The term 'football' is used throughout this book to refer to the sport of association football, often abbreviated to 'soccer'.

as yet under-researched fan sites: first, pubs showing the national team's matches to football fans during the 2006 World Cup and second, an Internet discussion forum for football fans analysed between 2008 and 2009.[2] Findings from studies in each setting were clearly interrelated and this evidence is used to challenge previous assumptions suggesting the rise in the use of the St George's Cross by English football fans signifies a rise in a specifically 'English' rather than 'British' national identity. Both the use of Elias and the use of evidence from previously under-researched aspects of fan culture make this book an original contribution to current literature.

A number of concepts are used throughout this book and it is therefore important to introduce them to the reader so that their intended meaning is clear from the outset.

Key Concepts

According to Smith (2010: 5–6), the concept of 'nationalism' has at least five different meanings, including: a process of formation, or growth, of nations; a sentiment or consciousness of belonging to the nation; a language and symbolism of the nation; a social and political movement on behalf of the nation; and, a doctrine and/or ideology of the nation, both general and particular. Within this book the main focus is on national identity, which is most closely aligned to the second of Smith's definitions of 'nationalism' as a sentiment or consciousness of belonging to the nation, rather than the organised political ideology or movement of nationalism that is referred to in Smith's last three usages of the term. Yet, it is also clear that many of these meanings overlap with one another and it is therefore often difficult to separate one from the other considering feelings of national sentiment or belonging within individuals are usually the result of the long-term development of nationalism.

'British' identity is not the topic of this book; however, it is the context within which 'English' national identity exists. The terms 'Britain' and 'UK' are used throughout this book and so it is important to briefly clarify their differences. 'Great Britain' is actually formed of the kingdoms of England and Scotland and the Principality of Wales, whereas the 'UK' is the United Kingdom of Great Britain and Northern Ireland (Groom, 2006: xv). These terms should not be confused with the term 'British Isles', which includes the Republic of Ireland and the Crown Dependencies (Isle of Man and the Channel Islands). The modern British state dates back to 1707 and the Treaty of Union between England and Scotland (Bryant, 2006: 23); although there had already been a version of the British Union flag flown a century before that in 1606 and there are over one thousand years of Union Jack prehistory (Groom, 2006: xiii–iv). The Union flag was conceived on

---

2 The abbreviation 'pub' is used throughout the book to refer to public house. This is discussed in greater depth in Chapter 3.

the banners of the ancient Britons and in heraldry according to Groom. Yet, the contemporary Union flag is made up of the crosses of St George, St Andrew and St Patrick, respectively the patron saints of England, Scotland and Ireland, and it was first flown on 1 January 1801, when the United Kingdom of Great Britain and Ireland came into existence (Groom, 2006: xiii).

Specifically 'English' national identity has undergone significant challenges post-1945 due to a number of global, European and British political, economic and social processes which mean this national construct has now reached a point where its very nature appears to be somewhat uncertain (cf. Colls, 2002; Kumar, 2003; Paxman, 1998; Scruton, 2000). Sociological, historical, cultural and political literature on English national identity suggests, in different but often interrelated ways, that any notion of a unified English national consciousness is undermined by competing conceptions of what it is and/or should be based upon. First, England has contained strongly felt regional and local identities at the expense of a clearly defined entity that can be separated from Britain (cf. Bryant, 2003; 2006; Colls, 2002; Russell, 2004). Second, although one should not underestimate how divided Wales, Scotland and Northern Ireland are, even the existence of English national identity is more problematic considering it has been significantly challenged through being synonymous with Britishness since the first successful Act of Union with Scotland in 1707 (cf. Colley, 1996; Kumar, 2003; 2006a; 2006b; McCrone, 2002). Whilst this literature is discussed in more detail in Chapter 2, Colls's (2002: 6) summary of the situation is that the term '"England" is always up for debate, of course, but in recent years the debate has become critical … . The English stand now in need of a reassessment of who they are'. The rationale for using football fan culture to understand English national identity is important to explain in more detail.

The Relationship between English National Identity and Football Fan Culture: Who Are Ya?

In this book English football and the practices of its fans are regarded as a microcosm through which to observe the current 'problems', or what Aughey (2007) refers to as 'anxieties', surrounding English national identity. In 1801, within his *Sports and Pastimes of the People of England,* Strutt (1903: xv) wrote that in order to form 'a just estimation of the character of any particular people, it is absolutely necessary to investigate the Sports and Pastimes most generally prevalent among them'. Although originally published over two centuries ago, this statement has no less relevance today. Whilst other scholars have recognised the significance of football in the study of national identity, for instance, Hobsbawm (1990: 143) stated that 'the imagined community of millions seems more real as a team of eleven named people', Elias (1986: 19) is one of the few modern social theorists to have recognised the value of studying sport to help understand wider social processes in detail, recognising that 'that knowledge about sport was knowledge about society'.

Elias (1986: 26) noticed that there are 'specialists in the study of sport, specialists in the study of society ... each group working as it were in its own ivory tower', and he sought to stimulate further sociological studies using sport as a lens through which to make particular aspects of societies more transparent because 'there are many problems which cannot be explored within the confines of a single specialism'. This Eliasian stance underpins the line of argument taken throughout this book that football fan culture illustrates current debates regarding Englishness at a time when the meaning of this national construct has become uncertain.

In *Britons: Forging the Nation: 1707–1837*, Colley (1996: 395) concluded that both war and religion no longer influence British culture to the degree either did before 1945, because successive

> wars with the states of continental Europe have in all likelihood come to an end, so different kinds of Britons no longer feel the same compulsion as before to remain united in face of the enemy from without.

The rise of 'Islamaphobia' following the terrorist attacks on London in July 2005 and the subsequent growth in popularity of right-wing political groups in England such as the British National Party (BNP) and the English Defence League (EDL), render Colley's conclusion somewhat dated. Aside from members of extremist groups, who despite their rise still represent a minority of the English population (Rhodes, 2011), the question remains: where do most English people get a chance to articulate or display national sentiment today? Carrington (1999:73) argues that given the

> decreasing centrality to public life of two of the key institutions that have traditionally helped foster a sense of national belonging – war and the Royal family – sport, and football more than any other sport, has increasingly occupied a central role in symbolising English nationalism.

It would be naive to argue that everyone who considers themselves to be English is a 'nationalist' or regards men's professional football as central to their national identity, and that is certainly not what is claimed here. The research that informs this book is limited to particular elements of Englishness – namely the identity of a largely white, working class, male football fan audience. This is reflected in the fairly homogenous characteristics of the samples of football fans used in the pub-based observation and online participant observation studies (see Chapters 4–6).

The historical context of international football in the UK means that the relationship between English national identity and football is particularly complex. Duke and Crolley (1996) recognise that nation-states usually have a football team to represent them in international competitions: members of Fédération Internationale de Football Association (FIFA) are the national Football Associations (FAs) of independent nation-states, and international tournaments such as the World Cup are contested by teams representing those national units.

However, Duke and Crolley also recognise that there is an exception to this rule when it comes to the United Kingdom.

According to Holt (1989: 161), it was not just in England where football had grown massively by the early twentieth century, 'football had become the major form of male entertainment in Britain'. Hill (2002: 14) states that sport

> has been responsible for maintaining some sense of Britishness, though by stressing the 'unity of diversity' of the British Isles rather than any commonality. Apart from athletics, which sponsors a team representing Great Britain in the Olympics, few sports have moved beyond a limited national field as the basis of their organization. Association football typifies this, with separate associations for each country.

Although Taylor (2008: 101) contends that football 'was a British game', he also states that 'there was no British cup, nor British league and (with the exception of early Olympic tournaments) no British team'. Whilst there was a Great Britain and Northern Ireland football team who competed in the London 2012 Olympic Games[3] – the first since the 1972 Olympics – Moorhouse (1996) states that football has helped maintain national divisions within the 'United' Kingdom and Ireland largely through having separate national FAs since the late nineteenth century.

After the first Football Association in the world was formed in England in 1863, the Scottish FA (SFA) followed a decade later in 1873 (Hay and Coyle, 2002). The Welsh FA (FAW) was next to be formed in 1876 (Johnes, 2002). Finally, the Irish FA (IFA) was formed in 1880 and governed football across the whole of Ireland prior to its division in 1921 (Cronin, 2002).[4]

In the late 1990s some sections of FIFA membership, particularly African states, questioned the UK's privileged position in world football in relation to them being allowed four separate FAs within one nation-state. The FAW responded to the challenge to their existence by introducing a national league of Wales in 1992/3 in order to establish its separateness from England. Scotland and Northern Ireland have for a long time had leagues of their own. In fact a

> similar progression is evident in all four countries with respect to the setting up of a football association, a cup competition, international fixtures and a national league. The one anomaly is the failure of the Welsh FA to establish a national league (covering north and south Wales) until 1993 (Duke and Crolley, 1996: 11).

---

3   The existence of a Great Britain football team at the London 2012 Olympics was highly controversial and this issue is discussed in detail in Chapter 5.

4   After the partition of Ireland in 1921 the IFA became the FA for Northern Ireland and remains so to this day (Cronin, 2002). In 1921 a new FA was set up for southern Ireland originally termed the 'Football Association of the Irish Free State' (FAIFS) which was formally recognised by FIFA in 1923 and later became known as the 'Football Association of Ireland' (FAI).

In highlighting cases such as that evident in the UK where the state does not equal the nation, Duke and Crolley argue that the existence of latent or submerged nations within a state provides the potential for political conflict. Politically unrecognised or unsatisfied nations/ethnies (ethnic communities) are particularly prone to resistance towards the centre.[5] England have maintained political power over the other home nations within the UK throughout history and international football has often been the site for Celtic resistance to such oppression because of the way it has always been organised.

Resistance of the other home nations to England has found expression via football perhaps most vehemently whenever England have played the 'Auld Enemy' Scotland (Haynes, 1996). Although the team only consisted of amateurs, England's first international football match was a friendly against Scotland in 1872 (Haynes, 1996). According to Hay and Coyle (2002: 280) this very first 'international fixture was a result of a joint initiative of the Queen's Park club and Charles Alcock, Secretary of the (English) Football Association'. After this, the two teams played each other, as well as Wales and Ireland, annually as part of the world's first international football tournament – the 'Home International Championship' which later became known as the 'British Championship' – from the 1883–84 season through to the 1983–84 season with intervals of five and seven years during the First and Second World Wars respectively (Coyle, 2002). Taylor (2008: 103) argues that during this period, football 'was probably more popular in Scotland than anywhere else in Britain'. This is demonstrated by the high crowd numbers at Rangers versus Celtic fixtures as well as Scotland-England matches (Taylor, 2008: 103).

To an extent at least, international football was able to unify the sectarian divide between Rangers and Celtic (and other clubs) for matches against the English and it was therefore a vehicle for the articulation of Scottish national distinctiveness (Holt, 1989: 258). However, at this time the same was not true of the English who were much more focused on 'expressing an attachment to community, town and even region but rarely to the nation' (Taylor, 2008: 105–6). The English obsession with international football had not yet begun. Similarly, Holt (1989: 272–3) states that

> 'North' against 'South' games were probably more engrossing than the home internationals. Beating a London club was something a Geordie could more readily appreciate than beating a Scotland side containing some of his own club's players ... the mentality that made the Scots so keen to beat England was much less apparent in English attitudes to the Scots ... English football was too self-absorbed to give itself whole-heartedly to the national cause. Club loyalties were too strong and the League programme too exhausting.

---

5 The 1960s, for instance, witnessed an upsurge in nationalist movements in places like Scotland, Wales and Catalonia, who were demanding greater autonomy from the states in which they are situated. Indeed in some authoritarian regimes football has been the only legal theatre for the expression of latent nationalism (Beck, 1999; Martin, 2004).

Although football has always held a special place as England's most popular national sport, the national team did not become associated with English national identity until after the Second World War (Polley, 2004; Porter, 2004). The English national team did not play teams from outside the UK (of which Ireland was also then a part) until a friendly against France in 1906. The first England match in a competitive non-British international did not take place until their World Cup qualifier, ironically against Wales, in 1949. England's first appearance at a serious international tournament as a non-amateur team was not until 1950 against Chile in the already twenty-year-old FIFA World Cup Finals tournament that had begun without the involvement of a UK team in 1930 (Glanville, 2010; Walvin, 1994).

Post-1945 the FA and the English media finally started paying attention to competitive international football. The involvement of the English national team in the World Cup competition was significant to this (Glanville, 2010). According to Carrington (1999: 72), as we are

> never likely to meet even a fraction of those whom we deem to be fellow nationals, it is through shared public displays and mass-mediated spectacles of nationhood – and few cultural events do this better than the hyper-mediated events such as the World Cup or the European Championships – that people come to see themselves as belonging to the same country.

A number of authors (cf. Holt, 1989; Porter; 2004; Moorhouse, 1996; Walvin; 1994) have suggested that for most of the first half of the twentieth century the FA and the national press were insular and self-absorbed in the fact that they had invented the modern game and thus felt no need to play against 'foreigners' from outside the British Isles. This also meant football fans had little understanding of or appetite for the international game before 1950.

A 'British' national football team has never competed in the World Cup Finals or European Championships, which have been the most regular and longstanding international football tournaments (Giulianotti, 1999; King, 2006; Menary, 2010). There is no other mainstream sport in which a non-amateur national team have *only* specifically represented *England* in serious international competitions (Robinson, 2008). Rugby union and cricket came to be key symbols of the British Empire due to their spread by English ex-public schoolmen in the late Victorian and Edwardian period (Holt, 1989), however, both British and English national rugby union teams have often competed in major international fixtures since the first international between England and Scotland in 1871 (Bowker, 1976). Similarly, even though cricket is often described as a quintessentially English game (Holt, 1989), and the first England test cricket international (against Australia) also dates to the 1870s (1877), the England cricket team also represent Wales and have always included Welsh players, as well as some Scots, throughout their history (Frith, 2007). This is why researching the actions and opinions of football fans rather than those of any other sport were chosen as the means through which to explore English national identity in the current book.

The following section of this introductory chapter explains how a myth regarding the relationship between English national identity and football fan culture has been created and that the aim of the current book is to challenge this myth. This includes a discussion of some of the key problems associated with previous academic research on the relationship between Englishness and football. These problems provide the basis for advocating the 'new' approach taken.

Euro 96 and the Construction of a Myth

The European Football Championships (Euro 96) was the first major international football tournament to be held in Britain since the 1966 World Cup Finals. There was great nostalgia for 1966; the one and only time the English have ever won a major international football tournament, due to Euro 96 being held on its thirtieth anniversary (Aughey, 2007; Crolley and Hand, 2002; 2006; Maguire and Poulton, 1999; Weight, 2000). Euro 96 is also widely considered to be *the* time when the majority of English football fans supposedly 'reclaimed' the St George's Cross flag from a minority of far right political groups, such as the BNP and the National Front, who had monopolised its use in football and other areas of society throughout the 1970s and 1980s (Carrington, 1998; 1999; Garland and Rowe; 2001).

Up to this point, the preferred flag of the majority of fans of the English national football team had been the British Union flag. Yet pressure was put upon England to establish their own distinctive 'national' identity because they played Scotland for the first time in the group stages of a serious international football tournament (Haynes, 1996). This meant that the British flag suddenly became redundant as it would symbolise the union between both nations, rather than their individual national characters (Perryman, 2006: 294). The fact that the English national team still used the British national anthem 'God Save The Queen' was also questioned, but remains the case to this day despite the Scottish, Welsh and Northern Irish using their own distinctive 'national' anthems whenever their teams compete (Robinson, 2008).

In his book *Patriots: National Identity in Britain 1940–2000*, Weight (2000: 708-10) discusses the centrality of Euro 96 to the construction of a 'separatist' Englishness in the face of growing Scottish and Welsh calls for levels of devolved political independence and the long-standing but intensifying cultural distinctiveness claimed by the 'Celtic' nations within the UK. Weight (2000: 709) specifically states that

> Wembley was a sea of St George's crosses and red-and-white-painted faces. There is no more potent symbol of how the English shed their Britishness than the comparison between the flags waved in 1966 and those waved in 1996.

In fact, Weight is just one of numerous academics, journalists and politicians to have regarded the increasing use of the St George's Cross by football fans since

Euro 96 as evidence of a supposed rise in a specifically 'English', rather than 'British', national consciousness. Carrington (1999: 76) also recognised this, stating that

> the abandonment of the Union Jack for the St George Cross was seen by many as a positive re-affirmation of an English nationalism in response to the collapse of a coherent British identity.

Yet, to date little empirical evidence has been used to substantiate the assertion that a coherent and specifically 'English' national identity is intended by all contemporary English football fans. This idea has therefore been constructed as a myth.

Problems with Previous Research on Englishness and Football

Drawing most significantly upon the 'figurational' or 'process-sociological' approach advocated by Elias, who argued for the sociologist to be a 'destroyer of myths' (Elias, 1978: 50), the aim of this book is to explore the precise nature of the relationship between English national identity and football fan culture and to challenge the emergence of this alleged English identity. This was motivated by a number of problems with previous research in this area, which require further elaboration.

There are some examples that appear outside the sport-specific literature regarding British and English national identity that draw upon the actions of football fans to help explain the confusion of Englishness with Britishness. For example, Groom (2006: xvi) recalls that he was

> talking to a German recently who was taken aback to learn that the Scots had their own football team: she assumed that 'Eng-er-land' were cheered on by the whole of the British Isles – not least because English football supporters often carried the Union Jack.

Even though the German woman in question must have known little about football considering England have played national teams representing the other 'home nations' on multiple occasions since at least 1872 (Haynes, 1996), the fact that Groom chose to refer to the actions of football fans to make his point provides some evidence that he considers football fandom to be an important manifestation of English national identity. Moreover, Kumar (2003: 275*n*) suggests that the

> recent flaunting by the English of the St George's Cross at football matches presumably indicates a rise in specifically English as opposed to British national consciousness – or at least recognition of the distinction between them.

Although it should be a testament to the relative unimportance of football in Kumar's mind that he see fit to mention this merely in passing in an endnote to a chapter, the main point is that both of these authors provide little evidence for such anecdotal claims.

In a similar fashion Burdsey's (2007) study on the under-representation of British Asians in English football at best speculates on the interplay and confusion between Englishness and Britishness. Burdsey (2007: 97) states that

> like the use of the St George flag ... it is an English symbol that is being used to represent a British identity. A British team does not compete in football (although it has been mooted for participation in the Olympic Games), yet if it did, it would be very interesting to observe how its presence alongside or instead of an England team might influence patterns of support and affiliation.

Although Porter (2004: 46) goes some way to providing historical evidence to suggest that British decline since the Second World War can be reflected in representations of English football, he provides rather less conclusive evidence to reinforce the bold assumption that, following 'the fortunes of the national football team helps to determine how English people see themselves and make sense of the world in which they live'. More recently, King (2006) has suggested that we are witnessing the rise of an English national consciousness among football fans that is a reflection of advancing processes of globalisation, European integration and devolution, which have led to a supposed decline in Britishness. The heightened appearance of the St George's Cross at football matches is again regarded as an obvious way in which a rise in English national consciousness is occurring. King (2006: 253) states that at the

> now famous World Cup semi-final against Germany in Turin in 1990, in which England was eventually eliminated on penalties, television broadcasts showed the England fans chiefly waving the Union Jack, with only a few St George's flags in evidence. In the course of the 1990s, however, England fans have increasingly preferred to use the red and white Cross of St George. This flag denotes a specifically English identity.

Yet again, evidence from the actions and opinions of fans themselves is not used to substantiate this assumption. Although Robinson's (2008: 221, emphasis in original) essay specifically argues that English football should be regarded as a suitable means through which to study English national identity, she does not provide any empirical evidence to suggest that the heightened use of the St George's Cross is intended by English fans to represent a unified Englishness when she states that

> English football does not reflect England, but actually brings it into being. In almost no other area is the distinction between England and Britain as absolute

and clear-cut. England has no distinctive political manifestation (Parliament is British), it has no national dress, no national anthem and even its patron Saint is neither English nor uniquely its own. The English (as opposed to the British) have few of the cultural or political trappings that have come to be associated with the nation. However, in sports, and especially in football, an England team represents England, not Britain, making football *the* location to examine an emerging national consciousness – whatever that may be ... . In football, if nowhere else, the English *are* England.

In contradiction to Robinson's claims, there is evidence from Abell, Condor, Lowe, Gibson and Stevenson (2007) to suggest that English football fans' articulations of support for the national team do not even necessarily represent their wider feelings of national sentiment. Importantly, King's (2006) and Robinson's (2008) work in relation to English football fans was observational, whereas Abell et al. conducted interviews with English individuals. According to Abell et al. (2007: 113), English national identity

> is not an all or nothing affair. People can display immense emotional involvement in the fate of the England football team, without expressing any such concerns over the nation as an imagined community.

Yet, these interviews, on the whole, were not conducted with English football fans, but members of the general public and as such it is difficult for the authors to justify their conclusions. More empirical evidence is required from the actions and opinions of English fans themselves.

Paradoxically, in earlier work using detailed ethnographic data, King (2000; 2003) suggested that recent processes of European integration and globalisation have led to a core group of fans of the elite English club Manchester United F.C., a team that regularly play in European competitions, to reject English national identity and form allegiance to their local identities by choosing to support their club team over and above the English national team. This may therefore be an example of how fans use football to articulate their local identities because they do not feel entirely comfortable with Englishness, but it is solely based on the views of fans of Manchester United. The justification for regarding this group of fans as representative of the majority of the English football fan base is unclear, particularly as it is usually fans of lower league clubs who appear to have a greater presence at the England national team's fixtures (Gibbons and Lusted, 2007). This is mentioned by both King (2003; 2006) and Robinson (2008), but is not explored in any depth by either.

Thus it seems academics have tended to rely on their own observations and interpretations of English national identity alone, rather than combining these with those of fans themselves. Perhaps the only exceptions are Perryman's (2006) *Ingerland: Travels with a football nation* and Pearson's (2012) *An Ethnography of English Football Fans: Cans, Cops and Carnivals*. The fact that these are both key texts in the study of English football fan culture is not questioned here. However, each of these works contains gaps which the current book seeks to repair.

Perryman's *Ingerland* provides a detailed, but admittedly personal, account of the author's own experiences as an English football fan and his interactions with other fans between 1996 and 2006. Near the beginning of the book, Perryman (2006: 11) confidently states: 'We wear the same shirt, fly the same flag, cheer for the same team .... But what do they know of I-N-G-E-R-L-A-N-D who only this England knows?' Although this kind of 'insider' account is useful as it provides evidence from English fans themselves on English national identity (among other related issues), it is entirely devoid of sociological theory and as such, links between theory and evidence are entirely absent. Elias (1978) argued that if social scientists are to increase knowledge of the social processes that shape the human figurations in which people participate – nations, classes, ethnic groups and so on – we must ensure theory and empirical evidence are used together wherever possible. Moreover, Perryman does little to ensure the reader that the contents of his *Ingerland* have not been influenced by his own biases. In considering the generalisability of his work, Perryman (2006: 5) states the following:

> I can't prove it; that would be a different sort of book, demanding all sorts of surveys and questionnaires. But everything I know about England fans, have seen with my own eyes, and come to believe in with a faith that sometimes comes close to missionary zeal, convinces me that these hundred or so fans whose stories I recount represent more about England than many who write about us realise.

Although this kind of 'insider' account does indeed add a valuable insight that was lacking in the vast majority of previous academic studies on English football fan culture, Elias (1987) argued that sociologists must take what he refers to as a 'detour via detachment' to ensure they do not become too 'involved' with the subject matter under investigation. Therefore, although being entirely objective or completely detached from the object of social research is impossible (Elias, 1987), there is a need to re-examine the link between English national identity and football fan culture by using a combination of empirical evidence and a clear sociological theoretical framework.

Thankfully, Pearson's (2012) book is much more robust methodologically and theoretically. Based upon sixteen years of ethnographic research with fans of Manchester United, Blackpool and the England national team, Pearson's book is undeniably the most comprehensive truly academic study ever produced on English football fans to date. Pearson's book contains evidence from observations of English fans themselves on a broad range of issues, including: identity; hooliganism; social control; policing; alcohol; gender; sexuality; race; disability and the impact of technology.

Whilst this wide-ranging approach highlights the importance of many contemporary debates regarding English football fan culture and sets the agenda for future areas of research in a number of related fields, it is not specifically focused on exploring the sociological relationship between debates regarding English national identity and football fan culture. Also, whilst useful in highlighting key ways in which technological innovations have impacted English football fan culture, the penultimate chapter of Pearson's book does not provide detailed empirical evidence from these new figurations of football fans. The current book seeks to cover both of these areas in greater detail. Finally, as per most other research on aspects of English football fan culture, Pearson's book is not written from within the Eliasian theoretical perspective which is another distinctive feature of the current book.

A 'New' Approach: Elias, English National Identity and the Changing Nature of Football Fandom

Why Elias?

The work of Elias is central to this book and has informed the research process both theoretically and methodologically. Elias's distinct sociological approach has been adopted principally because Elias himself, and the 'figurational' sociologists whom he influenced at Leicester University, most effectively highlighted the following: the centrality of national identity at the current stage of human social development (cf. Elias, 1991; 1996; 2000); the process through which English national identity has moved in order to reach its current phase of development (cf. Elias, 1991; 2000; Elias and Dunning, 1986; Elias and Scotson, 1994); the sociological significance of sport, specifically football, for understanding the impact of wider societal developments upon English national identity (cf. Dunning, 1999; Elias, 1971; 1986; Maguire, 1999; 2005; 2011a; Maguire and Poulton, 1999; Maguire, Poulton and Possamai, 1999); and, how to engage in empirically led, theoretically and historically informed sociological research (cf. Elias, 1978; 1987).

The Eliasian concepts of 'changes in the we-I balance' (Elias, 1991) and 'diminishing contrasts, increasing varieties' (Elias, 2000) were found to be extremely useful for explaining the findings of the two empirical studies conducted (see Chapters 4–6). Whilst these particular Eliasian ideas have been explored in relation to the globalisation and Europeanisation of sports, including football, principally by Maguire and colleagues (cf. Maguire, 1999; 2005; 2011a; 2011b; 2011c; 2011d; Maguire and Poulton, 1999; Maguire, Poulton and Possamai, 1999), these studies have largely relied upon depictions of English fans in the media. Whilst representations of Englishness via football in the media are important to consider when exploring the relationship between English national identity and football fan culture (Gibbons, 2010), Elias's ideas are yet to be applied to empirical research on the actions and opinions English football fans themselves regarding the topic of English national identity.

The Changing Nature of Football Fandom

What constitutes football 'fandom' has itself been contested by academics in the past and this seems to have acted as a barrier to researchers studying 'new' aspects of fan culture (Dixon, 2013). This could be a reason why the actions and opinions of English football fans regarding national identity have not been researched in enough depth by sociologists of football in the past. A cursory look at debates regarding definitions of fandom reveal reasons why some fans' voices might have been hidden from view in previous research (see Gibbons and Dixon, 2010 for more on this).

Wann, Melnick, Russell and Pease (2001) suggested distinguishing between sports 'fans' and sports 'spectators/consumers'. The latter group here were used to refer to individuals who may actively witness a sporting event in person or through the media, but who do not have the same degree of involvement with a sports team or athlete as the former category of sports 'fans' might. Furthermore, Wann et al. (2001) argued that sport spectators/consumers could be divided into two groups: 'direct' versus 'indirect', where 'direct' sports consumption involves personal attendance at a sporting event and 'indirect' sports consumption involves watching sport through the mass media or consuming sport via the Internet. In addition, fans are considered by Wann et al. (2001: 2–4) to be either 'Highly' or 'Lowly' identified with their team/club due to the 'types' of fandom practices they engage in. Some practices, such as attending games in person, wearing team colours and actively yelling for a team were viewed as more 'authentic' and signified a greater affiliation with a sports team or club than others here.

More specifically, there have also been a number of typologies created by academics that have attempted to explain football fandom along similar lines of authenticity. Two of the most prominent academic typologies include Redhead's (1993; 1997) view of football fans as either 'Participatory' or 'Passive' and Giulianotti's (2002) admittedly 'ideal-type' taxonomy of spectator identities in football. Giulianotti's is perhaps the most comprehensive and widely utilised theoretical model indicating specific characteristics of his different 'types' of football spectator who he claims exist along a horizontal axis of 'Traditional' to 'Consumer', split in the middle by a vertical axis running between 'Hot' to 'Cool' forms of fandom. Relationships with and proximity to football spaces (such as to club stadia and the local community); means of consuming football (such as in person versus via the media); interactions with other fans about football (face-to-face versus using new media communications); and, other aspects that are meant to depict levels of solidarity and identification around a football club, supposedly help determine whether a fan is categorised as being one of the following more to less authentic 'types': 'Supporter', 'Follower', 'Fan' or 'Flâneur' (Giulianotti, 2002).

Despite being the most comprehensive and widely utilised typology to explain football fan identities, at least one section of Giulianotti's four-part taxonomy should be re-visited and questioned in terms of its accuracy and empirical underpinnings. That is, Giulianotti's (2002: 31) 'Cool/Consumer Spectators:

Flâneurs' category of fan. Giulianotti (2002: 38) briefly acknowledges that the term 'Flâneur' dates back to the sixteenth century, used by Charles Baudelaire in the mid-nineteenth century, reworked by the sociologist Georg Simmel, later drawn upon by Walter Benjamin and subsequently debated by cultural theorists. Drawing these together, Giulianotti (2002: 38) defines his flâneur category of football fan as someone who

> acquires a postmodern spectator identity through a depersonalised set of market-dominated virtual relationships, particularly interactions with the cool media of television and the Internet.

Here Giulianotti makes a generalised assumption about the ways in which fans use television and the Internet. Through classifying them as non-interactive, Giulianotti suggests that forms of new media consumption are merely 'virtual' and essentially 'passive' forms of communication that supposedly inauthentic 'flâneurs' use to experience football in a detached manner, instead of engaging in more 'real' and authentic forms of fandom like attending matches in person. Indeed, Giulianotti (2002: 39) argues that the 'cool/consumer seeks relatively thin forms of social solidarity with other fellow fans'.

It is clear that Giulianotti ignores the vast amount of what might be considered 'authentic' football fans who, *as well as* attending games in person, *also* watch 'live' football on television at home or in pubs or contribute to Internet discussion forums, blogs and email loops and use the Internet as just one form of communicating with fellow football fans and/or showing solidarity with their clubs. Indeed, Boyle and Haynes (2004: 141) argue that 'fan websites, or e-zines, are created from a labour of love motivated by passion and heavily tied to the construction of cultural identities'.

The kinds of assumptions created by such typologies about the assumed 'inauthentic' nature of 'new' aspects of fan culture have merely constructed what Elias (1978) termed 'false dichotomies' because they fail to recognise the complexity of reality. In contrast, Crawford's (2001; 2002; 2003; 2004) work conceives of fandom as much more complex than authors like Giulianotti have proposed. Crawford (2004) suggests that all of the aforementioned typologies of football fandom fail to recognise that fans who attend matches 'live' and who participate in what are considered 'traditional' and 'authentic' fandom practices are often *the same* fans who *also* watch matches on television and/or contribute to Internet discussion forums, blogs and email loops – 'new' aspects of fandom that are considered to be less 'authentic'. Crawford (2004: 33) summarises that whilst

> it is possible to identify different levels of commitment and dedication to a sport and different patterns of behaviour of fans, it is important that we do not celebrate the activities of certain supporters and ignore (or even downgrade) the activities and interests of others … . Rather than privileging the activities of certain fans over others, it is important, if we are to understand the contemporary

nature of fan cultures, that we consider the full range of patterns of behaviour of all fans, including those who do not conform to 'traditional' patterns or images of fan activities.

For the purposes of the current study, 'fandom' is simply defined along these lines. The term 'fan' is used throughout this book to refer to someone with an interest in football which leads them to choose to interact with others regarding football-related issues. It is argued that pubs and Internet discussion forums are both significant and legitimate social spaces within which English national identity is displayed and debated by fans in a number of varied ways. Bennett (2005a: 1) suggests 'it is precisely the inherent taken-forgrantedness of everyday life that renders it valuable as an object of social research'. Such a view is maintained in the current book. An attempt is made to provide a unique contribution to existing literature that takes into account the actions and opinions of football fans that interact within these 'new' social spaces in order to provide further understanding on the relationship between English national identity and football fan culture. Whilst the pub has traditionally been a place within which football fans interact, it is also considered 'new' because it has only recently been recognised as an alternative space within which to watch 'live' football instead of attending football stadiums (cf. Sandvoss, 2003; Stone, 2007; Weed, 2006).

The final section of this introductory chapter provides an outline of the structure of the remainder of this book.

Chapter Outline

The remaining six chapters comprise the following: Chapters 2 and 3 are reviews of relevant literature; Chapters 4–6 are discussions of the findings generated from the two research studies conducted; and Chapter 7 is a conclusion. The following provides a brief outline of the contents of each chapter.

In Chapter 2 theories of nationalism are considered and the merits of using the work of Norbert Elias to study English national identity are discussed. The 'anxieties' associated with contemporary English national identity are explained using an Eliasian sociological approach and the specific theoretical concepts that underpin the analyses undertaken in the later empirical chapters (4–6) are outlined. A critical appraisal of Elias's general sociological approach is also provided.

Chapter 3 is a review of existing literature which highlights what Elias (1978; 2000) would have regarded as 'unintended consequences' of global and European forces on English football and its fans since the late twentieth century. A brief history of changes to the structure of English professional football since the 1990s is presented and a case is made for examining the impacts of such changes on new areas of football fan culture which have not yet been thoroughly researched.

Rationales are provided for researching the pub and the Internet as spaces where fans display, articulate and debate national identity.[6]

Chapter 4 is based upon the author's field notes recorded from observations of fans taken within a sample of English pubs that were showing matches involving the English national team 'live' on television during the 2006 World Cup Finals tournament. Elias's (1991) essay titled 'Changes in the We-I Balance' as well as Elias's (2000) concept of 'diminishing contrasts, increasing varieties' are used to help explain the significance of the findings. It is concluded that the opinions of fans are required to either confirm or refute the author's observations.

Chapters 5 and 6 contain discussions of findings from a fourteen-month participant observation study conducted within a specific online fan community between 2008 and 2009. In Chapter 5 the ways in which English national identity was debated by fans through their discussions around two football-related issues are interpreted using Elias's (1991) 'changes in the we-I balance'. The prospect of the Great Britain and Northern Ireland Olympic team fielding a football team for the London 2012 Olympics and the possibility that Arsenal's Spanish goalkeeper, Manuel Almunia, might be chosen to represent the England national team due to becoming a naturalised British citizen, were found to be the key issues in which fans' opinions on Englishness were manifest. The 'anxieties' surrounding contemporary English national identity were clearly evident from such debates.

In Chapter 6 further findings from more 'everyday' or 'banal' (Billig, 1995) interactions between fans within the online community investigated are used to argue that the significance of club/locality-based attachments, as well as the diverse use of the St George's Cross, both highlight the challenges posed to English national identity by the globalisation and Europeanisation of elite-level English club football. It is argued that this can be explained by using Elias's (2000) 'diminishing contrasts, increasing varieties'. The 'myth' discussed in Chapter 1, which suggests the increased ubiquity of the St George's Cross at English football matches signals a rise in English identity, is directly challenged using these findings.

In Chapter 7 a synopsis of the empirical evidence discussed in the previous three chapters is provided. Empirical and theoretical reflections on the research process are offered and suggestions for future research in this area are given before final conclusions are drawn on what the book has revealed about the relationship between English national identity and football fan culture.

---

6   The specific methodological framework used for collecting and analysing the data drawn from both research studies that underpin the later empirically-based chapters (4–6) appear in the Appendix.

Chapter 2
Theoretical Approach for Understanding Contemporary English National Identity

Introduction

The current chapter provides a more detailed justification for using an Eliasian theoretical perspective in order to understand contemporary English national identity. In the first section of this chapter, Elias's distinct sociological perspective is outlined. In the next section Elias is considered as a theorist *par excellence* of the 'national habitus'. In the following section the specific 'problems' with contemporary English national identity are detailed and a case is made for using an Eliasian sociological approach for understanding the multi-layered complex nature of contemporary Englishness. The final section of the chapter alludes to common criticisms of Elias and provides counter-critiques in the context of this book.

The Sociological Perspective of Norbert Elias

Elias's 'figurational' or 'process' sociological approach focused specifically on 'how human beings and societies interconnect and develop' (Smith, 2001: 1). More specifically, Shilling (2011: 3) states that

> Elias's analysis of the long-term development of humanity, and the webs of interdependence woven between people, and between individuals and the environments in which they live, stands as a prominent example of the potential of sociology to pursue many of the most important issues of our time rather than capitulating to the short-term political concerns and economic agendas that permeate so much current work.

Elias (1978: 15) contends that, 'people make up webs of interdependence or figurations of many kinds, characterised by power balances of many sorts'. These 'figurations' are fluid and ever changing depending on the dynamics of the relationships people form and the situational context they exist in at a particular point in time. Elias (1978: 74) created what he terms 'game models' to help explain how power pervades in all human relationships. Through regarding power relations as analogous to human games, such as invasion sports like football, rugby, basketball or field hockey, Elias was able to show that all relationships are processes subject to change. In a 'game' of football for example, the relationship between teams and the individuals which make them up on the field of play is constantly changing depending on a number of related factors, including: who has possession of the ball; where players are positioned on the field; and, so on. Here Elias conceives of the way power operates as: processual; fluid; multi-dimensional; relational; and, situational, instead of being static; fixed; one-sided; and, uni-directional, as for example a classic Marxist conception of class relations maintains where members of the proletariat are always subordinate to the dominance of the bourgeoisie (cf. Marx and Engels, 1967). For Elias, in any given figuration all individuals have a degree of power in the interdependent relationships they form with one another. Elias (1978: 93) contends that a

> more adequate solution to problems of power depends on power being understood unequivocally as a structural characteristic of a relationship, all-pervading and, as a structural characteristic, neither good nor bad. It may be both. We depend on others; others depend on us. In so far as we are more dependent on others than they are on us, more directed by others than they are by us, they have power over us, whether we have become dependent on them by their use of naked force or by our need to be loved, our need for money, healing, status, a career, or simply for excitement … all relationships – like human games – are processes.

Since the European Middle Ages, if not before, webs of interdependency (figurations) have gradually increased in size to such an extent that today in the modern world, 'millions of people may have some relationship to each other and be dependent on each other' (Elias, 1978: 100). The task for sociologists, according to Elias, is to study these figurations in order to make them more transparent. This requires a necessarily developmental sociological approach because 'people's interdependencies change as societies become increasingly differentiated and stratified' (Elias, 1978: 134). Thus, it is important to conceive of figurations as if they are in a constant state of flux because people form interpersonal bonds with one another as well as with larger units of which they have become part (such as nation-states) as a result of the ways in which societies have developed. Elias (1978: 137) states that people's 'attachments to such large social units is often as intense as their attachment to a person they love'. Elias argues that throughout history units or alliances of people have always held the function of 'survival units' or 'attack and defence units'. Whereas they have previously been in the form of smaller groups such as tribes or clans, at the present stage of human development nation-states act as the main units into which people are bound. Such a unit

> knits people together for common purposes – the common defence of their lives, the survival of their group in the face of attacks by other groups and, for a variety of reasons, attacks on other groups. Thus the primary function of such an alliance is either physically to wipe out other people or to protect its own members from being physically wiped out (Elias, 1978: 138).

Elias's (1939/2000) seminal tome, *The Civilizing Process: Sociogenetic and Psychogenetic Investigations*,[1] is essentially concerned with making strong links between large-scale social processes that have occurred in Western Europe over the last millennium and visible alterations in the psychological make-up or 'habitus' of individuals. The term 'habitus' is closely related to the word 'identity' according to Mennell (1994), although its meaning is more complex. Habitus refers to a specific set of acquired dispositions of thought, behaviour and actions that are embedded in individuals through long-term socialisation into particular cultures as part of everyday life. According to Mennell (1994: 177),

> Habitus is a useful word in referring to the modes of conduct, taste, and feeling which predominate among members of particular groups. It can refer to shared traits of which the people who share them may be largely unconscious; for the meaning of the technical term 'habitus' is, as Norbert Elias used to remark, captured exactly in the everyday English expression *second nature* – an expression defined by the *Oxford English Dictionary* as 'an acquired tendency that has become instinctive'.

Mennell (1994: 177) goes on to clarify that:

> *Habitus* is closely related to the notion of *identity*. The difference is perhaps that 'identity' implies a higher level of conscious awareness by members of a group, some degree of reflection and articulation, some positive or negative emotional feelings towards the characteristics which members of a group perceive themselves as sharing and in which they perceive themselves as differing from other groups. But there is no great value in drawing fine distinctions here.

Although habitus is a term thought to have originated in the work of Aristotle, Bourdieu (cf. 1977) is most commonly associated with its modern usage in sociology (Scott and Marshall, 2009: 299). Yet it is important to clarify that the term 'habitus' was actually used in a sociological context prior to this by Elias in *The Civilizing Process*. Elias uses the phrase 'social habitus' which he contends exists within the personality structure of any individual human being and the idea of the 'national habitus' figures prominently in a number of Elias's works (cf. Elias, 1978; 1991; 1996; Elias and Scotson, 1994).

---

1 *The Civilizing Process* was originally published in German in 1939 as two separate volumes, *The History of Manners* and *State Formation and Civilization*. English translations of the separate volumes were not published until 1978 and 1982 respectively. Both volumes were eventually published together in English in 1994. A revised edition (2000) of the 1994 version is the text drawn upon throughout this book, however, a more recent revised edition (2012) titled *On the Process of Civilisation: Sociogenetic and Psychogenetic Investigations* is now available.

Theories of Nationalism

In order to begin to appreciate why Elias can be considered a theorist of the 'national habitus', it is important to consider what is known as the 'traditional-modern' debate, which has dominated literature on 'nationalism' to date (James, 2006). Smith (1998) suggests that there are many theories that academics have formulated to explain how nations and their 'nationalisms' have developed. Although it is not within the scope of this chapter to discuss all of these multiple variations, the most dominant paradigms are briefly outlined here before the Eliasian alternative is considered.

In sociological terms, a 'nation' is a community of history and culture, possessing a compact territory, whilst a 'state' has a unified economy and common legal rights and duties for its members (Smith, 2010). Related to this is the distinction between 'ethnic' and 'civic' nationalisms, where the former relates to ideas of the 'nation', and the latter relates to ideas about the 'state' (Hall, 1992; Smith, 1996). Yet the two are easily confused within the UK primarily because England (the nation) has often been regarded as synonymous with Britain (the state) throughout history (Colley, 1996; Kumar, 2003). Essentially, 'nationalists' operating within modern nation-states have aimed to put the 'roof' of statehood over the nation or multiple nations, as is the case in the UK, whereas others have pointed to the 're-invention' of traditions that are symbolic of the cultural and often ethnic history of the nation, for example, 'Celtic' ethnicity is used to underpin the nationalism of the Republic of Ireland (cf. Anderson, 1991; Barraclough, 1971; Bartrum, 2004; Hobsbawm, 1983; 1990).

The 'modernist' paradigm of nationalism contends that nation-states, nationalisms, and feelings of national identity amongst contemporary Europeans, need to be viewed as completely 'modern' in that they have been developed since what is known as the 'Age of Enlightenment', which began in the second half of the seventeenth century. Of particular importance following this period was what is known as the 'modernising' revolutions beginning in the mid-late seventeenth century – the French Revolution, the American Revolution, as well as the British Industrial Revolution. Modernists contend that nation-states and nationalism emerged through the modernisation of western society and state politics of the elite classes, and are therefore *not* deeply rooted in history. This is recognised as the most dominant paradigm to date and has largely stemmed from influential scholars like Gellner (1964; 1983) and Kedourie (1960). In outlining the modernist approach of the social theorist Weber in relation to Germany after unification in 1870, Bryant (2006: 15) states that he

> treats nations as constructions … . Each is constructed in a unique way and each has an identity of its own. A nation is a … community, and intellectuals are important in forming the language of solidarity, whereas the state is … an association, and an instrument of politicians. Nations usually, but not invariably,

need a state to protect their integrity and interests; states usually need (to forge) a nation if they are to command allegiance.

Smith (1996) describes how most (but not all) 'modern' nation-states are simultaneously and necessarily 'civic' and 'ethnic'. He observes that it is often assumed, by leftist theorists in particular, that ethnic sentiments of collective belonging that enter into the life of a state inevitably breed exclusiveness and intolerance leading to conflict. Marxist theorists often tend to claim that states are modern capitalist inventions that seek to divide workers of different nations and disguise their common interests (Smith, 1996; 1998; 2010). Hobsbawm's (1983:1) is an example of a Marxist interpretation of the production of nationalism as a political ideology because he regards the practices that are associated with modern nation-states as 'invented traditions', which he describes as a term

> taken to mean a set of practices, normally governed by overtly or tacitly accepted rules and of a ritual or symbolic nature, which seek to inculcate certain values and norms of behaviour by repetition, which automatically implies continuity with the past. In fact, where possible, they normally attempt to establish continuity with a suitable historic past.

In later work, Hobsbawm (1990) proposed that the ruling political elites who had power throughout the industrial and modernising periods created or 'invented' certain 'national' symbols such as flags and anthems to symbolise particular nation-states. Though, as Smith (1998) clarifies, Hobsbawm does not adequately explain that traditions are not only invented by elites and neither are they always successful in binding society as if it were a homogenous community. Traditions also need to appeal to the majority of people within a nation in order to be successful. It is important not to divorce romantic symbols from historically lived experience and, therefore, because national traditions necessarily need a connection to the past, it is perhaps more accurate to conceive of them as 'selected' rather than completely 'invented'.

Stemming from a similar Marxist position, Anderson (1991) seeks to emphasise the cultural and subjective aspects in producing modern feelings of national belonging or sentiment, which Hobsbawm leaves aside to some extent. Instead of nations and their nationalisms being 'invented', they are actually 'imagined' according to Anderson. Therefore, nations are modern cultural artefacts and not ideological for Anderson (1991: 5), who states that it 'would, I think, make things easier if one treated it [nationalism] as if it belonged with "kinship" and "religion", rather than with "liberalism" or "fascism"'. Anderson (1991: 6) defines the modern nation-state as being 'an imagined political community – and imagined as both inherently limited and sovereign'. According to Anderson, the reason the nation is 'imagined' is because citizens will rarely meet or hear about the majority of other people existing within their nation. Still they will imagine similarities between themselves and the wider community of people existing within the limited boundaries of their country.

Billig (1995) helps one understand how what Hobsbawm termed 'invented traditions' are used to maintain the 'imagined national community' Anderson theorised. Billig conceives of national identity as constructed through the nation being 'flagged up' in many areas of everyday life including social interactions, language, signs, and symbols. Billig recognises that representations in the national media and other areas of everyday life, although not overt, still act to 'flag the nation' on a subtle but routine basis. He argues that it is by continual reference to national symbols, such as flags or anthems, and aspects of a nation's history, such as successes in wars, that what he terms 'banal nationalism' occurs. In this regard, Billig (1995: 93) contends that small 'words, rather than grand memorable phrases, offer constant, but barely conscious, reminders of the homeland, making "our" national identity unforgettable'.

The opposing paradigm to modernism is that of traditionalism. Taking this perspective, primordialists attempt to understand nations and nationalisms from more physical notions of the nation as a territory. Primordialists have the view that ethnic ties, often from the ancient past, explain that 'nationalism' has been apparent for as long as people have been in existence. Geertz (1994) notes how new societies have created a shared sense of collective belonging through six essentially ethnic elements, including: assumed blood ties; race; language; region; religion; and custom.[2] These are what he calls 'primordial' ties. Perennialists, being similar to primordialists, derive modern nations from fundamental ethnic ties rather than from the processes of modernisation (Smith, 2010). Perennialists locate myths that relate to the ethnic majority in society and may often be formalised through civic commemoration in order to make certain citizens feel more like a community.

A further traditional approach to nationalism, which is outlined by Smith (1981), is ethno-symbolism. As its name suggests, this model aims to unearth the ways in which symbols of ethnic history, including myths and traditions, are re-used by modern nationalist ideologies. This is important as nationalist groups have used these as propaganda to gain power through appealing to dominant groups. For example, Hitler used the reverse 'Swastika' symbol (originally imported from Asian cultures where it was often depicted on Buddha as a symbol of prosperity and good fortune) to turn those who he felt best fitted the dominant ethnic category of 'Aryan' against a less powerful minority of German Jews (cf. Elias, 1996).

Hutchinson (1987) states that cultural nationalists in particular have an elusive ethnic agenda that endeavours to incorporate ethnic traditions into the modern world and unite traditionalists and modernists through the use of ethnic symbols, values and morals. Many examples of this have been evident in Northern Ireland, a nation that has traditionally been, and to an extent remains, divided politically and religiously and this has strongly underpinned and defined the relationship of many within the Northern Irish population to Britain. This politico-religious

---

2   Geerz is referring to post-colonial societies here.

divide means that the Protestant majority have traditionally been 'Unionist' or 'Loyalist' and as such have had strong affiliations to the British state, whereas the Catholic minority have traditionally been 'Nationalist' or 'Republican' and defied British rule and the 1921 division of Ireland (Davey, 2001). Bryson and McCartney (1994) highlight how members of these competing groups have used flags, emblems and songs that relate to their ethnic past, particularly in terms of religion, to demonstrate their allegiances. For example, in Northern Ireland the British Union flag has often been used by Loyalists and Unionists. In opposition, Nationalists have often used the Irish 'Tricolour' flag and maintain Catholic religious values in connection with the Irish Republic.

Finally, there are post-modernist approaches which focus upon how the modernist paradigm needs to be adapted or extended to include more recent themes, including: post-colonial perspectives; feminist critiques; and, the impact of globalisation processes on national cultures (Smith, 1998; 2010). Whilst space restricts a full outline of all of the multiple variations of these approaches, the latter theme of globalisation is perhaps most significant as it underpins an understanding of what has led to post-modern thinking.

On the topic of globalisation, Schlesinger (1994: 318) states that, 'the old model of national sovereignty will not do, given the reality of global interdependence'. According to Maguire (1999: 3), who draws upon the observations of the globalisation theorist Robertson (1995), globalisation is best understood as comprising

> long-term processes that have occurred unevenly across all areas of the planet. These processes – involving an increasing intensification of global interconnectedness – appear to be gathering momentum and despite their 'unevenness', it is more difficult to understand local or national experiences without reference to these global flows. Every aspect of social reality – people's living conditions, beliefs, knowledge and actions – is intertwined with unfolding globalization processes. These processes include the emergence of a global economy, a transnational cosmopolitan culture and a range of international social movements.

Although multinational production, migration, mass travel and mass communications have themselves developed over protracted periods, all of these processes have arguably gathered momentum since the 1960s due to technological advances. Many argue that the creation of what Albrow (1996: 114 cited in Kennedy, 2010: 1) termed 'World Society' is questioning the territorial boundaries that were formerly created in the nineteenth century by political elites to distinguish the 'domestic' from the 'foreign' and may have even replaced 'the desire to defend and expand the nation's influence in a world of competing states', the primary objective of 'state-led modernization' until the late twentieth century (Kennedy, 2010: 2).

Inglis and Thorpe (2012: 261) state that globalisation has *economic*, *political*, *social* and *cultural* dimensions and there are now a plethora of theories which fit within each of these four broad areas. It is not within the scope of the current chapter to discuss all of the multiple ways in which theorists have debated how global processes impact traditional ways of theorising 'society', this has been done in much greater detail elsewhere (cf. Inglis and Thorpe, 2012: 258–81). Drawing upon Robertson's (1992; 1995) original theoretical contributions to understanding cultural globalisation, Giulianotti and Robertson (2009:38) explain that the 'homogenisation-heterogenisation' debate is the 'axial problem in the sociology of globalization', and these authors go on to say that:

> Homogenization arguments generally posit that globalization is marked by growing cultural convergence at the transnational level. Conversely, heterogenization arguments contend that global processes maintain or facilitate cultural diversity or divergence.

From the homogenisation perspective, globalisation is viewed as a kind of monoculture using neo-Marxist terms such as 'Westernisation', 'Americanisation', 'grobalisation' or 'cultural imperialism' (cf. Giulianotti and Robertson, 2009: 38–9). Proponents of this view regard globalisation as a one-way process whereby dominant national cultures, and/or transnational corporations (TNCs) usually emanating from 'core' states, have effectively forced less powerful 'peripheral' states to reproduce their products or practices sometimes at the expense of their own 'national' traditions (cf. Wallerstein, 1974).

Alternatively, from the heterogenisation perspective, globalisation is viewed as providing opportunities for interaction between different cultures throughout the world, leading to the creation of 'new' or 'hybrid' products, practices or even identities. For example, in relation to the global migration of individuals which has led to the 'hybridisation' or 'creolisation' of cultural identities within many nation-states, Bhabha (1990 cited in Smith, 1998: 203) states that the

> great influx of ex-colonials, immigrants ... and asylum seekers has eroded the bases of traditional narratives and images of a homogenous national identity, revealing their fragmented and hybrid character. Today, every collective cultural identity has become plural.

The broad study of globalisation includes debates regarding contemporary European integration or 'Europeanisation'. Although European unification via oppressive domination can be seen in varied forms as early as the age of ancient Empires spanning the fourth century BC to the fifth century AD, and also throughout the Middle Ages via invasions, conquests, crusades and migrations (Roche, 2010: 53), the more recent, non-violent and voluntary development of what is now termed the European Union (EU), began directly after the Second World War. This twentieth-century form of European integration originally began because 'a group of resistance militants belonging to nine European countries met near Geneva and issued a joint declaration emphasising the solidarity uniting the peoples fighting Nazism' (Guibernau, 2011: 3). Guibernau (2011: 3–4) goes on to state that the desire for peace throughout Europe was originally what motivated this group of elites who blamed the political ideology of nationalism

> for the desire of nations to expand their boundaries, dominate other peoples, access and control resources beyond their borders, and ultimately foster chauvinism and the hatred of the different.

Despite differing views of politicians about whether this 'European project' should be regarded as 'intergovernmental' (a body that has power by virtue of agreements between governments) or 'supranational' (a body that can require governments to act in particular ways whether or not they so wish due to majority voting), it is difficult to deny that what constitutes 'Europe' has expanded dramatically over the course of the late twentieth and early twenty-first centuries (Henry, 2003). The goal of uniting European nations politically, economically, socially and culturally has grown significantly with broader globalisation processes and Europe has expanded via various agreements and treaties between an increasing number of 'European' nation-state governments (cf. Chryssochoou, 2001; Guibernau, 2011; Roche, 2010).[3]

The Sociological Perspective of Norbert Elias and National Identity

At this point it is important to state that despite Elias's (cf. 1991; 1996; 2000) clear focus on the link between long-term processes of state-formation, the development of national identity amongst Europeans and the persistence of 'nationalism' within an increasingly global and European age, his work still remains somewhat under-utilised in the diverse academic study of 'nationalism'. According to Delanty and O'Mahony (2002: 69), when considering

> Elias as a theorist of nationalism the most striking factor ... is how little cited he is in the literature on nationalism. Extensive treatment is to be found of the question of how modern is the nation with no reference to a celebrated sociologist whose life's work was dedicated to a line of inquiry that illuminates this question.

For instance, the edited volume titled *The SAGE Handbook of Nations and Nationalism* (Delanty and Kumar, 2006) – arguably the most comprehensive volume on the subject of nationalism to date – contains half a paragraph (Haugaard, 2006: 347–8) that refers to Elias's (2000) *The Civilizing Process*. Elias's vast work is not

---

3   At the time of writing, the amount of individual member states within the European Union is 28 (not including five candidate countries and a further three potential candidates), and 17 member states now share a common currency in the 'Euro' (Europa, 2013).

referred to anywhere else in the entire 45 chapter text. Moreover, although Elias (cf. 1991; 2000) specifically theorised about the development of globalisation and its impact on European nation-states as a long-term process, even recent texts focused on globalisation and Europeanisation often pay scant attention to Elias's contributions to understanding in this area (cf. Kennedy, 2010; Roche, 2010).

So why might this be? Delanty and O'Mahony (2002: 72) argue that Elias may simply be placed 'before his time'. Nevertheless, through focusing on both structure (in terms of European state formation processes) and agency (in terms of the affective impacts of national culture building on citizens within states) Elias

> is the theorist par excellence of the national habitus, a position that insofar as nationalism is increasingly seen as intrinsic to modernity, places his work at the core of the theorisation of modernity itself (Delanty and O'Mahony, 2002: 71).

Elias is neither a modernist nor a traditionalist. Nor is he even a postmodernist. Elias (2000) posits that nation-states are not entirely 'modern', and in fact, state-formation processes extend to a far earlier time than the onset of modernity. According to Elias's (2000) empirical research, modernisation is part of the overall process of state-formation, but it is reductionist to see it as *the only* process within state-formation, often the argument of the 'modernist' paradigm (James, 2006).

In the second volume of *The Civilising Process* Elias (2000) investigated how personality structure and standards of behaviour are linked to the broader structure of society in his enquiry into the 'Sociogenesis of the State'. This is where Elias differs significantly from Marx himself, as well as the other 'modernist' or 'Marxist' theorists alluded to above. Marx saw the rise of nation-states as a particular outgrowth of the modern period and especially of the rise of industrial capitalism, thus viewing it in purely economic terms. Smith (1998: 47) explains that for Marx

> the national state was the necessary terrain for the establishment of market capitalism by the bourgeoisie; only a nationally unified territorial state could ensure the free and peaceful movement of the capital, goods and personnel necessary for large-scale production, market exchange and distribution of mass commodities. The creation of linguistically homogenous nations was therefore a prerequisite of market capitalism, and hence it was inevitable that the further progress of capitalism depended upon the political and cultural development of what Marx called the 'leading nations'.

Unlike Marx, Elias's (2000) discussion of processes of European state-formation neither reduces this process to economics alone, nor does he see the rise of the nation-state idea purely as a consequence of capitalism. Instead Elias posits that such a process is not only more complex than a mere reflection of capitalism, but also that it occurred much earlier than the onset of modernity. Elias (2000) contends that it is more accurate to accept that state-formation, the social division of functions and lengthening of interdependency chains, the growth of towns, trade and money; all intertwine and reinforce one another. Any attempt to separate out one strand as the 'prime cause', or to represent history as a sequence of static 'stages', distorts the essentially processual character of social reality.

The 'monopoly mechanism' is one of three principal elements in Elias's (2000) discussion of state-formation and refers to two intimately related processes: the gradual concentration of the means of violence and taxation into the hands of a single ruler and administration in each territory; and, the enlargement of the territory through competition with and elimination of neighbouring rulers. Another is what Elias terms the 'royal mechanism', which refers to the internal balance of social forces within the developing state. The third of these elements is the transformation from 'private' to 'public' monopolies. These are not successive stages, all intertwine and other strands including the growth of towns, of money economy and trade, of intermediate 'bourgeois' strata, are also tied together within this overall process of development. This relatively blind or unplanned complex set of processes can be traced back as far as the beginning of the European Middle Ages, the end of the Roman Empire, where there were great migrations of people across Europe.

The following extract is from an essay titled 'Changes in the We-I Balance', within *The Society of Individuals*, where Elias (1991: 228–9) explains that at one time

> in the past there were adjustments in all people to suit the integration level of the clan. At other stages in the past tribes were the highest integration units to which the human conscience and feelings were attuned. It is not so long ago that states became the integration units which attracted, if in an ambivalent form, especially strong we-feelings and imposed a relatively high obligation of loyalty and solidarity on all their members. The we-image of human beings has changed; it can change again.[4]

For Elias, individuals and their figurations (collectives of individuals or groups such as: families; clans; tribes; ethnic groups; or, nations/states) complement one another in that they are part and parcel of the same phenomenon, what Elias (1991) called the 'society of individuals'. In short, Elias (1991) contended that the involvement or commitment expressed by the use of the pronoun 'we' is probably usually strongest in relation to family, domicile or native region, but it has also grown to be just as strong in relation to an individual's affiliation to a nation or state.

According to Elias (1978: 128), long-term and largely unplanned processes shape the figurations which link people, groups and institutions interdependently

---

4   'Elias (1991)' is used throughout this book to refer to his third essay titled 'Changes in the We-I Balance' which was originally written in 1987 but was published within *The Society of Individuals* in 1991. This has been done to avoid confusion between this essay and Elias's *Involvement and Detachment,* which was published in 1987.

to one another and this means that the identity of individuals is also impacted. Elias (1991; 2000) considered the fate of European nation-states in the expanding European project in this way. He argued that a central aspect of the development of Europe over the last millennium has been a tendency towards increasingly dense and complex figurations. As Mennell (1994: 178) summarises in relation to this aspect of Elias's work,

> various layers of habitus simultaneously present in people today may be of many different vintages. Strong identification with kinship groups and local communities historically preceded that with state-societies, while at the present day for most people the sense of national or ethnic identity is much stronger ... than any that they feel for supranational groupings, as Europeans for example or simply as citizens of the world. Earlier and later layers of identity may conflict with one another.

Elias (1991: 222) terms this conflict between 'newer' and 'older' planes of identity the 'drag-effect', but expects that incorporation into larger and more complex integration planes will gradually increase over time as

> in the transition from tribe to state, the resistance of tribal traditions rooted in the social habitus of individuals has little chance of enforcing the survival of the independent tribe, the possibility that personality structures may successfully resist the pressure of integration is considerably greater in the transition from nation states to ... post-national units.

Whether nations-states and 'nationalisms' associated with them are invented, selected or imagined, it is clear that they are social constructs that are linked to a quest for identification or belonging (Parekh, 2008). In a case study on the Germans, Elias (1996) referred to 'the national habitus' as a particular form of 'we-group' identification. Elias (1996) noted that the fortunes of a nation become internalised and deeply embodied as part of the second nature or 'habitus' of its citizens. As such, he contends that one of the most potent 'I-We' identities belonging to individual citizens in modern European nation-states like Germany, France and Britain, is that associated with 'their nation'. Elias also recognised that people in contemporary European nation-states have come to develop multi-layered identifications that are simultaneously: 'local'; 'regional'; 'national'; 'European'; and, even 'global'. It is these overlapping affiliations that form the flexible and complex network of the habitus of a person (Elias, 1991). Thus, instead of viewing a person's habitus as fixed and immovable, it is perhaps more appropriate to view habitus as a process that may be subject to change. When speaking of the close relationship between the term *identity* and the notion of *habitus*, Mennell (1994: 177–8) summarises that habitus and identification, being related to group membership, are always – in the modern world where people belong to groups within groups within groups – multi-layered ... In more complex societies there are always many layers, according to the number of interlocking layers in a society that are woven into a person's habitus: one is a Yorkshire-born English European ... the very long-term trend-line in the development of human society has been towards larger and larger networks of interdependent people organized in more and more interlocking layers.

Anderson (1991) and Hobsbawm (1983) have been used by many scholars to suggest that national communities are continually 're-imagined' or 're-invented' in the face of new political developments such as European integration. Although this may be true, few have realised the potential of Elias's contribution to this area. Mennell (1994: 176) states that according to Elias humans have never

been solitary animals: their self-images and we-images have always ... been formed over time within groups of interdependent people, groups that have on the whole steadily increased in size.

Elias (1991: 202) observed as a general trend that 'in the earlier stages [of human existence], the we-I balance first tilted strongly towards the we. In more recent times it has strongly swung towards the I'. Furthermore, in a study on a small community in England, referred to as 'Winston Parva', Elias and Scotson (1994) created the theory of 'established–outsider relations', which can help explain what Elias refers to as the 'we-I balance'. Elias and Scotson (1994: xliii) noted how a

person's we-image and we-ideal form as much a part of a person's self-image and self-ideal as the image and ideal of him- or herself as the unique person to which he or she refers as 'I'.

Thus, wider group identities (such as a nation, class or religion) cannot often be separated from an individual's personal identity, meaning that in the same moment any individual is both an 'I' and a 'we'.

Elias (1991: 209) also contends that powerful as the advance of individualisation has been in recent times due to globalisation processes, 'in relation to the nation-state plane we-habitus has actually strengthened'. This is because people regard themselves as individual representatives of a we-group (an Englishman or Welshwoman for example). In fact, the traits of national group habitus – what we call the 'national character' – are a layer of the social habitus built very deeply and firmly into the personality structure of an individual (Elias, 1991). According to Fletcher (1997: 99), a

major obstacle to the mutual understanding of nations is the obsession of European nations with their own past – at the expense of considerations of their future. This past has given them unusually strong national contrasting 'physiognomies' and deeply ingrained prejudices against each other.

Elias (1991; 2000) urges that the state's role as nation-state, is of relatively recent date and he posits that the emergence of European states happened gradually and in complex stages, not all of which were linear. It is of importance to note that absolutist states such as France at the time of Louis XIV (1643–1715) were ruled autocratically by kings and nobles. England, although never absolutist, was still ruled largely by the monarch with the aid of the upper classes at this time. They alone, as the established group, formed 'the state' and the mass populace were perceived only as a 'they' group and as 'outsiders' (Elias and Scotson, 1994). Even in the late nineteenth and early twentieth centuries, parts of the populace in France – first peasants, then the industrial proletariat – were excluded from the citizens' 'we' group image by the ruling classes – the nobility and the rising bourgeoisie (Elias, 2000).

Thus, these 'outsiders' perceived the state as a 'they' rather than a 'we' group. The more complete integration, or what Elias (2000) terms 'functional democratisation', of all citizens into the state within European multi-party states has really only happened in the course of the twentieth century – only with parliamentary representation of all classes and both genders did all members of the state begin to perceive it more as a 'we-unit' and less as a 'they-group'. 'Democratisation' can be defined as 'the gradual historical tendency towards more equal – though not wholly equal – power balances between different groups and subgroups in society' (Murphy, Sheard and Waddington, 2000: 94). For Elias (2000), this is part of the process of movement from 'private' to 'public' monopolies.

Furthermore, Elias observed that it was only during the course of the two great wars of the twentieth century that the populations of the more developed industrial European states – Britain, Germany and France – took on the character of nation-states in the modern sense of the word. This leads him to suggest that nation-states, 'one might say, are born in and for wars' (Elias, 1991: 208). For Elias this is the reason why, among the various layers of identity, the nation-state level of integration today carries such an emotional charge. The integration plane of the nation-state, more than any other layer, has in the consciousness of most members, the function of a survival unit, a protection unit on which depends their physical and social security in conflict between human groups.

Elias (1991) speaks of power shifts in relation to European states over the second half of the twentieth century and how during and after the Second World War two superpowers emerged in the form of the United States of America (USA) and the (now former) Soviet Union. These pushed smaller European states with more limited military and economic resources, particularly Britain and France, into a second rank position. This was unexpected, yet could have been seen as a probable, if not necessary, accompaniment to the defeat of Hitler. Therefore, in the same way, Elias predicted that in the course of the twenty-first century, a further shift in the balance of power to the disadvantage of individual European states and in favour of other states and groups of states with greater military and economic potential would occur. This is something which has definitely become apparent in the 'rapid economic growth taking place in China, India and other Southern countries with large, expanding populations' (Kennedy, 2010: 5). Essentially, Elias (1991: 232) argued that to speak of

> humanity as the overarching survival unit today is quite realistic. But the habitus of individuals, their identification with limited subgroups of mankind, particularly single states, lags … behind this reality. And discrepancies of this kind are among the most dangerous structural features of the transitional stage at which we now find ourselves.

Globalisation and European integration are therefore processes that must be understood as not simply uni-directional, as neo-Marxist homogenisation arguments contend, but instead they must be regarded as multidirectional. As such, it is far more accurate to conceive of the current challenges to national sovereignty posed by global processes as a necessary condition of both homogenisation and heterogenisation (centripetal and centrifugal processes). Globalisation and Europeanisation both mean there are a growing number of similarities between different national cultures within Europe and world-wide, but at the same time this has simultaneously led to a number of differences. For example, transnational communities now exist and there are a number of 'diasporic' or 'hybrid' identities such as 'Scottish Pakistani' or 'Irish American'. This is an example of what Elias (2000) referred to as 'diminishing contrasts, increasing varieties', a result of the comingling of different cultures throughout the globe. Maguire (1999: 51) summarises Elias's (2000) notion of 'diminishing contrasts, increasing varieties' by stating that the

> dynamics of global interchange are characterized both by tendencies towards a diminishing of contrasts, emulation, equalization and imitation, but also by tendencies towards increasing varieties, differentiation, individuality and distinction.

There are clear similarities between Elias's (2000) concept 'diminishing contrasts, increasing varieties' and the more well-known concept of 'glocalisation' theorised by Robertson (1995). Whilst Maguire (cf. 1993; 1994; 1999) recognised these parallels and sought to develop the sociological study of globalisation in relation to sport by drawing upon ideas from both theorists (as well as others), other authors have been more reluctant to do so. In their text *Globalization & Football*, Giulianotti and Robertson (2009) totally ignore both Elias's (1991; 2000) contributions to the study of globalisation as well as Maguire's numerous studies (cf. 1993; 1994; 1999; 2005; 2011a; 2001b; 2011c; 2011d) which have successfully applied Elias's ideas to understanding the globalisation of sport in a variety of contexts. Potential reasons for this disregard are not clear, but can be

Using Elias to Understand Contemporary English National Identity

As well as providing an excellent framework for the study of national identity in general, Elias's work is fundamental for understanding the specific nuances of contemporary English national identity.

The 'English' Question

As was alluded to in Chapter 1, Englishness has recently been called into question. Evidence of renewed interest in the topic of contemporary English national identity can be found in the large (and increasing) number of books that have been published on the subject. Most prominent of these within the public domain was *The English: A Portrait of a People* written by the BBC journalist Jeremy Paxman (1998). This title alone sold over 300,000 copies in just two years (Bryant, 2006). Such high sales figures suggest a popular demand to understand or establish what actually constitutes contemporary Englishness, and subsequent studies on notions of 'Englishness' or 'the English' from the 1990s onward have used a combination of historical evidence and sociological, political and cultural theory on 'nationalism' to attempt to show, in a multitude of different ways, how the English have come to define themselves (cf. Ackroyd, 2002; Aslet, 1997; Aughey, 2007; Body, 2001; Bond, Jeffery and Rosie, 2010; Bragg, 2007; Bryant, 2003; Byrne, 2007; Chen and Wright, 2000; Colls, 2002; Corbett, Holt and Russell, 2002; Curtice and Heath, 2000; Curtice, 2009; Davey, 1999; Easthope, 1999; Edmunds and Turner, 2001; Giles and Middleton, 1995; Haseler, 1996; Hastings, 1997; Heffer, 1999; Jones, 1998; Kumar, 2000; 2001; 2003; 2006a; 2006b; Langlands, 1999; MacPhee and Poddar, 2007; Mandler, 2006; Mann, 2011; Matless, 1998; McCrone, 2002; 2006; Scruton, 2000; Wadham-Smith and Clift, 2000; Wellings, 2002; Wood, 1999; and, Young, 2008).[5]

The reason for this renewed interest in the topic is that English national identity has recently (over the latter half of the twentieth century) been increasingly called into question by the culmination of a number of interrelated developments highlighting that Englishness has almost exclusively been based on Britishness throughout history (Colley, 1996; Curtice; 2009; Kumar, 2000; 2001; 2003; 2006a; 2006b; McCrone, 2002; 2006). According to Delanty (2006: 357), two key aspects of the present stage of human societal development are

> an apparent rise in nationalism and, on the other side, the increasing impact of global forces ... . Globalization can be seen as creating the conditions for new

---

[5] Even this list is far from comprehensive considering the vast amount of recent interest in understanding contemporary Englishness.

nationalisms, which arise as defensive responses to global forces, or it can be seen as a response by powerful nations to the nationalism of the periphery.

Both of these responses to global forces can be identified within contemporary Britain and have therefore impacted the English. The following processes have all called the English reliance on Britain into question: the devolution of the UK; advancing European integration; and, the declining global power of the British Empire.

Although most historians agree that there has been an 'England' and an 'English' since at least 937 (Colls, 2002: 380), contemporary English national identity became a topic of intense political and cultural debate prior to and following the election of a 'New' Labour government of the United Kingdom of Great Britain and Northern Ireland in 1997 (Bond, Jeffrey and Rosie, 2010). The government quickly imposed constitutional reforms primarily involving limited and varying degrees of political devolution being granted to Northern Ireland following the Good Friday Agreement in 1998, and to Scotland and Wales in 1999 following referendums. The level of devolution granted to these nations meant that a large question mark was drawn over whether the English could claim to have a politically defined 'nationalism' at all because no such power was devolved to England as a whole or to regions within its borders (O'Neill, 2004). Regional identity was claimed to be so strong in north east England that it had the potential to lead to an elected regional assembly with partially devolved political powers, similar to those afforded to Scotland and Wales. This was emphatically rejected in a 2004 referendum, with almost 80% of the North East public voting against the idea (BBC News, 2004; Curtice, 2009; Willett and Giovanni, 2013).

Cornwall is another English region with a very strong sense of regional identity (some even say a national identity of its own), where many are campaigning for a degree of political devolution (Curnow, 2006; Willett and Giovanni, 2013). Cornwall has only been integrated into England from around the fifteenth century (Hechter, 1975), therefore culturally Cornwall is a Celtic nation with its own language (a form of Bretonic, similar to that spoken in Brittany, France); its own history; its own 'national' flag (a black background with a white cross); and, its own culture (Payton, 2002). According to Laviolette (2003: 218), many of

> Cornwall's claims to social difference are grounded in various elements of landscape and material culture. These relate for instance to food stuffs, religion, sport, Celtic imagery and ritual, industrial and seafaring traditions as well as to an affiliation with significant art and literature influences. ... Many perceptions thus clash as to whether Cornwall exists as a land apart or as a quintessentially British periphery.

Referenda have often been mooted for Cornwall, but these have not yet come to fruition. It seems then that there is deemed to be no requirement for, or perceived benefits to, devolved governments of the English regions or even a national English government amongst the mainstream majority of the English population, even amongst Conservatives. O'Neill (2004) suggests this is largely due to fears over the further fragmentation of Britain as well problems associated with having a further tier of government bureaucracy. This means it is harder for the English to establish or even claim anything like the level of autonomous political 'national' power that Scotland and Wales now have (McCrone, 2002; 2006).

Developments in European integration or Europeanisation mean that many citizens of 'regions' or 'nations' that claim to be 'submerged' within nation-states that form part of the European Union (EU), now feel the need to reassert their distinctive 'national' identities in order to feel recognised within an expanding Europe (Delanty, 2006; Guibernau, 2011). Scotland is an example of one of these 'submerged' nations. Although Scotland was united with England to create the United Kingdom of Great Britain as a result of the 1707 Act of Union (Colls; 2002; Kumar, 2003), post-devolution Scots (and not only Scottish Nationalists) often prefer to assert a specifically Scottish (rather than British) identity in interactions with other Europeans according to research by Grundy and Jamieson (2007). The level of devolved political power gained by Scotland, and to a lesser extent Wales (Northern Ireland being more complicated), was arguably the result of the desire of 'Nationalist' politicians, particularly the Scottish National Party (SNP), and many of the voting population to be recognised as European nations, marking their heightened level of distinction from the traditionally more powerful oppressors within the UK, England (Bryant, 2003; 2006; Kumar, 2001; McCrone, 2002; 2006; O'Neill, 2004). As a further development to the devolution of the late 1990s, there will be a Scottish independence referendum from the UK on 18 September 2014 (BBC News, 2013).

Despite devolution and European integration, one must remember that 'British' has always been a multifaceted concept. According to Bryant (2006: 24), 'British'

> has always been a composite identity and it has long proved possible to extend it to cover citizens of other origins, from refugees in Victorian times to 'coloured' immigrants from the former Empire in the 1950s and 1960s. What one has in Britain is a civic nation that has proved capable of accommodating a large amount of difference.

The ending of the significance of the British Empire overseas presents another major challenge to contemporary Englishness. The beginning of the end of the British Empire began at its height in 1921 (when almost a quarter of the world's population was under some degree of British Imperial rule) with Ireland gaining de facto independence over its 26 southern counties and formally becoming the Irish Free State in 1922. This was followed in 1947 by the loss of the 'Jewel in the Crown' (India) and the majority of the African nations throughout the 1960s (Hobsbawm, 1995). Finally, the presence of British rule overseas eventually came to an end with power over Hong-Kong being passed to The People's Republic of China (PRC) in 1997.[6]

---

6   Britain does still hold degrees of sovereignty over three 'Crown Dependencies' including: Jersey, Guernsey and the Isle of Man, as well as over some fourteen 'Overseas

With the decline of the British Empire came an increase in immigration, particularly following the end of the Second World War. Immigration is more complex in England compared to Scotland and Wales considering England is the largest nation within Britain. A database was produced by BBC News (2009) from a report on immigration published by the Institute for Public Policy Research (IPPR) largely based on data for the 2001 UK census which shows that the percentages of people born abroad living in eight of the nine regions of England are all higher than those living in Scotland and Wales (figures for Northern Ireland were not included). When compared with immigration figures on Scotland (3.32%), the north east is the only region within England with a lower percentage of people born abroad (2.67%). However, even the north east of England has a slightly higher percentage of people born abroad than Wales (2.66%).

As a response to increasing immigration since 1945 that led to a greater number of ethnic minorities existing in England compared to the other 'home nations', some have felt the urge to (re)invent and (re)assert a specifically English identity. However, unfortunately this response has often been related to issues of 'race' and ethnicity associated with Britain's far right organisations such as the BNP, National Front and most recently the EDL who champion racist politics and an ethnically exclusive white Englishness (see Trilling's, 2013 book on the rise of Britain's far right for more on this).

Elias and Englishness

So what can Elias add to the study of contemporary English national identity? Using Elias (1991) it is possible to see that Englishness is multi-layered and in a current state of flux due to the move of the British nation-state unit towards the larger integration unit of the European Union, itself an aspect of wider globalisation processes. This is compounded by the related processes of devolution that have recently occurred within the UK. Rather than declining in importance along with the decline of the British Empire, English national identity can be more accurately described as going through a process of re-invention or flux.

Bryant (2006) states that the British state is becoming increasingly dissociated from the nations that make it up, and could now even be regarded as a fifth nation after England, Scotland, Wales and Northern Ireland. This is the problem with understanding contemporary national identity formations within the UK; has there actually been a strengthening of 'we' image in the UK? Drawing upon

---

Territories' including: Anguilla; Bermuda; British Antarctic Territory; British Indian Ocean Territory; British Virgin Islands; Cayman Islands; Falklands Islands; Gibraltar; Montserrat; Pitcairn Islands; Saint Helena (including Ascension, Tristan da Cunha); South Georgia and the South Sandwich Islands; Sovereign Base Areas of Akrotiri and Dhekelia; and, Turks and Caicos Islands. Former British Colonies now form part of a voluntary association of 53 independent sovereign states known as the Commonwealth of Nations. Mozambique is the only nation within the Commonwealth that was not a former British Colony.

two papers delivered by Elias in lectures to German audiences in 1959 (Elias, 2008a) and 1960 (Elias 2008b) respectively,[7] Fletcher (1997: 105) criticises the 'outsider perspective' of English social habitus painted by Elias for being 'quite stereotypical and idealistic' even for the time it was written. Fletcher (1997: 105–6) states that Elias

> often, but not always, conflates the national boundaries of England, Scotland and Wales when referring to 'England'. This effectively downplays the tensions between the various regions and over-emphasizes their harmonious relations, despite Elias's disclaimers that such tensions are exaggerated by natives to these areas. He also seems to neglect the differences between Welsh, Scottish, Northern Irish and English national identities, as well as the extent to which the we-images of these other countries are constituted in relation to English hegemony ... Nor does he [Elias] comment on the so-called North-South Divide which cuts an economic and cultural swathe through the middle of England.

It must be stated here that Elias, like many, is guilty of using the terms 'British' and 'English' interchangeably,[8] and although Elias clearly knew the difference between England and Britain (see Elias, 2008a: 216 for an example to qualify this), it is clear to see that he was downplaying the divisions between England, Wales, Scotland and Northern Ireland and never really mentioned the north-south divide at all. Instead he preferred to overplay what he terms 'the extraordinarily strong integration of the British people' in comparisons with other European countries (Elias, 2008a: 219). Therefore, Fletcher is correct in criticising Elias for not going into enough detail on the nuances underlying *Englishness* specifically, and this is something that is developed in the current book.

However, the fact that Elias did not specifically deal with the intricacies of English national identity is not a satisfactory basis upon which to disregard his theoretical approach when considering contemporary English 'anxieties' (Aughey, 2007). Elias (1991) recognised that the function of the effective survival unit is now visibly shifting more and more from the level of nation-states to the 'post-national' unions of states such as Europe and beyond them to global humanity (cf. Appadurai, 1994; 1996), when he stated that 'nation state units have in reality already relinquished their function as guarantors of the physical security of their citizens, and thus as survival units, to supra-state units' (Elias, 1991: 218). Elias argues that the social dynamic is either opposed by being slowed or blocked due to people clinging to their identity from an earlier stage of social development, labelling this tendency 'the drag-effect'. If one applies these ideas to UK devolution, there is also a further point to the drag-effect which is the reversion

---

7   Elias (2008a) and Elias (2008b) are the first English translations of these lectures which were originally only published in German.

8   This is a point made by the editors Kilminster and Mennell, in their notes on the translation of the text of the two lectures under discussion here (see Elias, 2008: xix).

of British people to an association with the nation (the smaller unit) rather than the state (the larger unit). Thus, the re-articulation of Welshness and Scottishness, for instance, is a different kind of collective response to European integration and devolution as it occurs in the same direction to that of Elias's drag-effect, just further or deeper. This is also evidence for what Elias (2000) termed 'increasing varieties' because UK devolution itself is a direct response to the 'diminishing of contrasts' between the nation-states of Europe, both politically and culturally.

Elias (1991) devised several long-term eventualities for European nation-states that he argued could occur as responses to further integrative forces. All of these, to a greater or lesser extent, have occurred or are now beginning to happen: to build a closer union with and greater dependence on the USA; to gradually increase the union of European member states in the form of a multi-lingual federation of states or a federal state; and a continued existence of European states more or less in their traditional form, as nation states, each of which is nominally independent and sovereign. It is the latter of these which Elias contends best matches the social habitus of the people belonging to them and is a reason for the drag-effect that is currently occurring. Moreover, Elias asserts that states such as the UK have developed continuously as relatively autonomous organisational units over several centuries (partly due to its island situation meaning citizens did not have to constantly defend its borders, as was the case in other states within continental Europe), and in the past century in particular there has been a strong advance of 'functional democratisation', integrating practically all classes into the state structure (Elias, 2000).

These developments have brought about a deep-rooted predisposition of the individual personality structures of people of all classes to live together in this specific form. Yet in the UK, a number of citizens prefer not to regard themselves as British but as English, Scottish or Welsh (Northern Irish being more complicated for the reasons discussed earlier in this chapter). Common language, a long history and cultural traditions binds individuals strongly to their nation in its traditional form instead of, or as well as, to their state (Curtice, 2009). The bond to the UK state is also challenged (or at least pluralised) by the competing national identities of the four home nations. This cultural bond is comparatively weak, or non-existent, in relation to the preliminary forms of the European state federation (Guibernau, 2011), and the preference for nation over state within the UK is a further extension of this.

Part of the importance of the 'we-habitus' within a survival group such as a nation is beyond actual physical existence. It is survival in the memory of the chain of generations. This is a point Anderson (1991) also makes in relation to how nations are 'imagined communities'. Elias (1991: 224) states that the

> continuity of a survival group, which finds expression in the continuity of its language, the passing down of legends, history, music and many other cultural values, is itself one of the survival functions of such a group.

Resistance to merging of one's own survival unit with a larger unit, or its disappearance into that unit, is undoubtedly due in large part to the feeling that the fading or disappearance of a state as an autonomous entity would render meaningless everything which past generations had achieved and suffered in the name of this survival unit (Elias, 1991). This points to the importance of national identity to individuals and perhaps to the resurgence of English national identity over British in the face of globalisation and European integration processes – an extension of the drag-effect and an example of the kind of heterogeneity paradoxically made possible by these seemingly homogenising processes. It has been easier for the English to identify with the nation-state (Britain) because they have always been the dominant nation or group within it (Kumar, 2003). Up until recent developments in UK devolution it was easy for the English and many non-British observers to forget the 'Celtic fringes' evident in the UK and to see Englishness and Britishness as more or less synonymous terms (Colley, 1996; Colls, 2002; Groom, 2006; Kumar, 2003).

It is becoming ever more apparent that the 'centripetal' and 'centrifugal' forces which Elias (2000) contemplated have both now simultaneously increased significantly leading to a diminishing of contrasts between individuals in Europe but paradoxically an increasing of varieties in terms of expressions of national sentiment within the UK. As Curtice (2009: 2) points out, 'the emotional glue that previously has helped to keep the United Kingdom together might begin to come unstuck in the wake of Scottish and Welsh devolution'. Pooling together the results of a number of different surveys on how British individuals described their identities in 1992, 1997, 1999, 2001 and 2003, Bryant (2006: 5–6) contends that when the peoples of

> England, Scotland, and Wales are asked to specify their national identity there are clear differences in the claims each makes with respect to Britishness or lack thereof … . In sum, England, Scotland and Wales have different national profiles. Devolution has been accompanied by a weakening of Britishness and a strengthening of Scottishness, Welshness, and Englishness, but … there remains majority acknowledgement of Britishness to some degree.

Whereas for the Scottish and Welsh, Britain no longer offers anything attractive economically or culturally post-Empire, many white English people (particularly older generations) cannot disassociate themselves from Britishness as it has become synonymous with Englishness (cf. Colley, 1996; Curtice, 2009; Kumar, 2003; 2006a; 2006b). Bryant rightly mentions that disassociation from Britain is also problematic for many British Asians and Black Britons who are more likely to use the term 'British' to define their identity because they owe much to the British Empire and post-war immigration into Britain in one way or another and cannot simply swap British for English, Scottish or Welsh identities in the same way many white Scots and Welsh have. Although here Bryant fails to recognise that British Asians and Black Britons are far from homogenous groups and do not only live in England and newer generations have much more complex diasporic identities (cf. Burdsey, 2006). Bryant (2006) also urges that there are more truly British families who are a mixture of English, Scottish, Welsh and/or Irish descent in England than elsewhere in the UK, who also have a reason to think of themselves as just as British as anyone else. Disassociation may also be difficult for Ulster unionists who have to identify with Britain, even if it is a Protestant Britain of the past.

Curtice (2009: 5), citing evidence from *British Social Attitudes Surveys* between 1997 and 2007, stated that the proportion of people in England stating that they are 'English, not British' has been consistently higher since 1999 than it was in 1997, 'suggesting that a sense of Englishness did awaken in some people in the immediate wake of the creation of devolved institutions in Scotland and Wales'. However, feelings of Britishness and support for the Union have *not* completely disappeared alongside this apparent rise in Englishness and the evidence suggests that an 'apparent initial trend in 1999 towards feeling more English and less British has not been sustained' (Curtice, 2009: 19). Curtice (2009: 7) also states that the proportion of English respondents who stated they are 'very proud' of their region has remained at one in four since 2001 and there is therefore 'clearly little evidence of an increase in attachment to the English regions since Scottish and Welsh devolution has been in place'.

However, in the summer of 2011 the IPPR conducted the first Future of England (FoE) survey which they claim was 'one of the most comprehensive examinations of English attitudes to questions of identity, nationhood and governance to date' (Wyn Jones, Lodge, Henderson and Wincott, 2012: 2). Among other aspects, the findings indicated that

> there is evidence to suggest that we are witnessing the emergence in recent decades of a different kind of Anglo-British identity, in which the English component is increasingly considered the primary source of attachment for the English. (Wyn Jones, et al., 2012: 3)

And that there is

> strong evidence that English identity is becoming politicised: that is, the more strongly English a person feels the more likely they are to believe that the current structure of the post-devolution UK is unfair and the more likely they are to support the development of an English dimension to the governance of England. (Wyn Jones, et al., 2012: 3)

This initial FoE survey was quickly followed up with a second survey conducted in November 2012 (Wyn Jones, Lodge, Jeffery, Gottfried, Scully, Henderson and Wincott, 2013). Part of the reason for the second survey was that 'summer 2012 saw Britishness well and truly to the fore during both the Queen's diamond jubilee celebrations and the London Olympic and Paralympic Games' (Wyn Jones, et al., 2013). Nevertheless, the findings of the second study supported those of the initial survey. As well as demonstrating a persistence of feelings of discontentment among the English regarding England's position within the post-devolution UK, in addition, the 2012 survey findings demonstrated that this is 'closely linked with hostility towards England's other union, the EU. Among the English, devo-anxiety and Euroscepticism are two sides of the same coin' (Wyn Jones, et al., 2013: 32).

Such findings are a response to some of the many unintended social dynamics that have altered British-English citizens' social reality from the end of the Second World War to the present day – namely European integration, devolution and decline of Empire (and associated immigration) – which have caused a loss in sovereignty and a further fragmentation or confusion of national identity (Paxman, 1999; Colley, 1996). There has been a noticeable transfer from solely using the term England to refer to Britain (the larger group) – towards distinguishing England from the other home nations and even from Britain itself – a movement further to what Elias (1991) termed the drag-effect and an example of the diversification of cultural identifications made possible by the diminishing of contrasts between nations (Elias, 2000).

A Critique and Counter Critique of Elias's Sociological Approach

Now that the relevance of Elias's ideas have been explained in relation to: understanding the development of national identity and habitus amongst Europeans; the persistence of nationalism within in an increasingly global and European age; and, for understanding the fragility of contemporary English national identity specifically, it is now necessary to highlight prominent criticisms of Elias's distinctive approach. This might help explain the relative absence of Elias in comparison to other social theorists whose work is more prominently utilised in these areas of study. This final section of the current chapter is focused upon summarising the main critiques of Elias's sociological approach whilst providing counter-critiques to further justify the use of Elias in this book.

As is the case for any social theorist, Elias's work has been interpreted in many different ways and it has certainly not been immune from criticism. Dunne (2009: 31) goes as far as suggesting that Elias's approach has previously engendered a 'somewhat hesitant or hostile' reaction from many in the sociological mainstream. According to van Krieken (1998: 74, emphasis in original), the reasons for this reluctance to accept Elias can be related to the following four major critiques of his general sociological approach:

1. the question of the *distinctiveness* of Elias's perspective;
2. his treatment of human *agency*;
3. his emphasis on historical *continuity* at the expense of discontinuity; and,
4. his understanding of the *politics of knowledge*.

First, regarding the claim that Elias's perspective lacks distinctiveness, Giulianotti (2004: 155, emphasis in original) states that Elias

> displays a lack of critical reflexivity through his minimal referencing of sociologists and other scholars who clearly influenced his thinking and terminology (most obviously Weber, Durkheim and Parsons). In downplaying these interdependencies, Elias provides us with a paradoxically individualistic and *homo clausus* self-portrait.

At first glance this appears to be a fair criticism. It is true to say that Elias does not often go into depth about other theorists who have shared similar ideas to him and this could potentially hinder theoretical debate. Indeed, van Krieken (1998: 76, emphasis in original) summarises that

> *nothing* in Elias's approach cannot be found in some other school of sociological or psychological thought. Certainly we should reject Elias's self-portrayal as the sole, lonely representative of particular ideas, and his refusal explicitly to acknowledge any alliance with other sociological theorists. His preference for radically *transcending* current sociological debates over *participating* in them tends to discourage theoretical debate, and there is a distinct aggressiveness in his attitude to other theoretical positions.

This criticism has also been levelled at Dunning and other figurational sociologists in light of their sometimes 'hostile' responses to criticisms from others (cf. Collins, 2006; Curry, Dunning, and Sheard, 2006). Yet, although Elias might be guilty of not explicitly discussing the work of the founding fathers of sociology – Marx, Durkheim, Weber and Parsons – each of these theorists are mentioned to varying degrees in aspects of Elias's work and so are many other theorists. This is the case in *What is Sociology?* (1978: 37) for instance, where in addition to mentioning Marx, Weber, Durkheim and Parsons, Elias also explains how influential the nineteenth century philosopher Auguste Comte was to the establishment of the 'science of society' or 'sociology'.

The real distinctiveness of Elias's perspective is not to be found in the difference of his ideas to those of his predecessors, but it is in the way he has synthesised their work to develop new theories, the best example being *The Civilizing Process* (2000), to which all the ideas evident in his vast works are quite clearly related. According to Smith (2001: 15), 'Marx, Durkheim and Weber all borrowed from others and they have all in turn been pillaged to good effect'. The case is no different when one looks at Elias's work so this is not a satisfactory reason to shun his sociological approach.

This perceived failure to explicitly engage with what are considered, 'the "holy trinity" of Marx, Weber and Durkheim', is perhaps a reason why Elias's work has until relatively recently been largely absent from 'mainstream' sociology (Shilling, 2011: 2), including the study of nationalism. Although it must be said that, more recently, Elias's process sociological paradigm has become more prominent within some of the more comprehensive introductory sociology textbooks (cf. Inglis and Thorpe, 2012), Giulianotti (2004: 154) was correct when he stated that 'Elias makes few impressions in textbooks and compendia for modern social theory courses'. However, Giulianotti (2004) is very much mistaken when one goes beyond looking at introductory sociology texts. Smith (2001: 13) clarifies that, 'Elias finally became fashionable during the 1990s', and he draws upon data from the *Social Sciences Citation Index (SSCI)* to show that the number of publications using Elias's work as a central theme has been on the rise. Whilst Elias was not used as much as Giddens and Bourdieu in work cited in the late 1990s, he was used more than both Parsons and Bauman according to Smith (2001).

Although admittedly a little outdated, Smith's *Norbert Elias & Modern Social Theory* (2001: 4) effectively shows that Elias's 'interests overlap to a high degree' with those of other modern social theorists including: Arendt; Bauman; Foucault; and, Parsons. Smith (2001: 5) specifies that there has been some dialogue between Elias and Bauman; and, Elias and Foucault, and that Elias dismissed Arendt's work and repeatedly attacked Parson's structural functionalist perspective, despite the latter two theorists ignoring Elias completely. Surely this is evidence that Elias actually *did* engage in theoretical debates and was not some kind of 'lonely maverick' on the fringes of sociology (van Krieken, 1998: 76). Whilst Bauman's work has since become much more popular in the first decade of the twenty-first century, largely due to Bauman's own diligence in producing new work, one must consider whether Elias's popularity would have grown even further had he not died in 1990 just as his work was becoming more 'fashionable'. Elias's death could also explain why there is not further evidence of him engaging in theoretical debates with his contemporaries. If he had lived past the 1990s and into the twenty-first century, it is very likely Elias himself, and the plethora of figurational sociologists whom he influenced, would have pushed his distinctive approach further towards the centre of sociology before now.

More recently there has been further evidence of Elias's growing significance within the sociological mainstream. Dunne (2009: 30) suggests that figurational sociology is currently 'being pushed further and further towards centre stage of the English speaking sociological world'. Even more recently, in 2011, figurational sociology was the sole topic of a monograph series of the well-established academic journal *The Sociological Review* titled, 'Norbert Elias and Figurational Research: Processual Thinking in Sociology'. Here Shilling (2011: 2), has little hesitation in stressing that

> Elias's legacy continues to stimulate a thriving programme of empirical work that introduces previously neglected processual perspectives into the study of a huge range of issues and subjects in the social science, arts and humanities.

Dunne (2009: 32) argues that too often, 'the idea that there is an Eliasian "sect" gets in the way of the ideas themselves, thereby blocking sympathetic and systematic access to them'. This certainly seems to be the task Giulianotti (2004) sets out to achieve. As such, Dunne advocates a greater focus on the sociology of Elias *itself* and it is to some criticisms of the figurational approach that the discussion now turns.

Whilst the first of van Krieken's (1998) main criticisms of Elias's general sociological approach was not really related to Elias's sociology at all, the second sort of criticism definitely is. Van Krieken (1998: 78) states that by focusing on the, 'unplanned and "blind" character of social development', Elias is often criticised for ignoring the potential of human agency. In later work, van Krieken (2003: 121) suggests that Elias has been criticised for 'neglecting the organized interventions of powerful social groups into the form and direction of civilizing processes'. In fact, Elias never said human actions were not important. He simply clarified that it is *more* important to consider individual actions within their specific social contexts and that collective actions, rather than individual ones, have usually been those that propel societal processes in one direction or another (Elias, 1978; 2000). Mennell (1992) clarifies that Elias argued that individuals and societies are two different dimensions of the *same* process of societal development. Moreover, *The Society of Individuals* (Elias, 1991) comprises three long sole-authored essays all focused on the nature of the interdependent relationship between societal structures and individual actions. Each essay was written at different points in Elias's career (1939; 1940–50; and 1987 respectively), clearing showing that the importance of human agency, how the agent relates to the plurality of people, and vice-versa, was considered to be a topic he considered worthy of his attention.

To say that Elias ignores human agency, is to fundamentally misinterpret his sociological approach. Essentially, Elias considered individuals and societies as inseparable. He was critical of both Durkheim and Parsons for tending to over-stress the importance of the structure of society in determining human actions. Even though the intention of Parsons's (1949) *The Structure of Social Action* was to provide a more balanced view on the relationship between society and the individual, Elias (1978) suggested Parsons was unsuccessful as he still over-emphasised the power of 'social systems'. Elias begins *What is Sociology* (1978) by addressing head-on the 'structure versus agency' debate that has dominated sociology and in some respects continues to this day, despite the advent of post-dualist, post-modern or post-structuralist claims (Smith, 2001).[9] Elias positions his sociological approach as sitting between 'structure' and 'agency' or what he prefers to term 'society' and the 'individual'. Elias (1978: 13) regarded both society and the individual as one and the same thing because society, 'often placed in mental contraposition to the individual, consists entirely of individuals, oneself among them'.

Elias (1978) argued that dominant forms of thinking have emerged since the late nineteenth century – including that provided by key social theorists such as Marx, Durkheim, Weber and Parsons – that often regards everything external to

---

9   Elsewhere Elias (1987: 29–31) also discusses the structure/agency debate, although it is within the context of his broader argument on involvement and detachment.

individuals as 'things' or 'objects', which are 'static' and 'unchanging'. Thus a term such as 'society' has been considered in the same way as inanimate objects like trees or rocks (Elias, 1978: 13). Such reifying ways of speaking or thinking are unhelpful for understanding the nature of sociological problems according to Elias. Instead he contends that concepts like society, family or school refer to groupings of individuals who have formed interdependent relationships with one another. In *The Civilizing Process*, Elias (2000) demonstrated that specific examples of human actions at particular points in history could be related to one another and that this was intimately related to the broader ways in which European societies were changing. Van Krieken effectively summarises that Elias does not disregard or ignore human choice or free will, but

> Elias's position concerning agency is simply one about the 'logic of collective action', about the real effects those choices and evaluations actually have once they enter social life, especially while human groups continue to compete with each other. It is the dynamics of *competition, conflict* and *interweaving* which constitutes the 'blindness' of social development and restricts the effectivity of human agency (Van Krieken, 1998: 80, emphasis in original).

Elias's approach has similarities with that of other sociological thinkers whose work became popular in the late twentieth century, specifically Bourdieu (cf. 1977; 1984) and Giddens (cf. 1984). All three theorists are interested in overcoming the 'structure' versus 'agency' debate and they each contend – albeit in slightly different ways – that neither the abstract structure of society, nor specific social actions of individuals exist independently of one another. All three argue that both structure and action are intimately related and dynamic (rather than static) in nature. Some of these affinities are explored further in Chapter 7.

The third main criticism of Elias's perspective is related to the second. It has been claimed that Elias has focused on long-term developments at the expense of 'attending to the particular discontinuities and breaks in long-term trends' (van Krieken, 1998: 80). Whilst this criticism is justified in that Elias *does* tend to consider instances of discontinuity in broad social processes as somewhat *less* significant than longer-term trends, it was not his intention to completely disregard or hide what Bourdieu and Wacquant (1992 cited in van Krieken, 1998: 80) referred to as 'critical breaks' or 'fundamental ruptures'. Whereas the post-structuralist Foucault (1974) spoke of different 'epistemes' or knowledge-systems which replace one another at different eras or epochs in history, in his essays on the sociology of knowledge and the sciences, it is clear that Elias's more processual position conceived of civilising and decivilising 'spurts' or 'shifts' as being essential aspects of long-term processes of social development (cf. Kilminster and Mennell, 2009).

Despite what some authors such as Giulianotti (2004: 155) have contended about Elias simply ignoring instances of *de-civilised* behaviour because they did not 'fit' within the civilising process, Elias (2000: 157) explicitly states that the 'civilising process does not follow a straight line', and he goes on to state that on a smaller scale there are 'diverse criss-cross movements, shifts and spurts in this or that direction'. From closer reading of Elias's later works (cf. 1991; 1996) it is also clear to see that he was quite often concerned with *decivilising* counter-trends and *centrifugal* or dis-integrating forces rather than *centripetal* or integrating forces at work in society. Elias's (1991) notion of the 'drag-effect' with his essay 'Changes in the We-I balance' is a clear example of this. Mennell (1990: 205) demonstrates the theoretical significance of Elias's concept of decivilising processes and highlights their potential for explaining real historical examples of 'what happens when civilising processes go into reverse', including the Holocaust, in which Elias's own family were torn apart, as well as the collapse of the Roman Empire, the Thirty Years War and the 'Wild West'. The concept of decivilising processes is discussed further in Chapter 7.

The fourth and final criticism highlighted by van Krieken (1998: 81) relates to Elias's understanding of 'the politics of social scientific knowledge as well as the practicalities of sociological research'. For Elias (1987: 3–4),

> the very existence of ordered group life depends on the interplay in people's thoughts and actions of impulses in both directions, those that involve and those that detach keeping each other in check ... it is the relation between the two which sets people's courses.

Elias (1987) argued that the ongoing debate in the natural and social sciences between 'subjectivity' and 'objectivity' had created what he termed a 'false dichotomy'. Although he used similar terms – 'involvement' relating to subjectivity and 'detachment' relating to objectivity – Elias (1987: 4) argued that the connection between the two poles was a continuum rather than an absolute, mutually exclusive or zero-sum relationship because as

> tools of thinking ... 'involvement' and 'detachment' would remain highly ineffectual if they were understood to adumbrate a sharp division between two independent sets of phenomena.

This depends of course on the object/subject in question, the prior experiences of the individual with them and the publically accepted ways of thinking/acting around them in a society. This is highly related to what Elias (2000) argues in *The Civilizing Process* – the ability to reflect on one's own thought-processes via the long-term development of a gap between impulse to act and the act itself is something that can be observed only at more recent stages of human social development within Western societies. This contrasts with the instinctive emotional reactions that characterised the majority of the behaviour of similar individuals living in the Middle Ages, although that is not to say that acting on impulse does not still characterise some human behaviours today (Elias, 1987; 2000).

When considering this in relation to the discipline of sociology, in *Involvement and Detachment* Elias (1987) was essentially concerned with how to achieve 'valid' knowledge about society whilst investigating it from within (Kilminster, 2004). Elias (1987: 12) illuminates this through discussing the similarities, but more importantly, the differences, between the natural and social sciences, stating that the

> general aim of scientific pursuits is the same in both fields ... it is to find out in what way perceived data are connected with each other. But social as distinct from natural sciences are concerned with conjunctions of persons ... . The task of social scientists is to explore, and to make people understand, the patterns they form together, the nature and the changing configuration of all that binds them to each other. The investigators themselves form part of these patterns. They cannot help experiencing them, directly or by identification, as immediate participants from within; and the greater the strains and stresses to which they or their groups are exposed, the more difficult is it for them to perform the mental operation, underlying all scientific pursuits, of detaching themselves from their role as immediate participants and from the limited vista it offers.

Elias (1987: 48) goes on to clarify his ideas on the 'double-bind' or the 'circularity' of the relationship between involvement and detachment by discussing an illustration from Edgar Alan Poe's 'Fisherman in the Maelstrom'. To summarise, the story describes two fishermen brothers caught in the midst of a storm (maelstrom) at sea. The storm had created a whirlpool and the wreckage as well as the brothers were being swirled around its edges. Whilst the elder of the brothers was paralysed by fear and remained cowering in the boat, the younger brother managed to control his fear and began to think not about his impending doom, but about the movement of the pieces of the wreckage being swirled around with the boat. Elias (1987: 45–6) unveils the rest of the parable most succinctly in the following way:

> In short, while observing and reflecting, he had an 'idea'; a connecting picture of the process in which he was involved, a 'theory', began forming in his mind. Looking around and thinking with sharpened attention, he came to the conclusion that cylindrical objects went down more slowly than objects of any other shape, and that smaller objects sank more slowly than larger ones. On the basis of this synoptic picture of the regularities in the process in which he was involved, and recognizing their relevance to his own situation, he made the appropriate move. While his brother remained immobilized by fear, he latched himself to a cask. Vainly encouraging the older man to do the same, he leapt overboard. While the boat, with his brother still in it, descended more rapidly and was, in the end, swallowed by the abyss, the cask to which he had tied himself sank very slowly, so that gradually, as the slope of the funnel's sides became less steep and the water's gyration less violent, he found himself again at the surface of the ocean and eventually returned to the living.

So, it was only through standing back from the situation and making efforts towards detaching himself from his own involvement in it, that the younger brother was able to create an effective strategy for survival. Although the above story illustrates the way human thinking has developed to deal with naturally occurring phenomena, it can also help one understand how social scientists should deal with the socially constructed subjects of their investigations according to Elias. Elias (1987: 6) urges social scientists to make what he terms a 'detour via detachment'. That is, first to recognise that absolute objectivity is impossible in the study of human interactions because the researcher is *always* involved to some extent in the subject of their studies because they

> cannot cease to take part in, and to be affected by, the social and political affairs of their time ... in order to understand the functioning of human groups one needs to know, as it were, from inside how human beings experience their own and other groups, and one cannot know without active participation and involvement (Elias, 1987: 16).

Yet, secondly, Elias encourages social scientists to strive to be as detached as possible from their subjects of study in order to find adequate answers to their research problems or questions, as far as possible avoiding having their vision clouded by their own inevitable involvement. This is by no means a simple task and Elias spends a great deal of time deliberating on the complexities of taking such a detour via detachment, before eventually conceding that the best social scientists can do is to work on a hypothetical continuum where

> one marginal pole is formed by properties of persons and their situation characteristic of complete involvement and complete lack of detachment (such as one might find in the case of young babies), and the other of properties characteristic of complete detachment and a zero-point of involvement (Elias, 1987: 33).

Elias's (1987) call for sociologists to take a 'detour via detachment' is problematic because what Elias (1978) terms social 'myths' are the product of power relations and claims to be able to look at sociological issues in a detached manner are considered by many sociologists to be fictional: '*social science necessarily takes sides in political struggles*' according to Bourdieu (Bourdieu and Wacquant, 1992 cited in van Krieken, 1998: 81, emphasis in original). Similarly, in regarding 'detachment' as a way of controlling social situations, Arnason (1987: 450 cited in Dunne, 2009: 48) contends that 'the concept of control is not culturally neutral'. What Arnason means is that no sociologist can ever be completely 'value-free'. Dunne (2009: 51) points to the need for figurational sociologists to 'have to engage with moral and political questions if they hope to implement moral and political controls'.

Within the sociology of sport, Elias's approach has also been hotly debated. As one of the few modern social theorists (other than Bourdieu) to consider sport as an important social practice (cf. Guttmann, 2000: 248), Elias, and the figurational sociologists whom he influenced, have been subjected to criticism from many sport sociologists who prefer to rely upon the 'classic' sociology of Marx, Weber and Durkheim (cf. Giulianotti, 2004). Criticisms from within the sociology of sport therefore largely follow those discussed in each of the four areas above. However, there have also been some more specific critiques. For instance, the figurational study of football hooliganism has perhaps been subjected to most scrutiny considering this topic was what 'The Leicester School' (a group of figurational sociologists inspired by Elias himself) became most well-renowned for studying (Bairner, 2006). The figurational approach has also been criticised by historians of sport such as Collins (2006) who claimed that in theorising about the historical development of a number of modern sports, sociologists of 'The Leicester School' were simply trying to make history 'fit' into the theory of the civilising process. This stimulated a swift riposte from figurational sociologists Curry, Dunning and Sheard (2006). Although the specificities of all of these critiques are outside the scope of this book, they are mentioned in Liston's (2011) comprehensive exploration of the contributions of figurational sociology to the study of sport and leisure.

Now that the Eliasian sociological approach has been related to understanding contemporary English national identity, in the next chapter recent challenges to English football fan culture are discussed in more detail and further justification is provided for analysing the actions and opinions of English football fans in 'new' figurations.

Chapter 3

The Unintended Consequences of Global and European Forces on English Football Fan Culture[1]

Introduction

In the first section of this chapter existing literature that highlights what Elias (1978; 2000) would have regarded as 'unintended consequences' of global and European forces on English football fan culture since the late twentieth century, are discussed. This is used as the basis upon which to introduce two 'new' and as yet previously under-researched figurations of football fans: those who watch football in pubs and fans who interact in online discussion forums.

Changes to English Football since the 1990s

English elite level men's professional club football was subjected to significant changes in the 1990s. Whilst these changes were partly brought about by the reaction of the British government to events involving English football fans that culminated in the 1980s, they were also what Elias (1978; 2000) would have termed 'unintended consequences' of wider societal changes brought about by European integration and globalisation processes. The 'new' ways in which English fans 'consume' football – at both elite club and international levels – has also shifted significantly (cf. Dixon, 2013; Millward, 2011). This is largely (although not solely) due to the increasing centrality and ubiquity of televised football worldwide (Sandvoss, 2003), a process that requires further explanation in order to justify the methodologies for the two research studies that underpin Chapters 4–6 of this book.

---

1 Parts of this chapter have appeared in print previously as Gibbons, T. and Dixon, K. (2010) Surf's up! A call to take English soccer fan interactions on the Internet more seriously. *Soccer & Society*, 11 (5), 599–613. Reprinted by permission of the publisher (Taylor & Francis Ltd, http://wwwtandf.co.um/journals).

The End of the Terraces[2]

In order to appreciate what happened to English football in the 1990s, it is first important to briefly outline some of the influential events of the 1980s. The 1980s was a time of significant despair regarding what the English game had become – a symbol of a declining nation and a far cry from the World Cup 1966 victory according to Porter (2004). The 1980s has also been regarded as a 'decade of disasters' by Johnes (2005: 18), whereas Russell (1997: 208) even goes as far as suggesting English football had reached 'crisis point' by 1985.

The Football League remained an inward-looking institution refusing to recognise the financial benefits televising 'live' football could offer (King, 2002; Sandvoss, 2003). According to Russell (1997), match day attendance figures fell to their lowest point ever in the 1984–85 season largely due to a 'moral panic' relating to hooliganism (Dunning et al., 1988). This was reinforced by the press as well as many government ministers at the time (Johnes, 2005; King, 2002). Pitch invasions, riots and battles between rival groups of fans were rife and a fan was even stabbed to death in Birmingham on the final Saturday of the season. On the very same day (11 May 1985) a fire broke out at a packed Valley Parade football stadium, home to Bradford City F.C. The fire began during a match between Bradford and Lincoln City F.C. on the day that Bradford were also celebrating winning the Third Division trophy and promotion to the Second Division. A total of 56 fans lost their lives and 265 others were injured.

The Heysel stadium disaster occurred at the European Cup Final between Juventus and Liverpool in Brussels in the very same month as the Bradford Fire (29 May 1985). A total of 39 fans died (32 Italians, four Belgians, two French and one Briton) after a wall and then a fence collapsed following the pressure put upon them by large numbers of fans retreating from a 'series of consecutive charges' on the part of a hooligan contingent of Liverpool fans (Chisari, 2005: 79). English clubs were banned from European competition for five years by UEFA (Union of European Football Associations) and Liverpool were banned for a further two-years due to the violent actions of their fans, some of which were later found guilty of manslaughter by Belgian Courts (Chisari, 2005: 87). By this time, the British Conservative Prime Minister, Margaret Thatcher, was vocal in her disapproval of English football and its fans (Johnes, 2005). Public levels of despair and disgust about English football added to wider feelings of 'British national decline' at this point according to Russell (1997) and Porter (2004).

The most significant English football crowd disaster of the 1980s occurred on 15 April 1989 at the FA Cup semi-final between Liverpool and Nottingham Forest at Sheffield Wednesday's ground in Hillsborough (Scraton, 1999). At Hillsborough

---

2   The title of this sub-section takes its name from Anthony King's *The End of the Terraces: The Transformation of English Football in the 1990s*. This was originally published in 1998, but the version drawn upon within this book is the revised edition published in 2002.

fences had been erected around the perimeter of the pitch due to fears of hooligan behaviour. This meant that fans were literally fenced in to open-top, cage-like pens. Tragically, 96 fans, all supporting Liverpool, were crushed to death against these fences which had had their gates locked by the police due to the perceived hooligan threat posed by Liverpool fans.

Following allegations made by police in the national press that hooligans were to blame for the disaster, Lord Justice Taylor (1990) led a public inquiry and found that Liverpool fans were not to blame. A key recommendation of the 'Taylor Report' (1990) was that all football stadia in the top two divisions became 'all-seater' by the 1994–95 season (King, 2002). According to King, this was something the Thatcher government insisted upon to avoid further embarrassment and the fact that the disaster was shown 'live' on television, fuelled the general public consensus that something had to be done to ensure such disasters did not happen again.

Seating was designed to attract a more disciplined and respectable family audience rather than violent young males. However, King (2002: 100) argues that although

> Taylor applauded the attempts of certain clubs to encourage the attendance of families, nowhere did he argue that these families should come from more affluent sections of society ... . On the contrary, throughout his report, Taylor was concerned about the cost of his recommendations and assured the reader in a number of places that the price of tickets would not increase sufficiently to exclude fans who had attended the game in the past.

The Chancellor of the Exchequer, John Major, who later went on to succeed Margaret Thatcher as Prime Minister, was a football fan himself, unlike Thatcher. Major was largely responsible for making money available to help clubs in England, Scotland and Wales to pay for the costs of stadium redevelopments. Yet King (2002: 102) points out that the 'Taylor report suggested that £130 million would be required to renovate all the grounds in the League, but the methods which Taylor suggested were hugely inadequate to the that task'. King (2002: 102) goes on to conclude that despite 'his socially inclusive intentions, the cost of Taylor's demand for all-seater stadia has had to be borne, at least partially, by the paying spectator'. Ground redevelopments turned out to be far more expensive than Taylor envisaged and the cost of ticket prices increased substantially in the 1990s as clubs had to find ways of paying for them as well as ever-increasing players' wages. The latter was originally the result of the abolition of the maximum wage in 1960, but players' wages increased as the re-invention of English top-flight football was to gather momentum as a breakaway league for the most successful teams eventually came to fruition at the beginning of the 1990s. The English Premier League (EPL) grew in stature and attracted the best foreign talent pushing wages up even higher (Taylor, 2008).

Johnes (2005: 20) states that the changes to stadia that were forced upon the football industry by the British government compelled it to reassess its finances, its treatment of its consumers and, indeed, its whole image and future. Hillsborough thus became a catalyst not only for the rebuilding of Britain's stadiums, but also for the reinvention of the game itself. It focused ideas for a breakaway league and contributed to a chain of events that led to the Premier League, a lucrative deal with Sky television and the current fashionableness and wealth that pervades the upper echelons of football.

As summarised here, from the Taylor Report (1990) onwards the image of English football started to change. Yet it has been suggested that political changes to the structure of the English game were being considered almost a decade before (King, 2002). As early as 1981 a number of more popular and successful First Division clubs began to realise that the inward-looking philosophy of the Football League was a 'barrier to both their sporting and financial aggrandizement' (Russell, 1997: 210). On 30 September 1985 what were known as the 'Big Five' English clubs – Arsenal, Everton, Liverpool, Manchester United and Tottenham Hotspur – unveiled plans to form a break-away league consisting of only the top clubs in the country in order to concentrate television and sponsorship revenues rather than having to share them with lower-level clubs who did not attract as large an audience. Following long negotiations with clubs, the League eventually agreed to reforms that would be in the interests of the largest clubs and the proposal to form a breakaway league was subsequently dropped as it was agreed that 'the First Division sides were to take 50 per cent, those in the second 25 per cent and members of the Third and Fourth the remaining 25 per cent between them' (Russell, 1997: 210–11). Although this momentarily satisfied First Division clubs, the financial potential of forming a breakaway league meant it was an idea that never really went away.

One hundred years after the Football League had begun in 1888, in the summer of 1988 the terrestrial television company 'Independent Television' (ITV) offered to sponsor a breakaway league in order to capitalise on the expanding satellite TV industry. This second attempt at a breakaway league was again averted by the Football League who this time agreed to give First Division clubs an even greater 75 per cent share of the revenue gained from TV and sponsorship. Ultimately, the expensive all-seater stadia demanded by the Taylor Report (1990) was what focused the attention of all elite clubs to the need for a breakaway league. In order to assert their dominance over the Football League as the governors of English football, the FA published its *Blueprint for the Future of Football* in 1991, which included at its core, plans for the 'Premier League'. The 'FA Premiership' officially began on 15 August 1992 after all 22 First Division clubs announced they were removing themselves from the Football League (King, 2002; Russell, 1997).

British Sky Broadcasting (BSB, now simply marketed as 'Sky') is a satellite TV channel which is just one small part of the former media conglomerate 'News

Corporation' owned by the billionaire Australian entrepreneur Rupert Murdoch.³ In the early 1990s Sky was struggling to become popular in the UK and desperately needed to develop an effective marketing strategy in order to properly compete with terrestrial TV for viewing figures. Murdoch recognised that capturing the rights to broadcast 'live' sport, and football in particular, would secure thousands of subscriptions from English fans and boost advertising income from sponsors. When ITV's contract to broadcast live football in the Football League was due for renewal in May 1992 Sky managed to outbid ITV winning a five year contract with exclusive broadcasting rights over EPL football. According to Russell (1997: 214–15), from this point forward the majority of the domestic English football-watching population

> have found themselves denied access to live coverage of top English club fixtures unless they have a dish-owning neighbour, friend or relative, or frequent one of the pubs or clubs quick to spot the potential of satellite TV sport. Moreover, for TV and live fans alike, satellite schedules which spread the fixtures over three days, and also sometimes over different parts of those days, have accelerated the fragmentation of the fixture list that terrestrial TV had begun from 1983. This has brought disruption to lifestyles as fans struggle to accommodate ... breaks from tradition.

Thus EPL football was fundamental to Murdoch's expansion of Sky TV in England because 'once subscribing to Sky Sports, dish-owners would then buy subscriptions to their other services. Football was a route to other sections of the viewing public' (Russell, 1997: 214).⁴

The 1990s therefore led to significant changes in the ways in which English professional club football was organised, administered and depicted to fans. English fans of EPL clubs – although not necessarily fans of clubs from the lower echelons of English football (Clark, 2006; Gibbons and Lusted, 2007; Mainwaring and Clark, 2012) – finally began to be regarded as 'consumers' rather than 'yobs' due to the increased money in the game and the positive way football was being

---

3 From 28 June 2013 News Corporation was split into two companies: '21st Century Fox' covering the entertainment arm of the business and 'News Corp' covering the publishing side. At the time of writing Murdoch is still chairman of both companies and Sky is owned by 21st Century Fox.

4 Sky remained dominant over the broadcasting rights of 'live' Premier League football until 2006 when rival satellite subscription company 'Setanta' won the rights to air a proportion of games following a ruling by the European Commission who insisted that the Premier League allowed at least two broadcasters to have a 'viable and meaningful' share of football TV rights so that viewers (fans) had greater choice (BBC News, 2006). However, Sky still maintained the lion's share. Setanta financially imploded in 2009 and forfeited their rights to a proportion of games to the global satellite subscription channel ESPN. In June 2012 the telecoms company British Telecommunications (BT) won the rights to air a proportion of games for three seasons from August 2013 and began to seriously challenge Sky's twenty-year dominance of the market by offering BT's sport channel free if customers sign up to their Internet broadband service.

depicted in the press (cf. Crawford, 2004; Horne, 2005). Russell (1997: 211–12) stresses the priority of club over international football for top-level clubs in England in the early 1990s by stating that the

> successful establishment of a breakaway league stemmed from the fact that it was proposed by an outside body, the Football Association, rather than by a group of rebel clubs. This gave the scheme far more credibility, partly because, at least initially, it allowed the succession (*sic*) to be cloaked in national as well as self-interest. The FA's initial proposals had emphasised the benefits accruing to the English international side if an elite league of just 18 clubs, the number proposed in the original discussions, was introduced. Clubs would thus lose eight games per season, leaving the leading English players fresher and fitter for international commitments. Whatever the FA's intentions, this plan was rapidly diluted when it became clear that few of the chairmen of existing First Division clubs were willing to be excluded from these lucrative developments, even in the interest of the national side … . The notion of the Premiership serving English national interests has been further eroded by the influx of overseas players.

Yet it is also important to note that the relative success of the English national team in the 1990 World Cup Finals (held in Italy and known as 'Italia 90') also helped the image of the game within England following the disasters of the 1980s. A record number of terrestrial TV viewers tuned in to watch England versus West Germany in the semi-final of 'Italia 90' shown live on the BBC. England lost on penalties, but they went home national heroes. According to King (2002: 104),

> the 1990 World Cup echoed the effect which the 1966 World Cup had had 24 years earlier, when there had been a similar public interest in the game. The successful performance of the England team, and especially the role played in that success by Paul Gascoigne, attracted very large television audiences. In the UK, 25.2 million viewers (nearly half of whom were women) watched the semi-final … . Italia'90 led to an interest in football among sections of society which had previously shown little interest in the game.

King (2002: 104) even goes as far as suggesting that due to the BBC using the voice of the Italian opera singer Pavarotti in its coverage of the tournament, football became 'connected with high culture and, therefore, it was being strategically constructed as an appropriate entertainment for classes who were traditionally uninterested in football'. As Gibbons (2010) found, huge numbers of English fans were pictured in photos in the national press waving the St George's Cross as they gathered around the national team's bus as it toured London following England's exit from Italia 90. This was surely symbolic of a sense of renewed national pride in football and English national identity more generally following years of British decline.

Although England did not qualify for the 1994 World Cup Finals tournament, the fact that Euro 96 was held in England and was exactly 30 years after the 1966 World Cup win meant that English interest in football remained high during the 1990s. In addition, advances in European integration added further complexity to the relationship between English football fans, clubs and the national football team. As was discussed in Chapter 2, the legitimacy and authority of the nation is challenged by global and European integration processes (cf. Hall, 1992; Held, 2002; Smith, 1996), which in turn can accentuate both local and transnational frames of reference. Such transnationalism is evident in the rampant *global* commercialisation of EPL football since the early 1990s (Giulianotti and Robertson, 2004; 2009; Hamil, Michie, Oughton, and Warby, 1998). Elite clubs are now increasingly dominated by overseas players, coaches and owners mirroring the growth in international labour migration, resulting most notably from the 1985 'Heylens case' and the 1995 'Bosman ruling' that aligned European football into existing European legislation on free labour movement (Lanfranchi and Taylor, 2001; Maguire and Pearton, 2000). Such European level processes have transformed English elite level clubs into cosmopolitan sites, whereby fans consume 'images, concepts, lifestyles and ideas from well beyond their immediate communities [so they] can come to identify with groups beyond their [national] borders' (Held, 2002: 53). This is an example of what Elias (2000: 382) referred to as 'Diminishing Contrasts, Increasing Varieties', a concept that the research of Maguire (cf. 2005) has drawn upon significantly in relation to football (among other sports).

Europeanisation

One of the main foci of recent research on English football fandom has been related to Europeanisation. In the early 1970s members of the European Union were beginning to realise the need to establish and develop a collective political identity (Chryssochoou, 2001). In 1973, the year the UK entered into the European 'common market' of the European Economic Community (EEC) under Edward Heath's Conservative government, the EEC produced a 'Declaration on European Identity' that aimed to project a unified Europe to the rest of the world (Guibernau, 2011). Over the 1980s and 1990s the EU along with the Council of Europe appeared to make further attempts to create a sense of 'European identity'. Alongside this, sporting bodies such as the European Olympic Committees and UEFA also made a concerted effort to engender a notion of a 'pan-European' identity (Levermore and Millward, 2007). Despite this, Euro 96 did little to help solidify a shared sense of 'Europeanness' in the minds of English football fans, as studies on English press reporting of the tournament have shown (cf. Maguire and Poulton, 1999; Maguire et al., 1999; Garland and Rowe, 1999).

According to Levermore and Millward (2007: 160), informal interactions between supporters of 'G14' football clubs in European competitions (such as the UEFA Champions League) have been more successful than other more official attempts to establish a European identity,[5] or at least a European consciousness because

> although it cannot be calibrated, this informal/unofficial interaction of sport at the European level is probably more successful at developing a European sense of belonging, than half-hearted attempts at an official level have to instigate any form of European identity (whatever way it is defined).

Using evidence from fan contributions to e-zines (the equivalent of fanzines on the Internet), Levermore and Millward suggest that many fans of G14 clubs (they refer to Liverpool fans for the most part) interpret their team's position in the pan-European Champions League as more important than their team's position in national competitions like the EPL or the FA Cup. As the authors indicate themselves, this is somewhat similar to what King (2003) suggested in his earlier book on football and European identity, *The European Ritual*. In speaking of the importance of the 'locale' to his sample of Manchester United fans, King (2003: 201) suggested that the

> increasing place which Manchester has in the imagination of these men means that the city is frequently employed as a common symbol which the fans invoke to define appropriate behaviour in their relations to others; this is intrinsically connected to the transformed economic circumstances in the 1990s in football and in society more widely. Consequently, in Manchester's growing importance to these men, the outlines of an emergent identity which highlights regional or local urban interests and affiliations above national ones can begin to be traced.

King goes on to suggest that these Manchester United fans would rather travel to watch their club play in European competitions over domestic ones, and this is again the case with Levermore and Millward's (2007) and Millward's (2006) studies on Liverpool fans. King (2003: 203) suggests that

> familiarity with Europe is significant because it could potentially play a part in the development of a supranational European identity, where these United fans genuinely begin to see themselves as primarily Europeans rather than as British.

He also goes on to clarify that 'their notion of themselves as Europhiles cannot be taken as evidence that they think of themselves as distinctively European in the supranational way' (King 2003: 204). Furthermore, King (2003) provides convincing evidence to suggest that one of the major effects of the concentration

---

5 The G14 was the name given to a lobbying group consisting of some of the top European football clubs, including: Juventus; Liverpool; Real Madrid; Milan; Barcelona; Inter Milan; Bayern Munich; Ajax; Manchester United; PSV Eindhoven; Porto; Paris Saint-Germain; Marseilles; and, Borussia Dortmund (King, 2003: 152).

of power among the largest clubs in Europe, such as: Bayern Munich; Juventus; Real Madrid; and Barcelona, has been the growing antipathy that fans of other clubs direct towards them. But the radical commercialisation of Manchester United and its dominance over domestic competitions in England has provoked levels of unmatched hatred (Mellor, 2000; 2004). According to King (2003), the chant 'Do you come from Manchester?' sung by fans of other English clubs asserts the view that the commercialisation of Manchester United has rendered the club 'inauthentic' since it is largely supported not by local working-class fans, but by middle-class fans, from outside Manchester who only attend because the club is successful. King argues that this rejection of Manchester United is a half articulated resistance to the new global forces that are reconfiguring Europe, marginalising some cities and regions whilst favouring others.

Whatever the rationale behind the claim that Manchester United is an inauthentic club, it has seriously threatened the status of this network of masculine fans organised around fanzines and groups because at the very moment of the club's superiority, their support has not been recognised by their rivals at other clubs. King (2003: 205–6) states that it is local rivalries that have

> transformed the consciousness of Manchester United fans, precipitating an increased emphasis on the locale and on European competition … . In the face of these local rivalries and the accusation of inauthenticity, this network of masculine United fans have re-emphasised their Mancunian identity in order to reassert their status.

King cites evidence that shows how many Manchester born Manchester United fans have now become aggressively opposed to fans of the club not born in Manchester. Although, some supporters seemed happy to recognise proper out-of-town supporters who accorded with the masculine norms of the Mancunian fans in King's sample, so long as they did not advertise the fact that they were not from Manchester by displaying flags at European games with the place name of their disparate origins emblazoned on them.

In addition to this new emphasis on the locale of Manchester, King also argued that there was a widespread rejection of the England national team among his sample. Through rejecting associations with the England football team, these fans have developed a distinction between themselves and other English football fans and have thus made a critique of English 'nationalism' according to King. This sample of Manchester United fans no longer see 'English' as an identity which encompasses them, but rather only an expression of the particular interests of regionally located groups. For King's (2003: 210) Manchester United fans

> English nationalism is the appropriate identity of the South (which has benefited from the free market policies of national governments, particularly under Thatcher) or those small clubs (often in the South) whose fans' only hope of foreign travel (and status) is with the England team … . It should be noted

that these United fans are not rejecting appeals to all forms of nationalism or allegiance to the British state but rather they are specifically withdrawing themselves from relationships with masculine football fans from other clubs who support the England team.

Although he does not recognise it himself, King's (2003) book provides strong evidence for Elias's (2000) concept of diminishing contrasts and increasing varieties and also Elias's (1991) discussion on changes in the we-I balance whereby older and newer planes of identification have a tendency to conflict with one another. Instead, King (2003) prefers to utilise Appadurai's (1994; 1996) ideas relating to the significance of locality despite the increasingly globalising world – something Appadurai refers to as 'post-national'. King's argument is also informed largely by the work of Castells (1998) and Sassen (1991) who argue that cities have now become increasingly disembedded from the national contexts in which they are situated and are part of transnational networks that pay little attention to national borders. More recently, Millward (2011) has drawn upon Castells to identify the 'new' ways fans talk about football in what he refers to as the 'transnational network society'.

Whilst Elias (1991; 2000) did not speak of this development specifically, 'the question of whether national cultures and identities are being *weakened, strengthened* or *pluralized* by globalisation processes' is one which an Eliasian approach can also help to illuminate through allowing for all three possibilities (Maguire, 2011a: 978). Maguire (2011a: 991) suggests that sport occupies a 'contested terrain' which is used to display multiple layers of identity and global flows are producing a number of unintended consequences relating to the diversification of links between sports and cultural identities. The responses to global culture highlighted by the practices of King's (2003) sample of Manchester United fans illustrate these 'countervailing trends' of diminishing contrasts between groups and increasing varieties amongst them (Maguire, 2011a: 991).

Although King (2003), Levermore and Millward (2007) and Millward (2006) focus predominantly on the fans of the largest English clubs – Manchester United, Liverpool and (to a lesser extent) Arsenal – these authors also make some small reference to fans of smaller clubs or those at lower or less prominent levels in the structure of English football. King (2003) highlights how some Southampton fans recognise the development of transnational forces within football. Yet he stresses that their response is to concentrate ever more closely on their own club's success in its local and domestic context. Similarly, Levermore and Millward (2007) pay passing reference to comments made by Oldham Athletic fans that suggest they are far more hostile towards the impacts of deregulated European football competition and hold more xenophobic views towards non-English teams and players whilst also proudly voicing support for the national football team. Millward (2006: 391) concludes his exploration of Liverpool FC fans' narratives regarding Europeanisation by arguing that some of the most exhilarating dimensions of English football culture are rooted within the narratives which emerge at the lower professional and amateur levels. Therefore, it seems as if a football-based European identity, based upon favourable fan narratives, is highly exclusionary.

Yet he provides no evidence to support this claim. The reader is thus left pondering how European integration and globalisation affect those at lower levels of English football. Thus far few authors have made much of an attempt to address this issue by exploring the opinions and behaviours of fans of less prominent or lower league teams despite the fact that longer-standing *local* affiliations appear to remain an integral component of football fandom around the world (cf. Armstrong and Giulianotti, 2001; Tomlinson, 1991). Andrews and Ritzer (2007: 137) argue that many globalisation theorists have regarded cultural forms and practices as operating in a constant tension between global and local, and thus have regarded these as mutually exclusive categories, yet,

the *local* has been so effected by the *global*, that it has become, at all intents and purposes, *glocal* ... . Thus, the processual and empirical continuum through which we conceptualize globalization is bounded by ... *glocalization* ('the interpretation of the global and the local, resulting in unique outcomes in different geographic areas').

Giulianotti and Robertson (2004: 546) refer to 'glocalisation' as a process 'whereby local cultures adapt and redefine any global cultural product to suit their particular needs, beliefs and customs'. They define contemporary elite English football clubs as 'Transnational Corporations' (TNCs) characterised by their promotion of local symbols, folklore and traditions to re-brand their products to a *global* market place. Such cosmopolitan processes have had significantly less impact on lower league clubs and fans that have largely remained sheltered from such transnational developments (Clark, 2006; Gibbons and Lusted, 2007; Mainwaring and Clark, 2012).

This book is underpinned by in-depth studies within two relatively 'new' research settings in order to mirror some of the recent changes in football fandom discussed above. The first study involved observations of how English fans displayed and/or articulated their Englishness in pubs during World Cup 2006. The second involved gathering opinions from fans regarding the relationship between English national identity and football which arose from a fourteen-month participant observation study conducted within a specific online fan community. Both fans that congregate in pubs to watch 'live' football on television and those who interact in online forums, are examples of what Elias (1978) referred to as 'figurations'. The task for sociologists, according to Elias, is to make such figurations more transparent.

The Pub as a Setting to Observe Fans' Displays and Articulations of English National Identity

Jennings (2011: 214) notes that the traditional English pub has been in decline since the beginning of the twentieth century, meaning that in the mid-1990s 'more than a quarter of rural parishes were without a pub'. However, Jennings (2011: 215) goes on to state that since the 1950s, there has been an 'expansion of places to drink other than pubs'. As such, 'the 'pub' came to cover a highly diverse set of premises' according to Jennings (2011: 219), and is therefore used within this book to refer to social clubs, bars and nightclubs, as well as more traditional public houses.

A notable omission from Jennings (2011) otherwise comprehensive history of the English pub, is the role sports like football have played in attracting people to pubs. Stone (2007) and later Dixon (2013) identify the pub as a primary site where football is embedded in fans' everyday lives. Pubs have been a central aspect of English football fan culture for decades. Pubs, usually (but not only) those situated in close proximity to football grounds, are often visited by fans travelling to watch matches in stadia both before kick-off and after the final whistle. They are key socialising spaces within which pre- and post-match analysis takes centre stage in discussions amongst fans. Pubs are also often sites for identity displays (both local and national) and some have been at the centre of battles between rival hooligan firms. Many football fan/hooligan memoirs, novels and films have depicted pubs as 'the' spaces within which they regularly congregate (cf. Gibbons, Dixon and Braye, 2008).

Whilst not an entirely 'new' space for football fans to interact (Stone, 2007), the pub has recently become an alternative venue in which to watch 'live' football according to Weed (2006; 2007; 2008). Observation of fans in this setting could thus help elicit information on the significance of 'everyday' fandom practices to the display of national identity. The pub has become an important collective site for the English football audience according to Weed (2007: 408), who suggests, 'the concept of a shared experience is at the crux of understanding the attraction of the pub as a sport spectator venue'. Weed (2006) offers two factors that might account for the noticeable rise of the pub as one of the most popular venues for watching 'live' football in England since the early 1990s: first, the move of live EPL football coverage exclusively to the subscription only satellite television company BSkyB in 1992, and second, the changes to football stadia brought about by the Taylor Report (1990) that introduced safer, more family-oriented football grounds throughout the 1990s, which has arguably contributed (along with rises in players' wages) to vast increases in ticket prices to attend live matches (King, 2002).

Drawing upon evidence from 'Mintel Leisure Intelligence' in 2003, Weed (2006:77) suggested, 'more people – 9.1 million in 2002 – watched live sport on television in a pub or bar than paid to watch sport live at the event (8.7million)'. The lack of atmosphere at contemporary football grounds, due to the introduction of new 'all-seater' stadia, CCTV, stewarding and ever rising ticket prices to pay for the cost of these safety developments (as well as growth in players' wages), means the pub has been considered by some to be more attractive as a venue for watching live football (Williams, 1998). Whilst Weed's evidence is now somewhat out of date, a ruling of the Court of Justice of the European Union (CJEU) in October 2011 on the broadcasting of EPL football matches in pubs, highlights the continued significance of the English pub for watching 'live' football.

Karen Murphy is an owner of a pub situated in the southern English coastal city of Portsmouth. Mrs. Murphy used decoder cards imported from Greece to show EPL matches 'live' in her pub. Mrs. Murphy was prosecuted by 'Media Protection Services Limited' for the use of what was deemed to be an 'illicit' Greek decoder card and QC Leisure (the main supplier of foreign decoders to pubs and the general public for both commercial and domestic use in the UK) was sued for copyright infringement by the EPL. Mrs. Murphy and QC Leisure both raised important questions about the relationship between the EU principles of free movement of goods and services and what are extremely lucrative European broadcasting rights which were referred to the CJEU by the English courts. The result was a CJEU ruling that national legislation which prohibits the import, sale or use of foreign decoder cards is contrary to EU law on the freedom to provide services and cannot be justified (Curia, 2011; Geey, 2011). Whilst the English High Court endorsed the CJEU ruling on 24 February 2012, the EPL are still determined to attempt to prosecute publicans who use European Economic Area foreign satellite systems for breach of copyright in both the domestic civil and criminal courts (Scott, 2012). Whilst the 'Murphy ruling' does not relate to the broadcasting of international matches as these are deemed of national significance and as such are still usually shown on terrestrial television channels, it acts to highlight the continued importance of the English pub as a venue to watch 'live' football, a fandom practice which is set to continue (Dixon, 2013), yet one which is still under-researched.

The 2006 World Cup Finals tournament was held in Germany and, as always (cf. Perryman, 2006; Pearson, 2012), a large contingent of English fans travelled (despite the fact the majority of them did not have tickets) to watch the England national team progress through the group stages to the quarter-finals of the competition.[6] At the same time, as is usually the case (Weed, 2006; 2007; 2008), a larger number of football fans preferred to remain in England and watch the tournament on television either at home or in public houses across the nation. Whilst some academic studies exist on the behaviour of English football fans in Germany during World Cup 2006 (cf. Hay and Joel, 2007; Vincent et al., 2010), there is a lack of studies exploring fan behaviour back home. Thus, the pub was deemed a legitimate space in which to conduct research for the purpose of observing how English fans displayed national identity during the 2006 World Cup. The methodology for this pub-based observation study is detailed in the Appendix.

---

6   One report suggested as many as 70,000 English fans descended on Nuremberg and 60,000 on Stuttgart, the majority of whom watched games in fan parks outside stadiums (Armstrong, 2006).

The Internet as a Space for Accessing Key Debates between Football Fans on English National Identity

According to figures from the Office for National Statistics (2013), in 2012 33 million adults accessed the Internet on a daily basis and this has more than doubled the 2006 figure of 16 million. Of course one needs to be aware of what has become known as 'the digital divide' here. Katz, Rice and Aspden (2001) found that differences in access to the Internet persist across gender; age; household income; education; and race. BBC technology reporter Jane Wakefield (2010) has commented upon the fact that the digital divide is a 'global issue'. Using statistical evidence from the International Telecommunications Union (ITU), Wakefield (2010) highlights the large discrepancies in Internet access between the richest and poorest countries. Nevertheless, in the West, Internet communications are advancing and this is often linked to the technological revolution more generally.

Although the rapid rise of the Internet has largely been driven by businesses recognising its power to reach a global customer base, it is also important to recognise that its growth has significantly increased communications between disparate groups of people. It is easy to regard the Internet as leading to increased homogenisation between individuals and groups across the globe. However, the Internet can also be regarded as creating opportunities for 'new' or 'hybrid' cultures and practices that would not have been possible without it. Thus, the Internet is perhaps best regarded as an example of Elias's (2000) 'diminishing contrasts, increasing varieties'. Along such lines, Lee (2005: 50) states that: 'The Internet enhances the potential of interaction that transcends the time-space barrier at an unprecedented scale and scope'. Email loops and online message/ discussion boards are examples of what Mann and Stewart (2000: 2) refer to as CMC (computer-mediated communication).

Far from creating a dualism between 'online' versus 'offline' interactions, where offline communications are deemed 'real life' and online activities discarded as 'virtual' and thus inconsequential, social scientists now recognise that social, economic and cultural interactions occur simultaneously in 'cyberspace' and make up an extension of the everyday lives of many (Bell, 2007). Wellman et al.'s (2001) results indicated that the more time people spent online, the more they were actively involved with organisations and politics offline. There is evidence to suggest that the Internet provides an extension of everyday life for many people (A. Bennett, 2005; T. Bennett, 2005; Haythornthwaite, 2001). This is perhaps the main justification for conducting ethnographic research online as well as offline. More traditional ethnographic methods such as face-to-face interviews were not utilised in this book primarily because fans that inhabit online discussion forums remain in need of further research (Gibbons and Dixon, 2010; Millward, 2011). As 'new' social spaces in which figurations of fans regularly interact, these sites were considered important for exploring the relationship between English national identity and football fan culture. The choice to engage in participant observation within a specific online environment therefore requires further justification.

A number of academic journals dedicated to producing research on aspects of new media or online research are now in circulation. However, it is important to re-visit some of the earlier influential work on conducting research on the Internet in order to justify the use of an online participant observation study in the research underpinning Chapters 5 and 6. Hamelink (2000: 10) in his pioneering text *The Ethics of Cyberspace* states that the

> spaces of the physical and virtual world are closely inter-connected. The social relations that obtain in the physical world do not disappear in the virtual world. Features and qualities of people do not dissolve as they enter the virtual world. It needs to be noted that expectations about the different and totally new nature, the openness and equality of life in CyberSpace tend to be exaggerated and require considerable qualification.

According to Markham (2005: 794) 'meaningful and significant relationships and social structures ... thrive in text-only online environments'. Moreover, Garcia, Standlee, Bechkoff and Cui (2009: 53) state that while

> there exists a huge body of research on the Internet and computer-mediated communication (CMC), only some of this research is qualitative, and of this, an even smaller portion is ethnographic ... most ethnographers still conduct studies firmly situated in the 'offline' social world. To continue to effectively explore some of the main and enduring concerns of ethnographic research (such as the nature of specific social worlds and subcultures; the construction of identity; the beliefs, values, and world views underlying human action and social life; and the experience of everyday life) ethnographers must incorporate the Internet and CMC into their research to adequately understand social life in contemporary society.

Hine's (2000: 9) *Virtual Ethnography* provides a very strong argument for considering the Internet to be a plausible 'field site' for ethnographic research because it *is* a 'place' where cultures are created, maintained or transformed. Yet the issue of the lack of face-to-face interaction in online research and its necessity in most traditional 'offline' ethnographies, is a major one according to Hine (2000: 43–4) because ethnography 'has traditionally entailed physical travel to a place, which implies that face-to-face interaction is the most appropriate'. The main reason why physical travel and tales of arriving in the field have played such an important part in traditional ethnographies is because they have given the ethnographer 'authority' over the reader to speak about the specific field of investigation because 'the ethnographer has been where the reader cannot or did not go' (Hine, 2000: 45). However, Hine urges that the key aspects of ethnography which give an ethnographer authoritative accounts are *not* actually associated with physical travel. Through explaining how access to the field was negotiated, by observing interactions and via communicating with participants – all arguably more essential means of experiencing a particular culture – ethnographers who use Internet spaces as their research sites can still clearly maintain authenticity from both readers of their accounts and participants in the field of research. Whether

> physical travel is involved or not, the relationship between ethnographer, reader and research subjects is still inscribed in the ethnographic text. The ethnographer is still uniquely placed to give an account of the field site, based on their experience of it and their interaction with it (Hine, 2000: 46).

Moreover, in relation to research on Internet behaviour, Joinson (2005: 22) suggests that an

> accumulating body of experimental evidence, first person accounts and observation research has shown that Internet-based communication can be characterized as highly socialized – perhaps even more social than face-to-face interaction ... there is evidence that Internet communication can lead people to identify highly with relevant social groups and identities ... . The prognosis for an Internet relationship is just as healthy as that for one formed face-to-face.

Research into Online Communities

Schimmel, Harrington and Bielby (2007) suggest that research on sports fans remains largely isolated from research on other kinds of fans. It is therefore no surprise that academics unrelated to sport have often reported the value of researching online communities and there is already a well-established literature on this topic. According to Ridings and Gefen (2004), online communities have existed for over two decades. They cite 'the WELL' (Whole Earth 'Lectronic Link), started in 1985, and 'Usenet newsgroups' with early versions dating back to 1979, as being the first interactive communities on the Internet. The first book to provide an in-depth discussion about the nature and purpose of online communities, highlighting 'the WELL' as the first of these, was Howard Rheingold's (1993) *The Virtual Community*. As one of the original members of this community, Rheingold is still clearly well respected on 'the WELL' website. The following is the opening paragraph from the site's front page that explains the significance of 'the WELL':

> It is widely known as the primordial ooze where the online community movement was born – where Howard Rheingold first coined the term 'virtual community'. Since long before the public Internet was unleashed, it has quietly captivated some accomplished and imaginative people.[7]

---

7   See http://www.well.com (Accessed Nov 2010).

Ridings and Gefen (2004) cite four motivations for people to join online communities: information exchange; social support; friendship; and, recreation. With advances in Internet communications technology over the last 20 years these kinds of 'virtual' communication have received increasing attention from scholars as they offer a potential communication outlet for fans to relate to one another and discuss common interests (cf. Baym, 1997; 2002; Smith and Kollock, 1999).

Such online social networks allow the social researcher to 'observe a self-defined and ongoing interpretive community' according to Jenkins (1995: 53). There is a long-established body of research on online discussion groups that became ubiquitous (particularly in the US) from the 1980s, such as the aforementioned 'Usenet newsgroups' and interactive forums around television shows like *The X-files* or *Twin Peaks* (Hills, 2002; Jenkins, 1995; Lee, 2005). Although these kinds of online interactions are often criticised for their difference from face-to-face communications for being more narcissistic than traditional interactions with few communal rules, social norms and obvious personal attachments which lean to classify long-established community experience, they still provide an example of communication between fan groups and individuals through a new medium which should not be ignored by researchers who want to find out more about how social identities are maintained through fandom (Menon, 2007).

Fans use the Internet to interact with one another within specific domains. With direct reference to the consumption of 'old' and 'new' media as a constitutive part of everyday life, Abercrombie and Longhurst (1998) viewed fans in general (not just those who interact on the Internet) as audiences who discuss topical media discourse which is freely available. Likewise Hughson and Poulton (2006) and Crolley and Hand (2002; 2006) demonstrate the importance of the media in setting the public agenda for football fans specifically. Whist considering fans of any kind in this way implies that they are passive, the way fans consume football is changing and this does not mean that fans are engaging in less authentic forms of fandom, just different ones. Hills (2007) urges us to remember that fans in general represent a dedicated, *active* audience; they are consumers who can also be 'new media' producers (officially or unofficially) through the production of online discussions, e-zines and blogs, for instance.

The growth of the Internet has been rapid and the use of the Internet by fans of television serials and sports teams, especially in the USA, have been considered by academics (End, 2001; Jenkins, 1995; B. Wilson, 2007; W. Wilson, 2007). However, the potential usefulness of the Internet as a place for analysing ways in which football fans interact and debate key issues in football, often in ways which act to maintain their social identities, has only been partially recognised (Gibbons and Dixon, 2010; Millward, 2011).

The Internet and Football Fan Culture

Fans often develop a sense of emotional investment and even ownership over a football club and rather than passively accepting the ways in which their club is managed, they have been known to campaign for change (Harvey, Horne, Safai, Darrell and O'Neill, 2014; Kelly, 2004; Menon, 2007). Examples in English football include: the Charlton fans' 'Back to the Valley campaign' (Maguire and Possamai, 2005); fans' opposition to the previously London based Wimbledon FC's move to Milton Keynes (Auty, 2002); and, fans' opposition to Malcolm Glazer's takeover of Manchester United (Brown, 2007; Pratley and Taylor, 2005). In each of these cases the Internet aided communication between campaigning fans of English football clubs. Yet, according to Auty (2002: 273): 'Although the impact of the Internet has been thoroughly examined in almost every other sphere ... it appears that no-one has fully analysed the impact of the web on football'. As a proponent of research into Internet communities, B. Wilson (2007) has noted the usefulness of the Internet when investigating sport-related social movements. B. Wilson (2007: 462) quite rightly points out that within the sociology of sport, 'there is a dearth of research investigating links between the Internet and sport-related activism'. Whilst both Auty and Wilson highlight important issues here, the point of the online study conducted in the current book was to use the Internet as a tool to gather data from football fans rather than fully analyse the impact of the web on football fandom.

Sandvoss (2004: 42), as part of a discussion of 'sport online as a post-modern cultural form', attends to the practical uses of the Internet for sports fans and discusses popular Internet functions divided into three main areas (derived from a European football survey). First, 11% of all Internet users and nearly a fifth of all football fans (18%) regularly use the Internet to gain immediate access to results, match reports, and current news/background information. Second, the Internet is used to follow live sporting events via video, audio and textual commentary by up to seven per cent of football fans. Finally, the purchasing of merchandise and gambling through online activities formed a third, yet marginal group of online services. Although Sandvoss (2004: 42) is primarily concerned with a more theoretical discussion about the coverage of sport and the development of communications technology, he provides valuable information about the everyday use of the Internet by football fans as they attempt to gratify an instantaneous thirst for information when he states that the

> use of the World Wide Web as a means of accessing background information highlights the nature of the Internet as a medium of scope, granting an unrivalled wealth of instantly accessible information.

The account of Internet use reported by Sandvoss draws particular attention to passive activities such as watching, listening and reading, rather than interactive elements of fandom expression. So, while it is clear that fans are using the Internet in large numbers for practical purposes, it is the significance of interactions and Internet communications that are often downplayed if not entirely ignored by academics. For instance, researchers fail to identify the huge numbers of football fans who, through regularly contributing to web-based discussion forums and blogs, have built communities through which they not only discuss and voice their concerns on contemporary issues in football, but also call for and influence changes to aspects of the game/particular teams and/or articulate and form social identities (Millward, 2011).

In relation to the latter point, Edensor and Millington (2008: 173) agree that, 'football culture has become a pertinent field within which to explore contemporary formations of identity'. Evidence exists to suggest that football fans (just like other sports fans) all over the world use the Internet to interact with one another about many important issues. W. Wilson (2007: 395) makes precisely this point in relation to MLS (Major League Soccer) fans in the USA, concluding that the

> development and availability of information technologies such as the Internet ... certainly will facilitate the building of virtual communities of fans who want to follow specific teams and leagues.

Thus one might expect that involvement with Internet sites for football fan interactions would demonstrate a heightened level of fandom more generally, making fans located on the Internet a valuable resource for researchers (Gibbons and Dixon, 2010).

As was alluded to in Chapter 1, Crawford (2004: 30–33) argued that in previous academic literature, fans who follow sport via the mass media and perhaps do not solely interact face-to-face, but also do so around television and/or online, have usually been deemed to be less 'authentic' in terms of their support than fans who always go to matches in person. Crawford directly challenged the assumptions made by sociologists and psychologists of sport who endeavoured to create rigid typologies of sports fans based upon supposed norms of 'authentic' fandom practices. One of Crawford's key points was a counter-argument to assumptions made by these academics about the lack of authenticity of the 'types' of fans who interact on sport related issues via 'new media', including television and the Internet. Crawford (2004: 144) argued that rigid 'distinctions between 'virtual' (online) and 'real' (off-line) worlds are futile' because 'the uses and practices of the Internet are always located within ('real') everyday life patterns'.

Boyle and Haynes (2004) highlight this well by recognising the potential of the Internet for enhancing opportunities for 'interactivity'. It is clear that the Internet has become a key space for interactions between English fans and between fans and their clubs. Many fanzines set up in the 1980s in England are now e-zines and every club has official and unofficial websites with forums for fans to discuss various issues (Auty, 2002; Boyle and Haynes, 2004; Levermore and Millward, 2007; Millward, 2006; 2008; 2011). Nowadays, the ubiquity of these online message boards/discussion forums for football fans is difficult to miss. For instance, in an article within the January 2008 issue of *When Saturday Comes* (Plenderleith, 2008), comments from a total of twenty online discussion forums and blogs for both English and Scottish football fans were drawn upon to highlight the contrasting reactions of each nation's fans to the failure of both national teams to qualify for the European Football Championships ('Euro 2008').

Similarly, newspapers and other media organisations regularly place football-related stories on their websites and offer fans the opportunity to post their responses, stimulating interactions for all to see. For example, when the *Times Online* produced a short article (one-and-a-half A4 pages in length when printed) about the former British Prime Minister Gordon Brown calling for a return of the home nations football competition following the failure of England, Scotland, Wales and Northern Ireland to qualify for Euro 2008, 428 comments were posted within a 24-hour period from Internet users across the globe (Webster and Hines, 2007).

Examples of studies specifically relating to some of the spaces British football fans inhabit on the Internet do now exist. McMenemy, Poulter and O'Loan (2005) provide extracts from online interactions that clearly demonstrate fans of Glasgow Celtic and Rangers football clubs posting abuse about each other's politico-religious beliefs on message boards in 2003. The authors conclude that 'sectarian content does exist on boards that are there as discussion forums for footballing issues' (McMenemy et al., 2005: 500). The Internet could therefore be regarded as aiding in the articulation and perhaps even maintenance of particular layers of identity here.

The number of studies in the sociology of sport that have actually collected data relating to the ways in which English football fans interact using this medium are thankfully growing (cf. Hutchins, Rowe and Ruddock, 2009; Johnes, 2008; Kennedy and Kennedy, 2010; Kerr and Emery, 2011; Levermore and Millward, 2007; Millward 2006; 2007; 2011; Rookwood and Chan, 2011; Rookwood and Millward, 2011; Rowe, Ruddock and Hutchins, 2010; Ruddock, 2005; Ruddock, Hutchins and Rowe, 2010).[8] Cleland (2010) and Dart (2009) have also recognised that online fan message boards and blogs create or encourage interactions between soccer fans. The sociological significance of these online message board interactions has also been reflected in recent online surveys of soccer fans of the English game (cf. Cashmore and Cleland, 2012; Cleland 2013; Gibbons, 2011; Gibbons and Nuttall, 2012).

Thus, an Internet discussion forum was deemed a legitimate space in which to interact with and observe debates between fans of English football on issues relating to English national identity. The methodology for this online participant observation study conducted between June 2008 and September 2009 is detailed in the Appendix.

---

8   This list of studies is still growing and represents just some relevant examples.

Chapter 4
Manifestations of Englishness in Pubs during World Cup 2006[1]

Introduction

This chapter is based upon the author's field notes recorded from observations of fans taken within a sample of English pubs that were showing England matches 'live' on television during the 2006 FIFA World Cup Finals tournament. Observations of fans in this 'natural' setting helped to elicit information on the multiple ways in which football fans were displaying and/or articulating national identity at this particular point in time. Specifically 'English', 'British' and 'local' or 'club-based' identifications were observed around support for the English national team. Elias (1991; 2000) would have described this as evidence of the multi-layered identities apparent in citizens living in contemporary Western European states. Evidence for each of these layers of Englishness amongst fans is discussed in the following three sections. Elias's (1991) 'changes in the we-I balance' and Elias's (2000) 'diminishing contrasts, increasing varieties' are both used to summarise the findings and alternative theoretical explanations are also alluded to. It is concluded that the opinions of fans are required in order to either confirm or refute what was observed and to provide more detail on the reasons for such varied manifestations of Englishness.

The Dominance of the St George's Cross

During the 2006 World Cup Finals the display of the specifically English St George's Cross flag was ubiquitous, just as it was found to be in national newspaper representations of this tournament (cf. Vincent et al., 2010), and in studies of newspaper coverage of other international tournaments since Euro 96 (cf. Garland and Rowe, 1999; Maguire and Poulton, 1999; Maguire et al., 1999; Vincent and Hill, 2011). This was the case in the sample of pubs chosen as the venues in which manifestations of Englishness were observed. The following is an

---

1   Parts of this chapter have appeared in print previously as Gibbons, T. and Lusted, J. (2007) Is St George enough? Considering the importance of displaying local identity while supporting the England national soccer team. *Annals of Leisure Research*, 10 (3/4), 291–309. Reprinted by permission of the publisher (Taylor & Francis Ltd, http://wwwtandf.co.um/journals).

extract from field notes (10 June 2006) taken in a pub in Kirkby Stephen, Cumbria, during England's first match of the tournament against Paraguay.

> Almost everyone (both men and women) was wearing a replica England shirt or some kind of reference to England in the form of a t-shirt branded with St George's Cross flags or the three lions emblem. A few people also had St George flags wrapped around them … . Many people also had a small St George's Cross flag that can be clipped to a car window attached to their pint glass. I engaged in this practice also after my friend had gone over the road to the newsagent to buy us some.

The choice to display a specifically 'English' rather than 'British' layer of identity around the national football team was also observed for later matches. The following extract is taken from field notes (20 June 2006) from a large bar in Lancaster city centre where the England versus Sweden game was watched.

> Five minutes before half time I went to the lavatory upstairs and had a look around the upper level (this bar is organised on two levels, the top was a mezzanine floor with a large square hole in the middle around which a five foot high banister was erected). The upper floor was packed full of supporters with many St George's Cross flags draped over the sides of the ring banister and five deep rows of fans – like the old terraces at football grounds. It was even louder up here and fans seemed to be showing their support much more avidly – shouting at the opposition, leaning over the banister and swearing as if the Swedish supporters, players and referee were actually where the projector screen showing the match was. The bar at the back of this floor was decorated with St George flags and scarves, as if it were a mascot of some kind.

The second half of the above match was watched in a smaller pub in the same city. Another overt display of English patriotism was difficult to miss.

> We proceeded to run (as it was raining heavily) towards some of the other pubs with the idea of watching the second half somewhere we could sit down. As we left, I noticed a huge St George's Cross painted on the entire side of an end of terrace building that housed an Indian takeaway. The words, 'We believe … ' were written across the centre of the cross. The takeaway was situated opposite the large bar we had just come out of and this huge display of national identification was very noticeable as I stepped outside.

The significance of this overt display of Englishness may perhaps have been to deter any England supporters from venting their anger by attacking the takeaway, which they may otherwise have perceived to be 'foreign'. This kind of xenophobic practice has been observed in past tournaments (cf. Back et al., 2001; Burdsey, 2007), highlighting a kind of 'little Englander' mentality (Maguire, 2011a: 990).

English fans have often been labelled by the British national press as having a 'hooligan mentality' (Gibbons, 2010: 433). 'Ethnic assertiveness' was apparent in British national newspaper coverage of Euro 96 according to Maguire and Poulton (1999). Yet, the large display of the St George's Cross on the side of the Indian takeaway building may also have been created to show the 'white' English majority that the owners of the takeaway were celebrating being English themselves. If the latter was the case, it supports Burdsey's (2006; 2007) findings that increasing numbers of British Asians are expressing their support for the England football team and that the St George's Cross is slowly moving beyond being associated with an exclusively 'white' nationalism. This is not to say that both overt and covert forms of racism do not still pervade English football, clearly they do (cf. Burdsey, 2011). Towards the end of the first decade of the twenty-first-century right-wing organisations such as the EDL were beginning to gain prominence in England and particularly in the North West where the research was conducted (Jackson, 2011; Trilling, 2013). Links between English football supporters and such racist organisations that developed at this time 'have the potential to contribute to a climate of discomfort and/or fear in the live fan experience' according to Burdsey and Randhawa (2012: 106). Whilst no overt examples of racism were observed in the pub-based study, that is not to say that they did not exist nor that racism is no longer prominent.

During England's previous group match against Trinidad and Tobago, there were fewer overt displays of Englishness recorded (15 June 2006) from a small pub in Morecambe.

> Less than half were wearing any England merchandise – a stark contrast to the pub I watched the game at in Kirkby Stephen where almost everyone was wearing some form of England apparel.

Perhaps the main reason for this was that the kick-off time of the game was 5pm, meaning that many people had probably gone to the pub straight from work and had not had the time to 'dress-up'. Nevertheless,

> it was also apparent that hardly anyone was wearing a replica shirt, most were Lambretta or Umbro t-shirts or polo t-shirts with some form of St George's Cross or England reference incorporated in their design. There were a few St George's Cross flags on walls and some on bunting. A large St George's Cross was hung below the projector screen with signatures from the England players printed on it.

Field notes from a different small pub in Kirkby Stephen attended for England's game against Ecuador (25 June 2006) suggested that specifically English symbols were present but perhaps not as blatantly as observed in the larger or busier venues.

Only three people (all men) were wearing anything to do with the England team (two England replica shirts; one t-shirt with 'ENGLAND' written across it) and the pub had St George's Cross flags hanging from the ceiling of the bar area. Other than this, visual symbols relating to England were minimal – certainly compared with the bar in neighbouring Lancaster city centre where I watched the second group game.

Whilst the St George's Cross was by far the most popular national symbol displayed, it was *not* the only one. Elias (1991) suggests that spatial identities are multi-layered, yet the problem with English national identity is that the state layer is somewhat different to the national layer. As the following section highlights, the presence of attachments to a British-based Englishness were still apparent in a number of ways, even though World Cup 2006 took place ten years after Euro 96 where a specifically English national consciousness is said to have begun to take over from a British-based one (cf. Crolley and Hand, 2006; Weight, 2002).

The Display of a British-based Englishness

Robinson (2008: 216) argues that 'even though England and Britain can no longer be assumed to be the same thing, the two are completely and inextricably linked'. Yet, she later goes on to contend that in almost 'no other area is the distinction between England and Britain as absolute and clear-cut' as it is in relation to the English national football team (Robinson, 2008: 221). Whilst these quotations have admittedly been taken out of the broader context in which they were written, they highlight the complexities underlying the ways in which Englishness is attached to Britishness through football. Moreover, whilst Robinson (2008: 227) suggests that football is a good place to examine 'the 'problems' of Englishness', the evidence she uses about how English national identity has been depicted by football fans is overly superficial. Like both King (2006) and Kumar (2003), Robinson (2008) provides scant evidence of the diversity of ways in which English fans still display and articulate attachments to a British-based Englishness. This goes beyond the flags they fly.

The following is an extract from field notes (10 June 2006) taken in a pub in Kirkby Stephen, Cumbria, during England's first match of the tournament against Paraguay.

> Some fans ... had horns and megaphones which they used throughout the match for playing *The Great Escape* theme tune or more often a horn was blown a succession of times so that everyone could shout 'ENGLAND!' Megaphones were used for chants such as 'Ing-er-land, Ing-er-land, Ing-er-land, nah, nah ... '

As well as *The Great Escape* theme tune, the song *Ten German Bombers* was also sung by some of the fans observed. The following extract is from field notes taken after attending a large bar in Lancaster city centre for England's group stage match against Sweden (20 June 2006).

> During the second half, towards the end of the game when it looked as if England were going to win, a large group of about ten fairly young men next to us started singing a well rehearsed song called *Ten German Bombers* which referred to the British RAF shooting down the Germans.[2] This was clearly a reference to WWII and seemed to be articulated in response to (what turned out to be false) anticipation on the part of the commentators that England had a chance of meeting Germany in the second round of the tournament.[3]

These examples are illustrative of the continuing English reliance on British achievements – a practice evident in English national newspaper coverage of World Cup Finals since 1950 (Gibbons, 2010), which shows little sign of declining around the English national team. A number of newspaper reports before the 2006 tournament highlighted that references to the war were condemned by the FA; English footballers; and, members of the British government, even including the Prime Minister himself. It was also made clear that the German police would not tolerate 'behaviour seen as glorifying the country's Nazi past' (O'Neill, 2006: 33). Yet, despite this, English fans observed in pubs and those depicted in TV coverage of 'live' matches still made a number of references to the Second World War in songs and chants. Craven (2005), writing in the *Daily Mail*, mentioned both *The Great Escape* and *Ten German Bombers* in an article titled 'Don't mention the war!' The song *Ten German Bombers* has often been sung when the England team have played Germany. Its lyrics, according to the version in Locken's (2009: 14–15) *The Best England Football Chants Ever*, specifically state that 'There were ten German bombers in the sky ... ', ending with 'The RAF from England had shot them all down!' According to Craven (2005), the former FA chief executive, Brian Barwick, made specific reference to the song, stating there

> is this one chant about ten German bombers. In the context of where the tournament is, we'd like to ask supporters to question the logic of singing that, because we've moved a great distance and we'd like to continue to progress.

Similarly, Parsons (2005), writing in *The Mirror*, also mentioned *The Great Escape* and other anti-German songs. He argued that a 'residual resentment of Germany remains in our national consciousness' and that the British cannot forget the war because 'it is just too soon'. This evidence echoes Elias's (1991; 1996; 2000) argument that the identities of individuals living in European nation states is rooted in their national pasts, despite the advance of centripetal forces since the

---

2 'RAF' refers to the British Royal Air Force.
3 'WWII' is an abbreviation for World War Two.

mid-twentieth century which have attempted to integrate Europeans (Guibernau, 2011; Roche, 2010).

The Great Escape was a film produced and directed by John Sturges in 1963 about an escape by a group of Allied prisoners of war from a Nazi POW camp during the Second World War. It is based on a true story retold in a book with the same title written by Paul Brickhill. The theme tune to the film was coined by the American composer Elmer Berstein and has often been sung by English football fans around both domestic and international football matches. Fisch (2003) states that the

> theme from *The Great Escape* has been heard around relegation-threatened football (soccer) clubs in England for many years. It's usually sung in response to a good performance which might (against all the odds) save them. Its use spread to the national team when England played an away match against Italy in the World Cup qualification competition, needing a draw to ensure automatic qualification, with the Italians needing victory. Italy were hot favourites, but an unspectacular, hard-working performance by England was just enough to ensure out a draw. Since then, it has been a regular favourite with England fans, and in particular the small brass band that follows England everywhere! ... .
> Somehow *The Great Escape* encapsulates something about how the British (and in particular the English) like to see themselves – refusing to give up, fighting against the odds, proud, brave, and indomitable. Alternatively, it's typical of a nation living in the past, and refusing to engage with the modern world, preferring to wallow in xenophobia and past achievements.

The match the author is referring to was England's World Cup 1998 Qualifier in which they drew 0–0 with Italy in Rome on 11 October 1997. An article on the BBC Sport website (2000) explains that this match was the

> crucial World Cup qualifying decider with the winners guaranteeing passage to the France 98 finals while the losers were to be consigned to the play-offs. England needed just a point from the game and produced a thoroughly professional performance to keep the Italians at bay with Ian Wright going close at the other end when his shot hit the post. Angelo di Livio was sent-off in a game in which Paul Ince played partly with a blood-stained bandage while Paul Gascoigne, a favourite with former Italian club Lazio, had an influential part.

Bradshaw (2010), film critic for *The Guardian*, suggests English fans' continued use of *The Great Escape* theme tune is rooted in an English nostalgia for the Second World War victory when England could not be separated from Britain because

> the movie and that theme music celebrate bulldog spirit and cheerful, gutsy humour, with the underdogs never saying die and pluckily defying the might of the Third Reich. Singing it on the terraces is a cheeky provocation.

Cull (2002: 282), speaking specifically of the continued use of this theme tune by English football fans during the 1998 and 2002 World Cups, suggests that for

> England, as compared to Scotland, Wales and Northern Ireland, the war has remained disproportionately central to national identity if only because England lacks an England against which to define itself. The relationship between Englishness and the memory of the Second World War is complex, more especially as the war has become a time capsule containing the key elements of older conceptions of Englishness.

Finally, in agreement, Blake (1999: 117–18) states that similar to

> the *Dambusters* tune it [*The Great Escape*] is a reference to the Second World War ... celebrating in a very complex way victory over the Germans, 'The Great Escape' inhabits the same ideological world as the chant 'Two World Wars and One World Cup' ... English feelings of a certain sort, sung to American-derived music.

The singing of *The Great Escape* and *Ten German Bombers* during World Cup 2006 was an example of how the English fans observed did not see any difference between using 'British' and 'English' indicators of identity together. The fans observed singing these songs in pubs during the 2006 World Cup were the same fans who had clipped St George's Cross flags to their pint glasses only a few days earlier.

Moving away from the war, further evidence of the continued existence of and reliance on a British-based Englishness was evident by the fact the English fans observed in pubs often sang the British national anthem *God Save the Queen* extremely passionately in response to it being played in stadia before each England match. This was particularly prevalent in the larger and busier venues attended. The following extracts (presented in chronological order) are taken from field notes relating to the largest/busiest venues the author attended to watch England's group stage matches against Paraguay and Sweden respectively. The third extract is from England's quarter-final match against Portugal.

> Before the eagerly anticipated kick-off, what seemed like everyone in the pub stood up and sang *God Save the Queen* at the top of their voices and some people even had one of their hands on their chest. People seemed oblivious that this anthem is supposed to represent Britain, not just England.[4]

> Yet, before the game, many sang *God Save the Queen*, particularly those I could see around the front row mezzanine floor. Again, they seemed content to sing the British national anthem to represent England.[5]

---

4 10 June 2006, pub in Kirkby Stephen, Cumbria.
5 20 June 2006, bar in Lancaster city centre.

> I did not notice any Union flags or references to Britain although everyone sang *God Save the Queen* at the start of the match.[6]

Yet, it is also important to point out that fans observed in different pubs did not always engage with the British national anthem. This tended to be the case in the smaller and less crowded venues visited where blatant displays of national sentiment, be they specifically English or British, were not as apparent as in larger, busier venues. The following extract taken from field notes from the small pub attended in Morecambe for the Trinidad and Tobago game (15 June 2006) highlights this.

> There appeared to be less of a carnival atmosphere too compared with the pub in Kirkby Stephen where I had watched the Paraguay game, as there were no horns, flags or megaphones carried by fans. This may again be due to fans having less time to prepare and also less time for drinking before the game. In contrast to the previous pub, no one sang the national anthem *God Save the Queen* in this pub. People were either silent or chatting through it. Again, this may be due to fans not having had much of a drink beforehand.

Similarly, the following extract taken from field notes from attendance at a small pub in Kirkby Stephen for the Ecuador game (25 June 2006) reinforces this contention.

> The atmosphere was very relaxed and quiet. No one seemed to be worse for wear from drinking and not a lot was said during the first half of the game, apart from one man quietly humming and occasionally singing along to the horns played by the fans at the live event in Germany – the theme of *The Great Escape* with 'England!' shouted after each verse. Not one person sang the national anthem though.

These examples highlight that even though Union flags were not observed in any of the pubs visited during the 2006 World Cup, there were other ways in which some fans portrayed a British-based Englishness. This is the kind of 'drag-effect' which Elias (1991: 222–3) contended is symptomatic of the persistence among citizens of contemporary European nation-states of

> the feeling that the fading or disappearance of a ... state as an autonomous entity would render meaningless everything which past generations had achieved and suffered in the framework and in the name of this survival unit.

One must remember that the state definitely does not equal the nation when it comes to the UK. Nevertheless, what Elias explains here in relation to the 'drag-effect' has similarities to Anderson's (1991) conception of nations as 'imagined communities'

---

6 1 July 2006, bar in Keswick, Cumbria.

that survive in the minds of individuals partly due to having continuity with a nation's past achievements. Moreover, this 'wilful nostalgia' for a bygone era has been discussed by Robertson (1990 cited in Giulianotti and Robertson, 2009: 61) as a 'postmodern' aspect of globalisation. Giulianotti and Robertson (2009: 61) state that in football,

> postmodern nostalgia centres particularly upon the great players and teams of the recent past, and in the senses of loss that are expressed when contemporary international sides fail to match their predecessors' exalted standards.

Although Giulianotti and Robertson (2009) fail to recognise it, Robertson's (1990) concept of 'wilful nostalgia' has been applied by Maguire and Poulton (1999) and Maguire et al. (1999) to understand the dominant discourses presented in the English national press and other marketing during Euro 96 where many allusions were made to England's one and only World Cup win in 1966. Yet, as discussed by Gibbons (2010), even this apparently 'English' achievement was ironically then considered to be a 'British' victory.

On initial inspection, the persistence of the British we-image in the face of a more specifically English we-image appears to be moving in the opposite direction to the drag-effect Elias theorised as it is a larger integration plane (Britishness) being dragged alongside a smaller one (Englishness). However, on closer examination, this finding is still an example of conflict between two interrelated layers of identity both of which are of different vintages (Mennell, 1994). This suggests that English national identity is currently in a state of flux and this explains why a specifically 'English' national distinctiveness is not anywhere near as well defined as it is for the Scottish or Welsh.

If this were not complex enough, it was also apparent that 'local' and 'club-based' identifications were being displayed by English fans even though it was the national team that were competing rather than specific clubs. The following section seeks to highlight how this third finding provides evidence for both Elias's (1991) drag-effect as well as Elias's (2000) concept of 'diminishing contrasts, increasing varieties'. It is argued that both concepts allow one to see how processes of homogenisation and heterogenisation must be understood as simultaneous in order to fully understand the ways English fans seem to have reacted to the globalisation and Europeanisation of English football.

The Interplay between the Local, the Club and the English

Numerous St George's Cross flags that had been decorated with *local* signage and emblems were apparent in the pubs visited during the fieldwork (and these were also evident in large numbers in television coverage of German stadia during England's World Cup matches). Field notes (1 July 2006) taken in a pub in Keswick, Cumbria, during England's last match of the tournament reveal that these symbols were also displayed on fans' clothing and other decoration.

> Over the top of the staircase was perhaps the largest visual symbol of local identity attached to a St George cross I had seen yet – it was a huge six-by six-foot flag with a Carlisle United badge in the top left corner, 'Keswick Blues' in the top right corner, 'Pride of Cumbria' written in the bottom left corner, the three lions badge in the bottom right corner and, finally, 'CARLISLE UNITED' written in large letters across the centre of the red cross of St George .... I noticed at least three men wearing Carlisle United shirts and one wearing a Liverpool FC shirt. There was also a man wearing a T-shirt with 'Keswick Blues' on it across the background of a St George cross and a Carlisle United logo side by side. I also observed at least five males with their faces painted; one half with a St George cross and the other half with the Carlisle United logo on either cheek. (Gibbons and Lusted, 2007: 301–2)

Apart from the Liverpool shirt, such local displays were predominantly associated with towns or cities that are represented by clubs from lower leagues that operate in purely domestic competitions and are made up of largely British players, coaches and owners. Not only is the make-up of these clubs less international than those of EPL clubs, but they do not have anywhere near the same amount of global media coverage so almost never enter transnational spaces with their local club (Mainwaring and Clark, 2012).

Rather than registering a decline in support for the nation, these local displays appear to re-invigorate and re-define English national sentiment and as such are an example of Elias's (1991) drag-effect because local layers of identification are being 'dragged' alongside the national we-image. Thus, as well as British identifications being 'clung' onto by some English fans in relation to the English national team, there was also the 'drag' of local identifications. These layers underpin English national identity rather than challenge it. This has particular relevance in the context of recent devolution processes within the UK. The display of local fan identities might be assumed to be the source of some tension and be incompatible with national solidarity. Yet, a long history exists where local affiliations and rivalries have been accommodated within a national context both within and outside of football and other sports (see Edensor, 2002; Russell, 2004). Using cricket as an exemplar, in a speech to the IPPR, entitled 'A New England: An English identity within Britain', Rt Hon. David Blunkett MP (2005: 8) urged, we

> have an affinity with towns and counties which is not based on a region or province (created as an administrative or political unit), nor mobilized as a rallying cry for separation (as with the Basque country) but acts, rather, as a building block for patriotic sentiment. Coming from Yorkshire and being

English – and beating Lancashire at cricket – is a statement about our localism and our Englishness.

Exploring the problematic of local rivalries further, findings from the pub-based observations highlighted some tensions among English fans, yet they were largely portrayed in an environment of accommodation and jovial acceptance. The following episode, recorded in field notes (20 June 2006) immediately before England's game against Sweden, outlines such tensions.

> Prior to the game, the TV cameras focused on a few England flags situated around the ground in Cologne and the commentator read out the names of the localities and clubs that had been printed across them. Those that were considered southern, such as Wycombe, Bristol, and Pompey [Portsmouth] were booed by supporters watching in the pub as well as those that were less well known places / teams. Those from the northern counties like Cumbria, the north-east and Lancashire, were cheered and, predictably, when Morecambe [a town next to Lancaster] was read out, fans cheered the loudest. (Gibbons and Lusted, 2007: 303)

Clearly, regional and local tensions remain integral to the construction of Englishness. England's peculiar political history may contribute to the legacy and nature of local rivalries within the English nation – as David Blunkett appears to be suggesting – and yet similar tensions are evident in support for the Welsh national team between supporters of the big city clubs, Cardiff and Swansea (Rogers and Rookwood, 2007), while Scottish football continues to be dominated by sectarian tensions, most famously between Glasgow Celtic and Glasgow Rangers fans (Burdsey and Chappell, 2001).

Observations suggested that local identities were challenging the legitimacy of the English nation at times. When this occurred, national affiliations seemed to eventually envelop and suppress the local. In the following extract from field notes (25 June 2006) taken in a pub during the Ecuador game, one person articulates this suppression of localism within the national context.

> Towards the end of the match, when [David] Beckham was taken off, two of the men watching the game from the far corner appeared to be having a conversation about players in the England team and the clubs they played for. One man seemed to overhear this and said in a loud voice, 'It doesn't matter ... whether you support Leeds, Arsenal ... Sod off! It's all England, innit!' (Gibbons and Lusted, 2007: 303)

The display of the local can also have a particularly 'transnational' flavour emphasising the diverse frames of reference that are increasingly commonplace in the elite end of English club football (Giulianotti and Robertson, 2009). It is no coincidence that the following incident involved Manchester United – arguably England's most globally renowned club (Mellor, 2000; 2004). In the extract below, an English fan (1 July 2006) chose to verbally insult the player of the opposing Portuguese national team by referring to the player's English club attachment *rather than* to his nationality.

> After the Rooney-Ronaldo incident ... Rooney was sent off. After this one man shouted (after punching the wall!), 'Fuck off you Stretford cunt! I'll batter ya!' This was clearly a reference to the well-known Stretford End of Manchester United's stadium at Old Trafford and it was interesting how the fan chose to refer to the English club team Ronaldo played for rather than his Portuguese nationality – especially seeing as Rooney plays for the same club. (Gibbons and Lusted, 2007: 304)

Giulianotti and Robertson (2009: 108) touch upon the Rooney-Ronaldo incident, although they seem to only recognise how it acted to 'intensify nationalistic standpoints'. But both of the aforementioned observations actually highlight the diversification of contemporary identifications that reflect the simultaneously homogenising and heterogenising processes transforming the elite English club game. Even in a match between two national sides, the local still appears to complicate previously provided identifications based simply on nationality. This certainly provides evidence for King's (2003) thesis, but the latter example can also be explained using Elias's (2000) notion of diminishing contrasts, increasing varieties as it highlights two heterogeneous responses to global and European integrative flows (Maguire, 2011a).

It is important to highlight the variation in types of local or club-based layers of identity that interact with the national in English football, and, as in the latter instance, appear less able to be suppressed by national sentiment. The kinds of displays that celebrated local or club-based identities and were either accommodated by the nation or presented a challenge to it, were frequently portrayed by fans of lower level clubs. These teams largely operate within a domestic setting and almost never perform on a transnational stage (Mainwaring and Clark, 2012). Displays of Manchester United symbols, for example, were almost completely absent from the pubs chosen. This is surprising given the international status of United and the close proximity of Manchester to the location of the fieldwork (ranging from approximately 60 to 90 miles). Conversely, it is also unsurprising if King's (2003) findings are taken into account regarding how a core of Mancunian Manchester United fans have rejected the England national team. This again points towards the simultaneous homogenizing and heterogenizing tendencies brought about by global forces – something Giulianotti and Robertson (2009: 45) refer to as the 'duality of glocality' whereby local cultures respond to aspects of global culture and vice-versa. Although far less popular among globalisation theorists, this finding is equally well explained using Elias's (2000) 'diminishing contrasts, increasing varieties'.

The globalisation and commodification of the EPL has enabled many elite English clubs to operate consistently on a global stage, not only in the elite European club competitions, but also through the recruitment of *the best* players and coaching staff from all over the world – all displayed on TV stations with increasing frequency, and with an ever wider global audience (cf. Kerr and Emery, 2011; Millward, 2011; Rookwood and Millward, 2011). In addition, elite clubs are also branding themselves internationally and successfully breaking into new markets such as the Far East (cf. Manzenreiter and Horne, 2004; Horne, 2005; Rookwood and Chan, 2011).

While research on the impact of globalisation (and glocalisation) on supporter identities of elite clubs who regularly participate in transnational spaces (European competitions) is evident, the resulting impact on fans from leagues below the EPL is less clear. At this level, football competitions have remained purely domestic, with the personnel of lower league clubs largely British and often retaining a particularly local flavour through 'home-grown' players and local owners. In a study of northern English identity, Russell (2004: 273) suggested that English identity is 'something constructed in and experienced through the *locality*'. Local identities appear to remain central components of football fan culture whether as a result of globalisation or longer-standing parochial rivalries. At the same time, identifications with the national team seemingly appear as strong as ever, particularly in the months surrounding international competitions. According to Andrews and Ritzer (2007: 148), many

> researchers are transfixed with identifying, and subsequently seeking to rescue, the residues of the sporting local. The inference of such projects would appear to be that the organically local, sporting or otherwise, is somehow actively resistant to the forces of globalization.

Related to this, King (2003: 221) stresses that people experience multiple realities as opposed to singular ones and this provides support for Elias's (1991; 2000) claims and those made in relation to sport by Maguire (cf. 2011a). Though by focusing on only the largest football clubs, King (2003), Levermore and Millward (2007) and Millward (2006) fail to properly recognise the ways in which the identity of fans of clubs at lower levels of the English football league structure have been impacted by increasing European integration and globalisation processes. Moreover, they also fail to consider evidence of the competing conceptions of English identity that have been presented to, and demonstrated by, football fans since the 1950s when the England national team first began to compete in international football fixtures (Gibbons, 2010). Whilst King (2003) does go to some lengths to explain the rise of Manchester United in European football and successfully places this in what was occurring economically, culturally and socially throughout the latter half of the twentieth century, his analysis is overly focused on one English club and the views of a small contingent of fans from that club. Moreover, Manchester United are perhaps the most untypical club in English football and cannot be representative of others clubs, particularly when it comes to discussions of fans' actions and opinions.

Conclusion

The evidence provided in this chapter suggests that the overt display of the St George's Cross during World Cup 2006 offers a more complex picture of contemporary English national identity than has so far been proposed in relation to other tournaments since Euro 96. Observations confirmed that rather than being a homogenous, fixed expression of nationalist sentiment, supporting the England national team reflects how multiple layers of identification are simultaneously depicted by English football fans.

The evidence provided in this chapter shows specifically 'English', 'British' as well as 'local' and 'club-based' identifications that are often simultaneously displayed or articulated by different fans in relation to the English national team. Although none of these layers of we-image are 'new', their simultaneous appearance around the national team seems to have become more prominent since the 1990s and this is not something that has been addressed in enough depth by academics before now. Whilst the current ubiquity of the St George's Cross gives the impression that attachments to a British-based Englishness of the past are in a process of dissolution, the continued existence of songs relating to the Second World War and the unquestioned acceptance of the British national anthem amongst many English football fans suggests this is not the case. The English national team are not representative of a unified conception of Englishness as has been previously suggested by Robinson (2008), and English national identity is still defined by past British rather than specifically English achievements, despite the fact that this is not the case for any of the other home nations within the UK. This finding can be explained using Elias's (1991) notion of the drag-effect because identifications with Britain are being 'dragged' alongside those with Englishness. Post-devolution displays of what appears to be a specifically English national identity still often lag behind them displays of a British-based Englishness of the past.

There was also evidence of the continued importance of local and club-based identifications, and the ways they interact with national symbols and national football support. These local identities are themselves informed *differentially* by wider processes of social change, including globalisation and European integration which can be explained by what Elias (2000) termed 'diminishing contrasts, increasing varieties'. Attached to apparently homogenising displays of the English St George's Cross are a myriad of displays of local and/or club-based identifications. These multiple varieties are largely dependent on the type of club supported. The changes to the elite club game in England since the early 1990s (discussed in Chapter 3), which are perhaps best regarded as 'unintended consequences' of globalisation and European integration, have caused many fans of *elite* English clubs to diversify their support.

European integration, as well as the wider political devolution of the 'Celtic' nations within the UK has also prompted further displays of localism among English football fans. While these processes have not directly impacted upon fans of clubs from the lower leagues, who do not perform on an international stage and are largely British in make-up, such processes have encouraged these fans to utilise the global stage and profile that the England team perform on to display, negotiate, and symbolise their own, otherwise globally 'invisible', varieties of local identification. This is an aspect of fan culture that requires further research as it may help gain further insight into understanding the role of the local in the construction of contemporary Englishness via football.

Most research on local identities in football support appears to have followed one of two paths: local identities have either been analysed as somehow distinct from, and resistant to, national and global identities (cf. Andrews and Ritzer, 2007; Mainwaring and Clark, 2012), or they have been seen within the paradigm of the homogenising aspects of globalisation and European integration (cf. King, 2000, 2003; Levermore and Millward, 2007; Millward, 2006), where the display of the local is part of a wider emerging European transnational consciousness. Each approach appears to suggest that local identities offer a challenge to the authority and legitimacy of the nation. Yet Maguire and Possamai (2005: 60), in advocating an appreciation of Elias's (2000) concept of 'diminishing contrasts, increasing varieties', point out that 'the meanings and outcomes of local/global sport remain highly contested' and this certainly seemed to be what was observed in the actions of English fans in pubs during World Cup 2006.

An alternative explanation could be provided by Giulianotti and Robertson's (2004; 2009) global-realist approach, specifically the 'duality of glocality', which is also useful to begin to account for the heightened visibility of local identities that are displayed mostly *within*, rather than *beyond*, a national frame of reference in terms of support for the England national team. However, when considered together, Elias's (1991; 2000) concepts of the 'drag-effect' and 'diminishing contrasts, increasing varieties' offer clearer explanations of *both* the drag of Britishness and localism alongside Englishness *as well as* the display of support for the local and / or the club as a direct response to globalisation and Europeanisation. When applied to these findings, Giulianotti and Robertson's (2004; 2009) approach is not as clearly applied to the former as it is to the latter.

In summary, the argument and findings presented in this chapter appear to challenge longer-standing common sense notions that a post-Euro 96 increase in the appearance of the St George's Cross marks the beginnings of a unified 'English national project', one that will blindly follow the path of the other now devolved nations within the UK. Englishness, at least that which is constructed through support for the national football team, appears to be as much about representing British and local layers of identification as it is an expression of specifically English national sentiment. Rather than initiating the 'death' of the nation, the homogenising processes of globalisation and European integration that seemingly diminish the contrasts between people across nation-state borders, appear to re-invigorate English national identity via football, albeit in novel and somewhat fragmented ways – increasing varieties (Elias, 2000; Maguire, 1999).

The evidence provided in the current chapter suggests the relationship between English national identity and football fan culture is more complex than the rise in the display of the St George's Cross suggests. However, following Hills (1999, cited in Sandvoss, 2003: 177–8) it is acknowledged that observations of fans' actions are limited on their own without also assessing the views of fans themselves. The reasons why English fans have recently chosen to articulate and display their multi-layered identities around the English national team in the ways described above can only be accurately determined by taking what fans have to say themselves into account. This is the task of Chapters 5 and 6.

Chapter 5

Fan Debates on Team GB at the London 2012 Olympics and the Almunia Case

Introduction

To more fully understand whether the relationship between English national identity and football fan culture painted by the author's observations of fan's actions during World Cup 2006 were an accurate representation of English fans, it was deemed necessary to conduct a further study. This was the specific task of the fourteen month online participant observation study that underpins the current chapter and Chapter 6. In this chapter, the ways in which English national identity was debated by fans through their discussions around two football-related issues are interpreted in relation to Elias's (1991) 'changes in the we-I balance'. The two issues debated amongst fans which best highlighted their views on English national identity were the prospect of the Great Britain and Northern Ireland Olympic team fielding a 'British' football team for the London 2012 Olympics and the possibility that Arsenal's Spanish goalkeeper, Manuel Almunia, might be chosen to represent the England national team due to becoming a naturalised British citizen. In the following two main sections, findings relating to each issue are discussed under various sub-headings. These findings are placed in the context of previous research which was lacking evidence from fans themselves. It is concluded that these discussions highlight the multi-layered nature of contemporary English national identity in seemingly different but often interrelated ways.

GB Football Team for the London 2012 Olympics

The prospect of Great Britain and Northern Ireland fielding a football team for the London 2012 Olympic Games first became a topic of media attention even before London's bid to host the Games was successful in July 2005.[1] Soon after this an intense political debate began between the home nations of the UK that went beyond football, the Olympics and even sport itself, to the very core of 'British' national identity politics in the early twenty-first century (Ewen, 2012; MacRury and Poynter, 2010). As the host nation, the International Olympic Committee (IOC) expected Team GB to field a team for every event and football was to be no exception. The problem was that the UK has four separate national

---

1 The Olympic football team is referred to hereafter as 'Great Britain', 'GB' or 'Team GB'.

teams with four separate football associations for England, Scotland, Wales and Northern Ireland, each affiliated to FIFA independently (see Chapter 1 for more on this). This is a privileged position in world football considering all other nation-states are only permitted one national team and football association in order to be formally recognised (Menary, 2010: 18; Moorhouse, 1996).

Whilst a GB football team was fielded in eleven Olympic Games tournaments between 1908 and 1972, all players in the squads for many of these tournaments were English and before 2012 a British football team had not competed at an Olympic Games since 1972 (Menary, 2010: 290). This was said to be due to the English FA removing the distinction between amateurs and professionals in 1974 (Menary, 2010: 278). In 2009, the Scottish, Welsh and Northern Irish football associations signed an agreement stating they would not stop England fielding a GB football team as long as it was a one-off for the 2012 Olympics and assuming there was no attempt to pick Scottish, Welsh or Northern Irish players (Ewen, 2012: 307–8). The Scots, Welsh and Northern Irish had unanimously decided they did not want to be involved in the Games in order to retain their independent status as national teams in their own right. The fear was that if the separate nations within the UK competed together under the 'Team GB' label at the 2012 Olympics there would be little justification for them being allowed to compete as separate national teams in future international competitions such as the more prestigious FIFA World Cup. This is something many within FIFA and UEFA have long been calling for despite FIFA president Sepp Blatter's verbal reassurances that it would not happen (Menary, 2010).

Whereas pre-1974 the FA had made the decision to field a GB football team regardless of what the SFA, FAW and IFA wanted, the growth in the political power of the 'Celtic' nations within the UK following devolution processes of the late 1990s, meant that the Scottish, Welsh and Northern Irish now had the political power to stand up for themselves. What better way to flex this newly acquired political muscle than through the globally high profile lens of international football and the most popular sporting event on earth: the Olympic Games. The Team GB issue was essentially one of national identity, with the main concern being that fielding such a team signalled a loss of national distinctiveness for the individual home nations, including England (Ewen, 2012). From an Eliasian perspective, this issue highlights 'the close associations of sport with national cultures and identities' and that, particularly in the context of devolution of the UK, 'moves towards integration of regions at a political level are undermined by the role of sport' (Maguire, 2011a: 991).

A number of opinion polls, petitions and official/unofficial fan groups were mobilised (mainly via the Internet) to oppose the idea of a British Olympic football team. Perhaps one of the most prominent was the 'NoTeamGB.com' campaign, a collaboration that began in May 2006 between official fan organisations from Wales, Scotland, Northern Ireland and England.[2] The group attempted to lobby government MPs, the FA, and the British Olympic Association (BOA) by providing

---

2 However, it is important to point out that the 'NoTeamGB' campaign was organised by a Scottish fan group and its membership was dominated by Scottish and Welsh supporters.

evidence in the form of fan polls / petitions to demonstrate that the majority of fans within the UK were against a GB football team ever happening (Ewen, 2012).[3]

In June 2011 the BOA declared that they had made an agreement with the FA meaning that players from all four home nations were eligible to be picked to play for Team GB at London 2012 (Conway, 2012; Ewen, 2012). The decision meant that the SFA, FAW and the IFA were effectively silenced. Nothing new according to Menary's (2010) account of the history behind the GB football team, but the agreement contradicted that previously made in 2009 between the FA and the other national associations that the team would only comprise English players. In any case, current Olympic football rules mean that all teams must consist of an eighteen-man squad of fifteen players under the age of 23 and three players of 'open age' and that they must play for no money in line with the amateur ethos of the Olympic movement (Menary, 2010: 287). Such restrictions mean that national teams who compete in the Olympic football tournament are quite different in make-up to the national teams who compete in the FIFA World Cup or UEFA European Championships (Euros) which are competitions with no age or payment restrictions that gain much more global interest from fans.

On 28 June 2012, it was announced that Micah Richards (English), Ryan Giggs (Welsh) and Craig Bellamy (Welsh) would be included as the three 'over-age' players in the Team GB squad (Kelso, 2012a). The full squad was announced on 2 July and comprised thirteen English and five Welsh players, but no Scottish or Northern Irish players were selected (Daily Mail, 2012). Thus, as in previous Olympic tournaments (Menary, 2010), Team GB was dominated by English players and was therefore not truly representative of the United Kingdom of Great Britain and Northern Ireland. This was despite the fact that no players from the England squad for the Euro 2012 football competition (which took place after the Olympic tournament) were allowed to be picked by the 2012 Team GB manager Stuart Pearce to avoid players being tired and to reduce the potential for injury (Idessane, 2012). This acted to clearly highlight that the main focus of the FA was not success at the 2012 Olympic football tournament but at Euro 2012.

Both during and after the 2012 Olympics, the GB football team issue was a much less popular topic of debate in the national press than it had been prior to the tournament. This was largely due to the fact that the team only managed to progress to the quarterfinal stages losing 4–5 to South Korea following extra-time and a penalty shootout after a 1–1 draw. During the tournament there is some evidence that players in the squad, including the Welsh captain Ryan Giggs, as well as some members of the BOA, wanted Team GB to enter a football team

---

3 According to the noteamgb.com website: 'The NoTeamGB.com campaign is run by fans organisations from England (the English Football Supporter's Federation), Northern Ireland (Amalgamation of Northern Ireland Supporters Clubs), Scotland (Association of Tartan Army Clubs) and Wales (FSF Cymru) and we are united in our opposition to the creation of a Great Britain football team for the purposes of the 2012 Olympics or beyond' (http://www.noteamgb.com/Q-And-A-About-No-Team-GB.htm, Accessed Jun. 2011).

at future Olympic Games (Toney, 2012; Winter, 2012). The chief executive of the English FA is reported to have said that the FA would not support a future GB football team at the 2016 Olympics (Kelso, 2012b). The success of Team GB in other events, resulting in them finishing third in the overall medals table, meant that the football tournament was not the main focus of most national media coverage. This is rare considering men's football usually dominates the English / British national media and especially considering the England national team were competing in the Euro 2012 competition later on.

Considering the data for this study was gathered between June 2008 and September 2009, it provided an excellent opportunity to gauge the views of a sample of fans on the Team GB issue as it was very high on the agenda in the national news at that time. It is important to point out here that none of the home nations qualified for Euro 2008 which was the main international tournament occurring in 2008. This may therefore have impacted the findings.

The Team GB issue was raised by the author on two separate occasions, both within discussions about other related topics. For instance, the author began a thread about the 2008 Beijing Olympics and whether this event united the home nations and made citizens feel a sense of British unity. Other forum members raised the GB football team issue as a specific discussion topic with its own thread three times over the time period researched. Twice this was in response to what fans had heard in the media. For example, an English fan posted the following in response to a BBC article he had seen:

> December 16 2008 08:42
> 60:[4] Team GB ... Now I think all GB nations want this to happen, but the main problem yet again with most footballing matters is FIFA. Nobody can trust them at the moment they're saying it's ok but in 3 years' time that view might change. I guess it's easier in a way for them to have the UK competing as one team instead of 4. Now UEFA, and FIFA insist it won't affect us. I think team GB should sit down with lawyers and get this all in writing. [Male, English, West Ham United FC, aged 45]

The same fan began another thread titled 'Team GB Deal Agreed' after the announcement had been made in May 2009 that the SFA, FAW and IFA had agreed to have nothing further to do with the GB football team idea so long as the English FA agreed to only ask English players to join the team. This topic was also

---

4   The numbers used at the beginning of each quotation indicate the code that has been used to protect the identity of the forum members. '1' is the number code used to refer to the author. The identity of fans has been protected by using their assigned number codes rather than the fan's actual screen-name. '(Fan 1)' has been used to keep the author's screen-name anonymous as it has the potential to lead to the identification of the forum used and thus the identities of members.

specifically raised by an Australian fan as if the idea was almost hypothetical in nature and a GB football team was unlikely to occur.

The issue arose during discussions around many other topics and it became clear that English fans in the online community were divided not just on whether a GB football team would work and how it would look in practice – some stating that there should be a team entered and others stating reasons why this should not occur – but perhaps more importantly, what layer of identity football 'should' actually represent. For many English fans, this represented an opportunity to articulate their attachments to England, Britain as well as to specific regions/localities within England. As such, the same kinds of multi-faceted representations and displays of identity to those observed during World Cup 2006, were also evident here in discussions amongst fans. English national identity depicted by fans' discussions around these two football-related issues highlighted the multi-layered character of contemporary English national identity whereby smaller and larger, as well as older and newer, planes of identification were simultaneously interacting with one another (Elias, 1991). The information provided in what follows helps explain the possible reasons underpinning fans' preferences for associating themselves with some layers of identification over others. It also highlights the situational nature of this process. It seemed that these layers were readily swapped by some fans depending on the context, but were rigidly adhered to by other fans at all times.

Attachments to England and 'Anti-Britishness'

Some English fans seemed to be against Team GB simply because they had not experienced a Great Britain football team representing them. For instance, the English fans in the following discussion thread felt that Team GB would not work for football nor glean much interest from fans in the UK who were used to being divided into separate national teams:

> May 29 2009 11:09am
> 18: Only English players will be picked. [Male, English, Juventus FC, aged 28]

> May 29 2009 11:10am
> 61: Just for the Olympics. Still it won't be popular, people will laugh at it. [Male, English, FC Barcelona, aged 23]

This is a point also made by Kelly (2011) in reaction to the BOA announcement of June 2011 that a GB football team would be able to field players from Scotland, Wales, Northern Ireland and England meaning fans of the separate national teams – who have a long history of being divided (Moorhouse, 1996) – would be expected to unite to support Great Britain. Other members of the forum were against Team GB because they could not see how the team would equally comprise Scottish, Welsh, Northern Irish and English players in order to be truly representative of the UK. Later on in the same thread, fan 61 suggested:

> May 29 2009 11:24am
> 61: People forget that players could refuse to play for it. Considering England's history and what not. [Male, English, FC Barcelona, aged 23]

To which a Spanish fan replied:

> May 29 2009 11:25am
> 25: The first British teams at the Olympics were also all-English. [Male, Spanish, Real Madrid CF., aged 20]

After this, the author added:

> June 6 2009 12:23pm
> 1: Bet there will be more English fans supporting them than Welsh and Scottish.

To which an English fan immediately replied:

> June 6 2009 12:25pm
> 3: Only because there be (*sic*) hardly any Welsh or Scottish players in the squad (laughing emoticon).[5] [Male, English, Arsenal FC, aged 53]

There were also English fans that were completely adamant they felt no attachments to Britain whatsoever and as such would never support a GB football team. Many of these fans demonstrated familiar xenophobic views and some even demonstrated a kind of 'anti-Britishness' that supports the findings of the Future of England surveys conducted on the English population by the IPPR later on in 2011 and 2012 (Wyn Jones, et al., 2012; 2013). The following three examples are the views expressed by one fan on three separate occasions, clearly demonstrating hostility towards the other home nations:

> August 21 2008 09:39am
> 17: Team GB can f**k off unless its all English players. [Male, English, Arsenal FC, aged 20]

> October 2008 05:41pm
> 17: Hate the term British as well, I'm English and that's the end of it, no one is going to tell me I'm not.

> December 16 2008 10:19pm
> 17: F**k Scotland, Wales and Northern Ireland, we play as England or nothing.

---

5 'Emoticons' are on-screen expressions of feelings or gestures. They are presented in brackets to indicate when they were used in conversation.

Whilst these were the most extreme examples, two other English fans (3 and 30) demonstrated support for the sentiments expressed in the latter post and there were two others who were similarly keen to stress their anti-British stance:

December 17 2008 05:03pm
14: When I walk around the streets you see England flags waving, not Great Britain flags waving. England til I die! [Male, English, Notts County FC, aged 22]

December 17 2008 05:05pm
17: (Good posting emoticon) Same here. [Male, English, Arsenal FC, aged 20]

One of the fans who had previously highlighted support for the expression of English nationalism within this thread seemed eager to point out that the GB football team for the 2012 Olympics is not really an issue at all and that fans should not worry about it:

December 17 2008 05:04pm
3: I don't see what all the fuss is about, it's a one off at the end of the day. It seems a bit petty to be whinging about this. The only reason that seems to be given is that we don't compete in football as GB. This won't result in a future merger of the home nations in all internationals, so chill the fcuk (*sic*) out lads. [Male, English, Arsenal FC, aged 53]

This met with the following riposte from the fan who had posted the most extreme anti-British views:

December 17 2008 05:06pm
17: Because some of us don't agree with GB. [Male, English, Arsenal FC, aged 20]

The following exchange ensued between fans 17 and 19 about why the former held such anti-British views:

December 18 2008 02:14am
17: I'm English not British, I support England only. I don't want a [Team] GB either what's so hard to understand about that? [Male, English, Arsenal FC, aged 20]

December 18 2008 02:16am
19: Why are you so against the whole British concept? (Clueless emoticon). We fight wars as Great Britain. Do you agree with that? [Male, English, Arsenal FC, aged 21]

December 18 2008 02:18am
17: There is no need for us to be at war, but I think we should do everything independent (*sic*). [Male, English, Arsenal FC, aged 20]

This sparked debate between the author and fan 17 about the English political situation regarding devolution:

January 3 2009 10:42pm
1: What do you mean by 'everything'?

January 5 2009 02:54pm
17: Sporting events, government, basically everything that is done in the UK but with it being 4 independent countries instead. [Male, English, Arsenal FC, aged 20]

January 6 2009 04:04pm
1: So are you saying you'd vote for English devolution?

January 6 2009 09:42pm
17: I'd vote for England to break away from the UK anytime.

This was evidence that the Team GB issue went far beyond football and into UK post-devolution politics (Wyn Jones et al., 2012; 2013), as has been previously suggested by Maguire (cf. 2011a) and also by Ewen (2012). Building upon this, the author began a discussion thread on the topic of whether fans felt 'British' when the 2008 Beijing Olympics was occurring and whether the Olympics had the power to unite the home nations. Anti-British sentiments came out in response to this also, for instance:

July 30 2008 04:54pm
3: I'm English end of ... [Male, English, Arsenal FC, aged 53]

July 30 2008 04:58pm
9: (Good posting emoticon and St George flag emoticon). [Male, English, Birmingham City FC, aged 24]

July 30 2008 05:00pm
17: English as well. F**k the other 3 countries, should be like football and all have separate teams. [Male, English, Arsenal FC, aged 20]

July 30 2008 05:40pm
4: English, should be like Commonwealth Games, England, Wales, Scotland and Northern Ireland. [Female, English, West Ham United FC, aged 60]

July 31 2008 12:28pm
30: Englishman, not Britishman, that could imply I'm from Wales, Scotland or Ireland (surprised emoticon). Like it's been said, like the Commonwealth games it should be separate countries, also like the world cup. [Male, English, Manchester United FC, aged 51]

In response to these posts the author decided to bring up the issue of a GB football team within the thread about Britishness and Beijing:

> August 1 2008 04:01pm
> 1: So you guys wouldn't support a British football team in the Olympics? Have you always felt more English than British? What's the reason for this?

The response from many English fans was again largely against the idea of the home nations competing together and once again this went beyond football. For instance, one fan replied:

> August 5 2008 03:49am
> 17: Football is the country's biggest sport and we compete as England same with rugby and cricket. Also I've got nothing to do with Northern Ireland, Wales or Scotland. I'm English ... . I believe in the flag of Saint George not the union jack which I hate. Since England is the biggest country in the UK and the most powerful why is the union jack a blue background from Scotland instead of the white of England? ... . I don't believe in British though only English. [Male, English, Arsenal FC, aged 20]

In response to this, another English fan highlighted that fan 17 was a British citizen regardless of his anti-British views, stating the following:

> August 5 2008 01:10pm
> 47: You should probably rip up your passport then (fan 17). [Male, English, Queens Park Rangers FC, aged 24]

The author also asked fan 17 why he disliked the union flag and being classified as British so much, and this sparked the following discussion:

> August 6 2008 09:19pm
> 17: I've got no connections with Scotland, Wales or N. Ireland so I class myself as English. Also I was born in England so class myself as English and therefore believe in the flag of St George not union jack. [Male, English, Arsenal FC, aged 20]

> August 7 2008 09:09am
> 1: Is national identity important to you then? Or is it only important when it comes to football/sport in general?

> August 7 2008 03:58pm
> 17: National identity is very important for everything, inside sports outside sports. I look at it in this way, Britain is a collection of countries not a country itself, it describes me as much as saying I'm European, while English describes me much more. If someone from outside the UK said are you British? I would go 'I am

English'. Calling me British is like calling an American person Canadian or calling an Aussie a Kiwi, or even a Geordie a Mackem. [Male, English, Arsenal FC, aged 20]

Two other English fans (3 and 79) agreed with this statement. The author went on to ask member 17 the following:

August 9 2008 12:56pm
1: Of course it's up to you how you define your own national identity but whether you like it or not Britain is the political nation-state and England is a nation within this with no political power of its own. Would you be happier if England had a level of devolved power from Britain in the same way Scotland, Wales and Northern Ireland have?

To which he responded:

August 9 2008 06:35pm
17: I'd rather UK was abolished and each of the 4 countries had its own government with no powers in other three countries. [Male, English, Arsenal FC, aged 20]

There were other brief conversations between the author and individual English fans in this thread that highlighted somewhat ambivalent feelings towards the idea of the Olympics representing Britishness. For instance, in response to the author's initial post asking fans whether they felt British when the Olympics was occurring and whether the Olympics had the effect of uniting the home nations, one fan replied:

August 5 2008 09:05am
78: No and no. In general I suppose if I happened to see some athletics I might cheer for a British lass rather than a Bulgarian (don't have anything against Bulgaria, it's just an example!) but I don't cheer for the Brits no matter what.[6] It's just not THAT important to me. And the hypocrisy of the Olympics makes me vom (*sic*). A war or something might bring the Nations of the British Isles 'together behind the flag', but the Olympics, nah. [Male, English, Blackburn Rovers, aged 27]

The same fan later went on to say:

August 5 2008 07:51pm
78: I think the four nations should each have a team at the Olympics. And sure, I feel England deserves to have its own team at the Olympics. Why not? (Confused emoticon).

---

6   The term 'lass' is used in some areas of the UK to refer to a 'woman'.

Perhaps one of the best examples of English xenophobia came in response to the following post:

> August 6 2008 09:20pm
> 35: lol it's amazing that the people who haven't experienced even the UK, let alone interact and meet other people just come out and say, I'm English ... f**k everyone else ... . The ignorance.[7] [Male, English, Newcastle United FC, aged 22]

This was met with the following:

> August 7 2008 09:02pm
> 3: I'm English and yh fuck everyone else.[8] ENGLISH AND PROUD! Have you a problem with that? [Male, English, Arsenal FC, aged 53]

For some English fans the idea of Britain simply did not sit comfortably with how they perceived their own national identity. The anti-British views cited in this sub-section provide evidence of 'resistance by those within a national culture who still cling to more intense versions of the invented traditions that underpin their sense of identity' (Maguire, 2011a: 988). In relation to England specifically, and as alluded to in Chapter 4, Maguire (2011a: 990) has termed this anti-British reaction the 'Little Englander', which he defines as a 'strong defensive reaction to globalization processes, European integration, the pluralization of national culture and the assertiveness of the "Celtic fringe".' Thus, in this case the English layer of identification was being 'dragged' alongside moves towards a more inclusive Britishness (Elias, 1991).

Such findings are hardly surprising given recent devolution processes which have led to cultural divisions rather than unity between the nations of the UK. This can be aligned to the idea that for some at least, England is an emerging political community in its own right (Wyn Jones et al., 2012; 2013). Whilst UK devolution occurred after Elias had died and the complexity of the identities that exist within the UK was not a topic Elias himself wrote about in any detail (Fletcher, 1997), it can be explained using his concept of 'changes in the we-I balance' whereby identities of many different ages and sizes conflict with one another and national identity is challenged by global integrative forces. This is seemingly a clearer case of the 'drag-effect' Elias theorised than the drag of 'British' identifications alongside moves towards a specific Englishness observed in the pub-based observations (Chapter 4). Although both movements appear to be going in opposite directions, they simply emphasise the fluctuating nature of contemporary English national identity amidst broader European civilising processes. However, as was

---

7   'lol' is an abbreviation for the phrase 'laugh out loud'.
8   'yh' is an abbreviation for the terms 'yeah' or 'yes'.

the case in the pub-based study findings discussed in the previous chapter, the same was not evident for all English fans.

English Support for Team GB and Attachments to Britain

In contrast to the above, there were many examples of support for a GB football team amongst other English fans. The reasons for this were varied. Some fans thought that a GB team would simply be more successful than the separate national teams within the UK because the pool of talent that could be drawn upon would be larger if players of all UK nationalities were eligible to play. For example:

> December 17 2008 05:23pm
> 60: If we went into the Olympics as England we would come about 20th. Instead under GB we're about 5th in the world. 5th under team GB or 20th under England? I go for team GB. [Male, English, West Ham United FC, aged 45]

Some English fans also displayed similar sentiments after it had been announced that the GB football squad would solely comprise English players. For instance:

> May 29 2008 11:13am
> 60: Tad gutted it will just be English.

> June 17 2009 02:21pm
> 63: F**k the other nations FAs they're probably just worried that their players wont (*sic*) get in the squad (poking tongue out emoticon). It's so stupid that politics have spoilt an opportunity to show unity and give a great exhibition of football. The ¼ squad allocation would work perfectly to make it fair and with the right manager as well, I heard Fergie was interested if it was a GB team.[9] [Male, English, Arsenal FC, aged 23]

Other fans suggested that although they preferred separate national teams for the most part, as long as Team GB was a one-off for 2012 then they would get behind the idea and could not see a problem in playing as separate national teams for some competitions and being united under the British flag for others. For instance:

> August 11 2008 03:23pm
> I'd love to see a GB football team as a one-off for the 2012 Olympics, but away from that would prefer to keep separate sides. There is still plenty of room for people to celebrate their separate identities as English, Scottish, Welsh or Northern Irish as well as being British. [Male, English, Everton FC, aged 25]

---

9   'Fergie' is a nickname for the now retired Scottish Manchester United manager Sir Alex Ferguson.

The author then asked this fan:

> August 11 2008 06:26pm
> 1: So why would you prefer to see separate sides? Can you give any other e.gs of places where English, Scots, Welsh and N.Irish can celebrate their identities outside of sports?

To which he responded:

> August 11 2008 07:32pm
> 59: The 4 countries have always enjoyed a sporting rivalry, and I'd like to see that continue. Although I consider myself British I'd always support, for example, an English boxer over a Scotsman, just as I'd support a Scouse boxer over a Yorkshireman. Events such as Burns Night and the patron saints' days (are examples of places where separate home nations' identities can be celebrated). [Male, English, Everton FC, aged 25]

Another fan in this thread simply said:

> July 30 2008 07:16pm
> 47: It's sport, I'll be supporting the British team, just like I wish the separate home nations well in football. [Male, English, Queens Park Rangers, aged 24]

It was interesting to note the way in which some English fans often suggested football represented a more central aspect for confirming their national identity than other sports. Many stated that whilst they supported British teams or Welsh and Scottish athletes representing Britain or their individual nations in other sports, they could not do this for football due to the strong link it had to their national identity. The following discussion highlights this:

> December 5 2008 12:29pm
> 19: In the Tennis I like to follow Andy Murray (Scottish) and in the boxing I like Joe Calzaghe (Welsh). I don't see a problem in celebrating Britain's achievements in the sporting world outside of football. [Male, English, Arsenal FC, aged 21]

> December 5 2008 01:13pm
> 1: Interesting. Do you think there's a difference between individual sports like these and team sports like football then? Would you show similar support for Scottish and Welsh national football teams (or dare I say it, a 'British' football team)?

> December 6 2008 01:26pm
> 19: Not for football teams, because I follow England so it would seem strange to show support for more than one country. I think the idea of a British football team

isn't so bad as long as it stays in the Olympics. The England, Wales, Scotland, and Northern Ireland national teams have too much history, pride, etc., to make a British team work in things like the World Cup. I don't think many would warm to the idea. But in team sports such as Rugby I prefer the home nations to do well and would want them to beat the likes of South Africa, etc.

December 8 2008 05:49pm
1: So why do you feel differently when it comes to rugby?

December 9 2008 01:18pm
19: Don't get me wrong, I don't put on a Wales shirt and join in the national anthem, but I just prefer to see them do well over the southern hemisphere teams. Maybe because I'm not as into Rugby as I am with football so it doesn't seem strange to want another country to do well.

December 9 2008 04:36pm
1: I see, interesting. So is football the only sport that makes you feel like that?

December 9 2008 06:46pm
19: I would say so, yes.

Other English fans in this thread suggested that football was regarded as so important for affirming their national identity due to its popularity over other sports. This helps support Robinson's (2008) and Porter's (2004) arguments that football defines the English more than any other sport. In another discussion thread about Wimbledon 2008, a different English fan similarly demonstrated how his support for both English and British teams / athletes did not really relate to his conception of his own national identity or was somehow irrelevant to this:

July 3 2008 11:34am
7: If it was an Englishman against a Scotsman or Welshman I suppose I would support the Englishman. I don't necessarily feel a stronger affinity with English than British. [Male, English, Manchester United FC, aged 31]

July 3 2008 06:06pm
1: So would you be happy to regard yourself as English-British then? Is national identity important to you at all?

July 4 2008 11:25am
7: Yes, I have a little national identity but it doesn't really extend beyond what goes on on the sports field.

Such findings provide evidence for Abell et al.'s (2007) contention that people can display immense emotional attachment to the English national team *without* having a strong attachment to their national identity at all. This is similar to comments made by another fan regarding the link between football and national identity in a later thread about the use of the St George's Cross at football. It became apparent that for the fan in question, the British layer of identification was more important than English, yet neither was really regarded as that significant:

April 30 2009 09:33am
1: Are you patriotic outside of football?

April 30 2009 09:03pm
6: Not particularly, St George's came and went for me, like every other Thursday. [Female, English, Leeds United FC, aged 24]

May 5 2009 03:30pm
1: What about when it comes to Britain?

May 5 2009 03:33pm
6: Nope. I guess I believe in Britain a bit more, if that make sense. Like, I believe that people are British whereas I think stating you are English seems a bit self-indulgent. I'm not a flag-flying Brit though. I don't think I owe it anything.

May 5 2009 04:04pm
1: Interesting. So why do you feel 'stating you are English seems a bit self-indulgent'?

May 5 2008 04:11pm
6: Because I know that I am a British citizen in the eyes of the law, so that must count for something officially. But being 'English' ... less so. Yeah, you could argue that 'I was born in Leicester in 1963... I'm ENGLISH' but what's to stop you going a step further 'I was born in Bootle actually, I'm not English, I'm Liverpudlian'.

The multi-layered nature of English national identity was therefore illustrated again here. As Maguire (2011b: 999) states in relation to Elias's (1991) 'changes in the we-I balance', 'people have multiple identities that are formed and transformed in social interaction' and 'sport plays an important role in embodying multiple notions of identity'. This was reinforced by the fact that other fans could not understand why the UK could unite in times of war but not in football:

December 17 2008 07:32pm
19: I love it when this whole identity crisis debate pops up (laughing emoticon). I don't know why people are so against the Team GB thing. In the Olympics we compete under the Great Britain banner. Britain is hosting the 2012 games. We should enter a team for football as we are the host nation and it makes sense.

So that team should be Great Britain, surely? Then comes the whole, 'I hate England' or 'I hate Scotland' bollocks. We are stronger as four opposed to one. When we fight wars, we fight with our Welsh, Northern Irish or Scottish allies, why should sport be different? [Male, English, Arsenal FC, aged 21]

It must be noted here that this fan was in the British armed forces and as such was bound to defend an attachment to Britain, but others who were in agreement displayed similar sentiments about sport and war in general. For instance, one fan said the following:

July 4 2008 11:37am
18: Sport actually divides British people into regional thinking, whereas I would argue combat and warfare unifies British people into breaking down national barriers. [Male, English, Juventus FC, aged 28]

In a separate thread the same fan later said the following to highlight the situational nature of the link between sport and national identity:

December 9 2008 04:40pm
18: It is probably the only thing many people can identify with these days. Aside from war, and then we fall under the 'British' umbrella again.

Still others suggested that those who stress Englishness over Britishness are somehow deluded because the nations of Britain have worked together on a number of occasions throughout history. The idea that football in England is a substitute for war was also apparent in the observations study findings discussed in Chapter 4 as well as in previous research on British print media representations of Englishness (cf. Gibbons, 2010). It is a point that has been made by previous authors, although without using the views of fans themselves (cf. Carrington, 1999: 73).

There were also fans eager to point out that when it comes to ethnicity, the nations of Britain are all intertwined anyway and have been for hundreds of years. For example:

December 20 2008 05:57am
34: Most people in England probably have some Celtic blood in them. At any point I am not sure where we get our fierce English pride – most of the true Britons (original inhabitants of the land) were Celtic anyway. English in its truest form is mostly a mixed race of Romans, Normans, Saxons, Vikings etc. It's pretty amusing to me listening to people talk about English this, English that, we aren't Scottish we're English. I just don't get it. I mean I understand I am English first, then British. But I don't understand the hatred of Britain. [Male, English, Manchester United FC, aged 30]

This topic has been hotly debated in the literature on Englishness (cf. Young, 2008) and represents another of the 'anxieties' surrounding the idea of English national identity (Aughey, 2007). Fans whose parents were immigrants were also keen to stress that Britishness is a civic identity that defines them much more so than Englishness which has often been ethnically exclusive (Burdsey, 2007). For instance, one English-Italian fan with mixed parentage stated this, although also recognising that Britain is not as relevant as it once was:

> August 8 2008 02:50pm
> 18: For me the term 'British' is almost defunct now, it was a word that struck fear and commanded respect into outsiders and often pride in its citizens, but today it seems to be a term used to the same effect but with far less power. It only remains in essence because our laws are governed by the monarchy and a British government, the idea being of course that we are stronger as British than individually, in several areas. I consider myself British because I have mixed heritage but also a European for obvious reasons. [Male, English, Juventus FC, aged 28]

The discussion continued later on:

> August 11 2008 01:03am
> 7: I don't quite get why so many Scots get all anti-British and want out of the union. I mean the whole excessive patriotism seems a little outdated to me, it's like people are stuck in the past for some reason or other. The world's a small place... I mean I can't think of a good reason, even political, that would make the Scots hate the UK enough to want to leave and harbour such resentment towards the English. [Male, English, Manchester United FC, aged 31]

> August 11 2008 12:02pm
> 1: Do you see yourself as English and British then? Which one do you feel most affinity for?

> August 11 2008 01:12pm
> 7: English, but that doesn't mean I don't like being British.

The comments from fan 7 were made at an interesting time because the Scottish National Party (SNP) had formed a minority government (with Alex Salmond as First Minister) the year before in May 2007 and from August 2007 had begun making steps towards Scottish independence from the UK (BBC News, 2013). Such examples demonstrate how some fans recognised the increasingly outdated nature of national identity given the reality of global interdependence and the increasing drive of individualisation in developed Western nation-states like Britain (Elias, 1991). Elias stated that the balance is changing from the 'we' towards the 'I' as a result of globalisation. Individuals in Western European states are increasingly regarding themselves as part of humanity as a whole rather than as representatives of a more particular 'we' group.

In contrast, however, similar to findings from the pub-based study (Chapter 4), it was also interesting to observe how many fans amalgamated 'British' and 'English' achievements to reinforce the character of their 'we' group image. This was even observed in discussions about a Germany versus England friendly match on 19 November 2008 and became most clearly visible by the posting of lyrics to songs and chants linking the English national team with the Second World War, as was observed in fan behaviour during World Cup 2006:

> October 17 2008 06:28am
> 17: lets do what we do best and that's beating the krauts.
>
> > One nil down
> > Five one up
> > Two World Wars
> > And One World Cup
> > With a knick knack paddy wack
> > Give a dog a bone
> > Germany will f**k off home (cheeky emoticon). [Male, English, Arsenal FC, aged 20]
>
> October 17 2008 11:56pm
> 16: THERE WERE 10 GERMAN BOMBERS IN THE AIR THERE WERE 10 GERMAN BOMBERS IN THE AIR … . (cheeky emoticon). [Male, English, Aston Villa FC, aged 27]
>
> October 18 2008 12:01pm
> 14: How very un-PC of you (sticking tongue out emoticon). AND THE RAF FROM ENGLAND SHOT THEM DOWN, SHOT THEM DOWN, THE RAF FROM ENGLAND, RAF FROM ENGLAND SHOT THEM DOWN (cheeky emoticon). [Male, English, Notts County FC, aged 22]
>
> November 10 2008 11:37am
> 1: Funny how English and British victories often get amalgamated in football!
>
> November 15 2008 09:00am
> 61: That's because against Germany there haven't been enough of them. [Male, English, FC Barcelona, aged 23]
>
> November 16 2008 02:44am
> 19: (Good posting and laughing emoticons). [Male, English, Arsenal FC, aged 21]

November 20 2008 12:35am
14: F**k off to all you gloom merchants, we've just beat the Germans again! (Range of emoticons with St George Cross flags and a large photo of a bulldog with the union flag in the background). [Male, English, Notts County FC, aged 22]

The author asked fan 14 the following in direct response to this post:

November 24 2008 07:31pm
1: Do you use British symbols and political figureheads when England plays anyone else, or is it just the Germans?

There was debate about this and it was apparent that some fans were well aware of the distinctions between England and Britain but others could not see the difference:

November 25 2008 10:33pm
14: Don't see any political symbols (confused emoticon). [Male, English, Notts County FC, aged 22]

November 25 2008 10:35pm
60: I'm guessing he's talking about Churchill. Don't see the problem, greatest leader in British history. [Male, English, West Ham United, aged 45]

November 27 2008 2:10pm
1: Didn't mean any offence! I'm just interested in the way English achievements are often linked to British ones. All I meant was that Churchill was the British Prime Minister (political figurehead) and the symbol you used was the British bulldog with the British Union Jack. I was just interested to know if you usually refer to British symbols like those when England play / beat any other teams – or is it just Germany?

November 27 2008 02:12pm
18: Strange that isn't it, we choose to class British military success as English military success. [Male, English, Juventus FC, aged 28]

November 29 2008 09:07pm
14: Well I see the British bulldog as more representative of culture and personality, but obviously you can align it with the war. But I refer to them against most opponents as it's part of English culture, but even more so against Germany. 2 world wars and one world cup (cheeky emoticon). [Male, English, Notts County FC, aged 22]

As was found in the World Cup 2006 study, these findings can be explained using Elias's (1991) notion of the drag-effect because British achievements were being clung on to by some English fans in the face of opposition, particularly that from nations they had previously been at war with. This is an example of the 'wilful nostalgia' that Maguire and Poulton (1999) found was apparent in English national newspaper coverage of Euro 96. Drawing upon the work of Elias (1991) and Robertson (1992), Maguire (2011b) regards this as characteristic of many Western European nation-states that tend to live in the past and construct their national identities based on nostalgia for past glories. Whilst basing national identity on past achievements is not unique to the English, the fact that the smaller national unit (England) relies upon the larger state-based layer of identification (Britain) makes the English case somewhat unique because it is a movement in the opposite direction to Elias's (2000) civilising process. These findings therefore provide some further examples of how a British-based Englishness persists in the minds of many football fans, even at a time when global and European integration are at their height.

Local Attachments

In addition to attachments to England and Britain, there was also strong evidence of a north- south divide amongst fans that came out in discussions around the GB football team issue. This acted to further highlight the multi-layered nature of the contemporary English national we-image that Elias (1991) stated was characteristic of contemporary European nations, although has not been explored fully in relation to Englishness. Whilst many fans were keen to stress various links between regions / cities across the borders of the nations within Britain, other fans disagreed and felt they had more in common with other English people despite being geographically closer to cities / towns within Scotland and Wales. This was apparent on a number of separate occasions in discussions that emerged out of the Team GB issue. Perhaps the best examples to highlight the ways in which views differed, came in the form of the following extracts from a much longer discussion:

> December 18 2008 04:36pm
> 47: Scotland contributes more to the UK than most of the North of England, certainly more than Geordie land, maybe you lot should be kicked out (smiley face emoticon). [Male, English, Queens Park Rangers FC, aged 24]
>
> December 19 2008 02:07am
> 17: Except Newcastle is in England and Scotland aint (stupid emoticon). I don't give a f**k about the UK I care about England only. [Male, English, Arsenal FC, aged 20]
>
> December 20 2008 01:18pm
> 47: I think there are inherent links between all parts of this country … . I live in Bristol, and the South West of England in particular has very close links to Wales, much closer than any they have with Geordies or anyone up north. Lots of Welshmen in Bristol, plenty commute to and from Cardiff for work etc. Much

closer culturally arguably as well than with other parts of the UK. (On a side note, I haven't been further north than Leeds either).

January 7 2009 07:15pm
1: What about devolution of the English regions?

January 7 2009 07:16pm
17: Tbh the regions I don't mind because they're part of the country but Scotland, Wales and Northern Ireland are separate countries.[10]

January 7 2009 10:57pm
27: Decided by some kings 1000 years ago. It's just chance that your city isn't part of Scotland. [Male, Norwegian, Manchester United, aged 36]

January 9 2009 10:43am
1: So do you think you share much in common with people who live at the other end of the country?

January 15 2009 05:17pm
6: I think as a general rule, close proximity to Scotland = North. That is what I would work with. Therefore, close proximity to Wales = Liverpool = Not North. Etc., etc. [Female, English, Leeds United FC, aged 24]

January 15 2009 05:20pm
18: People north of the Midlands like to term themselves as Northern because they think it sounds cooler to be from the 'underprivileged' part of the country (smiley emoticon). [Male, English, Juventus FC, aged 28]

January 15 2009 05:22pm
6: I'm not ashamed to admit I'm a pauper (smiley face emoticon).

January 15 2009 05:33pm
18: Exactly (smiley face emoticon).

January 16 2009 12:20am
68: I disagree I've lived down south born and bred there its much better up north cost of living cheaper people more friendly and not so many snobs. [Males, English, Blackburn Rovers FC, aged 69]

In the above discussion, some English fans are clinging to older and smaller local/regional planes of their identities. These layers of identification exist simultaneously

---

10 'Tbh' is an abbreviation for the phrase 'to be honest'.

with attachments to England and Britain (larger and newer layers of identity) which other fans appear to show preference for. Both are examples of how

> sports represent individuals, communities, regions and nations, and a key feature of the sport process is that it is used by different groups, those more established, emergent or outsider groups, to represent, maintain and / or challenge identities (Maguire, 2011b: 999).

The north/south divide within England is somewhat neglected by Elias according to Fletcher (1997: 105–6), yet its very existence is evidence of how layers of identification that are of many different sizes and vintages are simultaneously present in people today (Mennell, 1994). Despite his lack of acknowledgement of the specificities of the English case, this kind of process is explained by Elias's (1991) notion of the drag-effect. This was also observed in relation to the Almunia case, albeit in slightly different ways.

The Almunia Case

Using the case of English-born footballers who have chosen to play for the Republic of Ireland national team, Holmes and Storey (2011: 266) argued that 'people can be quite happy to swap and switch their national affiliations and therefore to at least some degree, their own national identities' and they add that 'these insights cast further light on the multi-layered, dynamic, shifting and contingent nature of social identities'. In this section further evidence in support of this contention is provided through analysis of discussions amongst the figuration of fans under study concerning 'the Almunia case'.

Manuel Almunia is a goalkeeper born in the Navarre region of Spain who signed for the EPL club Arsenal F.C in July 2004. In July 2009 he became eligible to gain British citizenship through naturalisation considering he had lived and worked in the UK for five consecutive years. As Almunia had never been called up to play international football for Spain before 2009, he had the option to play for England if picked by the England manager, Fabio Capello.[11] As early as 2007 – but then more consistently from the summer of 2008 after England (and the other home nations) had failed to qualify for Euro 2008, a tournament which the Spanish national team later went on to win – the English national press began to focus attention on the fact that Almunia had announced on a few separate occasions that

---

11   At the time of writing Almunia still had never been called up to represent either the Spanish or English national squads. Capello resigned as England manager on 8 February 2012.

he would like to play for England if he was given the chance, but that this was only if he was not called up by Spain first.[12]

In the spring of 2009 the Almunia case again became a hot topic in the English press because the goalkeeper had arguably just had his best season yet for Arsenal and this happened to coincide with the England national team competing in qualifiers for the 2010 World Cup under massive pressure from the English press and general public following the team's recent failures. This was equally fuelled by the choice of English goalkeepers becoming increasingly sparse at the time due to a number of injuries and some poor performances.[13] The Almunia case is somewhat of an anomaly as whilst there are many past and present foreign EPL players who have remained in the UK long enough to be eligible for British citizenship, it is rare for such players to have never played international football considering their obvious talent. The only reason this is the case with Almunia is because there are two other goalkeepers who have kept him out of the Spanish national squad: Iker Casillas (Real Madrid) and Pepe Reina (Liverpool).

English fans were clearly divided on the Almunia issue and their discussions brought out a number of concerns relating to the construction and representation of English national identity around the English national football team. These reactions highlighted how Englishness is defined as an imagined community (Anderson, 1991), but equally how the defining characteristics of this we image are undergoing a period of flux (Elias, 1991). The issue was brought up as a specific topic on two separate occasions. The first time by an American fan (21) and the second time by the English founder of the forum, who is an Arsenal fan (3). The first time the topic emerged throughout the time period analysed was 1 May 2009. The second time the topic was raised was the day Almunia actually became eligible for a British passport after spending five years in the UK. Fan 3 quoted directly from (and posted a link to) an article in *The Sun* about this, using a number of happy emoticons that clearly demonstrated his support for the idea seeing as though Almunia was an Arsenal player. Although the topic did not arise often in other threads, it proved very popular and English fans in particular were keen to post their views.

Ethnic versus Civic

Whereas some fans stated that Almunia's Spanish heritage meant he should not be permitted to play for any other country, others stated that if he was eligible to play for England through obtaining British citizenship it should not matter what his ethnic heritage is. This sparked interesting debates over what 'English' should actually be based upon: ethnicity or British citizenship. For instance:

---

12 In international football, unlike some other sports, FIFA's rules stipulate that players only have one choice of national team. Once they represent one national side they are no longer eligible to represent another nation.

13 England did eventually qualify for the 2010 World Cup in early September 2009 after defeating Croatia 5–1 at Wembley.

May 1 2009 10:17pm
6: I don't see what the problem is. Almunia will be getting British Citizen because of his treaty rights – i.e. Because he's been self sufficient in Britain for more than five years. He works for his living and pays a lot of tax so I think if he's eligible, he's got as much right as any others to play for the country that he contributes to. Surely it's better to have a player who is good and who wants to play for England, rather than a third rate keeper who is preferred for no other reason than he happens to be born here. [Female, English, Leeds United FC, aged 24]

May 1 2009 10:21pm
18: Britain don't have a football team though (Fan 6) (smiley face emoticon). [Male, English, Juventus FC, aged 28]

May 1 2009 10:23pm
6: But he got his citizenship (or will get his citizenship) because he's been living and working in England specifically.

May 1 2009 10:26pm
60: Yeah but its not English citizenship its British. I don't like the idea, but tbh it wouldn't surprise me the way football is going. [Male, English, West Ham United FC, aged 45]

May 1 2009 10:33pm
6: Yes, but he gets it because he's been working in ENGLAND. Nobody has English citizenship. The likes of Wayne Rooney for example (b.1985), British by parents. Nobody is automatically British anymore. And nobody is an English citizen ever.

Fan 6 continued pushing the legal entitlement to British citizenship as justification that Almunia should be allowed to play for England, often highlighting EU rules on citizenship rather than those of the UK. Thus fan 6 was displaying her preference for a more integrated European identity. Fan 18 disagreed and would simply not accept that British citizenship was enough to qualify Almunia as English. This was particularly interesting considering one of fan 18's parents was an Italian immigrant and so one might expect him to have a more inclusive European based identity in a similar fashion to the fans discussed by King (2003), Levermore and Millward (2007) and Millward (2006).

Later on in the thread, fan 60 attempted to justify his defence of Englishness by declaring he was not British, only English. Fans 18 and 6 were keen to point out that whether he liked it or not, fan 60 was in fact a British citizen in a similar way to that observed in discussions relating to the GB football team. The same kind of debate arose again in a later thread once it had been announced that Almunia was now eligible to gain British citizenship via naturalisation. Here fan 9 attempted to justify Almunia playing for England due to his substantial tax contributions to the British government:

> July 12 2009 04:35pm
> 9: Almunia is now eligible for dual citizenship presumably, what more do you want? The guy has probably paid more into our country's tax system than I ever will in my life, he has therefore contributed more to this nation than I? [Male, English, Birmingham City FC, aged 24]

In support of this, fan 6 repeated the same question she had raised in the previous thread regarding British citizenship being a justifiable criterion for Englishness. This met with opposition from fan 18, but support from fan 63:

> August 2 2009 06:12pm
> 6: Okay then, forgetting about football for a second: do you think Almunia should be allowed to have British citizenship? [Female, English, Leeds United FC, aged 24]

> August 2 2009 06:15pm
> 18: Yes. And the answer to your next question is 'no', because he is therefore British and not English. [Male, English, Juventus FC, aged 28]

> August 2 2009 06:18pm
> 6: Everybody in the English national team is British. And he got his citizenship by living in England. Much like people who are born British derive their English national mentality from spending their life here.

> August 2 2009 06:22pm
> 18: Ok so if you went to Belgium and lived for two years, as is there requirement for citizenship, laughably, would you consider playing sport for their national side? Do you think that is right?

> August 2 2009 06:24pm
> 6: Why not? If I could get a job for them. They are kind enough to let me live in their country, who am I to turn my nose up at representing them?

Both fans in the above discussion had different but equally valid conceptions of what English national identity should be based upon. This discussion highlights how resistance to both 'pluralization processes and the integrative tendencies associated with globalization reflects the ability of national cultures to be responsive to global flows' (Maguire, 2011a: 988). These seemingly contrasting responses to the integrative processes at work within Europe that have allowed Almunia to become a British citizen via naturalisation, and as a result, be in a position where he could theoretically be picked to represent the English national team, are evidence of the diminishing of contrasts between national groups within Europe and the increasing varieties of expressions of identity that are simultaneously made possible (Maguire, 1999). Moreover, the English we-image is engaged in a transitional phase whereby older and newer conceptions of its essential characteristics are contrasting.

Talent versus Blood

Related to the above, English fans were also divided over whether 'talent' should override 'blood' and comparisons were made between Almunia and 'foreign' players in other national teams such as the Republic of Ireland, Italy and Spain. Various cases of foreign players / athletes representing English national teams for other sports such as cricket and rugby were also raised with some fans stating football should be regarded differently to other sports and others contending that there was no difference.

This debate highlights how Elias's (2000) civilising process does not follow a linear trajectory. Elias's (1991) 'changes in the we-I balance' can be used to explain how some English fans were responding to the Almunia case by defending their English national identity on the basis of the player lacking any English heritage (or 'blood'); whereas others were not concerned about this and were happy for Almunia to represent the English national team regardless of his Spanish roots. The following are examples of English fans being negative about Almunia playing for England on the grounds that they did not consider him to be English even if he gained British citizenship because he was not born or raised in England:

May 1 2009 06:29pm
13: I only want England players playing and managing England, so it's a big no-no from me. [Male, English, Leeds United FC, aged 25]

May 1 2009 06:34pm
15: He's a good keeper I'll give him that but even with British citizenship he will still be Spanish so it's a no from me. [Male, English, Chelsea FC, aged 44]

May 1 2009 07:23pm
18: No, he is not English in any way. [Male, English, Juventus FC, aged 28]

May 1 2009 07:57pm
39: I don't think someone without ANY connection to English blood should be playing in the team. [Male, English, Liverpool FC, aged 36]

May 5 2009 03:34pm
60: Almunia is Spanish however ya look at it and doesn't have a trace of English bloody anywhere, I wouldn't like to see him in a England shirt, in fact I would hate it, it shows desperation in my opinion, so his (*sic*) not good enough for them but he is for us. Sorry but fuck that. [Male, English, West Ham United FC, aged 45]

The same fan later went on to add:

May 5 2009 04:26pm
60: He's been a servant to the country paid his taxes etc. ... . But he's still Spanish at heart whether he's got British citizenship or not, ask the man when he gets it if he's English or Spanish he would say Spanish every time. I honestly would rather keep the team English rather than have a few foreign players who are deemed British as they have lived here however many years. I would rather be shite and 140th in the world but have an English side than be a top team in the world with a team with a few foreign players.

Some fans directly blamed the increased amount of non-English players in the EPL for threatening the very existence of national identification, which many felt national teams 'should' represent. For instance, when one fan stated:

May 1 2009 09:02pm
24: what about if it was Torres and not Almunia? Just say Torres hasn't played for Spain and has been here five years so qualifies. How many wouldn't want Torres for England?[14] [Male, English, Arsenal FC, aged 41]

Another was quick to respond:

May 1 2009 09:06pm
18: Interesting how the English sell-out mentality has crept from the clubs to the national teams. Scary really. Where's the pride in seeing a team of foreign players win a trophy for your country? What do people get out of that? Is winning all that counts? [Male, English, Juventus FC, aged 28]

In response to such comments, the author asked forum members the following two questions relating to foreign fans:

May 5 2009 03:28pm
1: This happens in other sports, athletics is a prime example with Kenyans running for various countries despite never setting foot in them, so why not in football? Also, English Premier League clubs no longer represent the localities in which they are based (foreign players, managers, owners and fans) so why should the national team?

To which Fan 18 was the first to reply with the following:

---

14 This fan was referring to the Spanish centre-forward Fernando Torres who played for Liverpool between 2007 and 2011 (at the time of writing Torres plays for Chelsea). Torres was a prolific goal-scorer in his first and second seasons at Liverpool and fan 24 was alluding to this in his post.

May 5 2009 03:32pm
18: I think football and other sporting teams are the last remaining media for fans to show national pride. But judging by some comments on here, it seems that the feeling is disappearing rather quickly. Perhaps due to the lack of success in particular in recent years. I can picture it now, England win the World Cup under Capello and it will be 'we are England, best team in the world, we don't need johnnies like Almunia in the team'. Oh ... [Male, English, Juventus FC, aged 28][15]

Here fan 18 highlights the hypocrisy surrounding support for the English national team on the basis of 'identity'. The Italian former manager of the England national team, Fabio Capello, proved a similarly controversial figure to Almunia in debates among English fans. Feelings towards Capello, the second non-English manager to manage the English national team,[16] were discussed and fans were divided on whether the national identity of players representing England was different to or the same as that of managers. For instance:

May 1 2009 07:23pm
18: No, he is not English in any way. [Male, English, Juventus FC, aged 28]

May 1 2009 07:35pm
3: Nor is the manager. [Male, English, Arsenal FC, aged 53]

May 1 2009 07:38pm
18: A coach is different, any nationality can coach a side.

May 1 2009 07:39pm
12: Managers who manage a country and players who play for **their** country are miles apart. [Male, English, Tottenham Hotspur FC, aged 49, emphasis in original]

May 1 2009 07:45pm
3: Lost our identity already so it don't *(sic.)* matter.

May 5 2009 04:12pm
60: I don't really like the idea of Capello but we have him there now so we have to lump it but I won't accept a Spanish player by birth and blood to be playing for the national team, there's one thing having a foreign manager but a player well I'm sorry that takes the piss, I couldn't give a fuck how long he has lived here ask him if he's Spanish or English he will say Spanish every time. This gets my blood boiling it really does. [Male, English, West Ham United, aged 45]

---

15 The term 'Johnnie/Johnny' is an abbreviation for the phrase 'Johnnie/Johnny foreigner' which refers to anyone who is not British.

16 Sven Göran Eriksson was the first non-British (Swedish) manager to lead the English national team.

English support for Capello was surprisingly positive at this time because he was relatively new as England manager and because England were winning. However, there were some English fans who felt the national team no longer represented them due to having a foreign manager, for instance:

> September 5 2008 11:48am
> 3: Win the world cup I'd never get behind them like at one time, England lost itself a soon as they put a Johnny in charge (popcorn eating emoticon). [Male, English, Arsenal FC, aged 53]

Then in a later thread the same fan wrote:

> May 5 2009 03:49pm
> 3: lost our pride once a johnnie took charge.

During the Germany vs. England friendly match English fans were praising Capello, but this seemed to be only because England won the match:

> November 19 2008 10:44pm
> 51: England looking a real outfit with Capello. Unrecognisable from team a year ago ... incredible what a class manager can do. [Male, English, Sporting Clube de Portugal FC, aged 35]

> November 19 2008 10:45pm
> 63: FT Capello we love you (emoticon flying St George Cross).[17] Time to celebrate (emoticon holding a beer). [Male, English, Arsenal FC, aged 23]

The same fan later relayed similar sentiments when England beat Ukraine:

> April 2009 10:00pm
> 63: KING CAPELLO (four emoticons with various St George Cross flags).

Regardless of the obvious contradictions regarding Capello and Almunia, many fans remained in opposition after the announcement was made that Almunia was eligible for British citizenship and some other members voiced their concerns:

> Jul 13 2009 07:53pm
> 60: He can fuck off he's Spanish. End of. [Male, English, West Ham United FC, aged 45]

---

17 'FT' means full-time here.

August 31 2009 01:20am
92: No I don't want a Spanish keeper in an England team it should be only for players born and brought up in England. Whoever thought of that idiotic idea? [Male, English, Tottenham Hotspur FC, aged 32]

September 15 2009 03:32am
70: Almunia is Spanish and although not being good enough to play for us, he would only consider playing for us as he is behind Casillas and Reina, who are still going to be playing when he retires. [Male, English, Liverpool FC, aged 24]

Comparisons were made between the large contingent of foreign players in EPL clubs with some fans saying national teams will become like clubs and no longer represent nations. For example:

August 2 2009 06:02pm
18: Ok so you think that anyone can play for any country, I think that basically destroys international football. It just becomes like club football. National football teams are a source of national pride and attention, it would be a waste of time playing as England or Spain or whoever with a team full of foreign players, it becomes invalid in itself, it therefore isn't England or Spain it is just a football team. I blame this attitude on the club game becoming so dependent on foreign players. Also if the national team was good people would have more pride in it and wouldn't even entertain the idea, which in itself is a sad indication. [Male, English, Juventus FC, aged 28]

There were however, also English fans who said they would welcome Almunia into the England team regardless of his nationality due to him being a proficient goalkeeper. Most fans in this camp were Arsenal fans who simply wanted to see another Arsenal player in the English national team. For instance, the forum founder (an Arsenal fan) even began chanting for Almunia at one point:

July 13 2009 04:01pm
3: He's big, he's mean, he's better than Robert green Almunia Almuniaaaaaaaaaaa! (waving emoticon) [Male, English, Arsenal FC, aged 53]

In response to the apparent contradiction between this fan's previous xenophobic attitudes towards anything non-English, and his support for Almunia playing for his beloved England, the author asked:

July 16 2009 11:08am
1: I thought you were fiercely patriotic about England? If he (Almunia) didn't play for Arsenal would you have a different view?

There was no response to this from fan 3. This seemed to be a good example therefore both of the contingent nature of national identity for this fan and the hegemony of his support for Arsenal over his support for England (the 'club versus country debate' is discussed in greater depth in Chapter 6). Drawing upon discussions on e-zine message-board websites for Liverpool and Oldham Athletic fans in 2005, Millward (2007) found that non-English players in the EPL seemed only to gain what he terms 'notional' acceptance among English fans that was often subject to their performance on the pitch. The same seems to be the case with managers taking into account the evidence provided above. Millward (2007: 604) suggested that,

> the increasing number of non-national European players in local teams might be one way in which national stereotypes are being eroded and a cosmopolitan consciousness may be developing.

This idea supports King's (2000; 2003) 'Europeanisation' thesis and Millward (2007: 618 emphasis in original) concludes, '*Outsiders*, such as *foreign players* are easy targets for criticism because they are 'different'.' It is also important to note Elias and Scotson's (1994) concept of 'established / outsider relations' in that English fans might regard themselves as being members of the established group and 'foreign' players represent a challenge to this we-group image, yet they could eventually be incorporated into it. What Millward (2007) refers to as 'true cosmopolitanism' might appear on the surface when it comes to English support for foreign players (and managers), yet underlying xenophobic attitudes still persist. Although Millward (2007) fails to recognise it, this is evidence for Elias's (1991) 'drag-effect' as national allegiances from English fans still seem to be deeply entrenched in the idea of 'blood ties' to England and these often reappear when fans are threatened by the challenges posed by European integration and wider globalisation processes. In relation to cosmopolitanism (heightened degrees of experience and awareness of cultural variety) Giulianotti and Robertson (2009: 58, emphasis in original) suggest that 'football crystallizes periods of *exceptional nationalism*, as well as its banal variant' drawing upon Billig's (1995) concept of 'banal nationalism' (discussed previously in Chapter 2).

Yet, this kind of 'Little Englander' viewpoint expressed by some could not accurately be applied to the views of all English fans. Another fan contributing to this thread said of Manuel Almunia:

July 13 2009 07:59am
24: I don't think he is good enough for Arsenal let alone England. [Male, English, Arsenal FC, aged 41]

To which a different Arsenal fan responded:

July 13 08:27pm
19: He'd definitely be first choice if he was allowed to play for England. I'm not trying to be funny or anything, but if you seriously watch his performance over the past two years he has greatly improved and he's a very good goalkeeper

now. David James will always fuck up while Robert Green and Scott Carson aren't good enough at international level. Whether you agree with him playing for England or not, I don't think you can argue that he wouldn't be good enough to be first choice. [Male, English, Arsenal FC, aged 21]

Yet another English Arsenal fan later clearly highlighted that he had club over country concerns regarding Almunia playing for England also:

August 3 2009 03:04pm
63: In some ways I personally would kind of hope Almunia would at least play a friendly for England and do it well, just to try and change this silly attitude. On the other hand if he made the smallest of errors he would be lamb to the slaughter and though I'd rather Arsenal had a proper class keeper, he is our current and being targeted would be very unfortunate. [Male, English, Arsenal FC, aged 23]

There were also examples of other fans that were happy to have Almunia playing for England. For instance, a Birmingham city fan wrote:

May 5 2009 03:52pm
9: He's better than any of the English lads. Let him play, all the other countries do it FFS![18] Look at Zidane, Viera, Klose, Podolski, Deco, Senna … I could go on. [Male, English, Birmingham City FC, aged 24]

Fan 9 also repeated this in response to Almunia actually becoming eligible for British citizenship whilst again adding that other national teams contain 'foreign' players so there is no reason why England should not do the same:

July 13 2009 04:05pm
9: I'd be happy for him to play for us. Why the fuck not, he's better than our current crop of shitters. Plus every other country does it, why shouldn't we? Look at the Brazilians in Portugal's team, or all the African born players in French teams over the years, or the polish players in the German side.

The post following this, from a Newcastle United fan, supported this view:

July 13 2009 04:06pm
38: I'm all for it … other countries do it, why shouldn't we? [Male, English, Newcastle United FC, aged 33]

However, these posts were met with a long riposte from fan 18 who felt it important to clarify the situation regarding 'foreign' players in other national teams stating that citizens of former colonised nations playing for the national teams of their

---

18   'FFS' is an abbreviation for the phrase 'for fuck sake'.

'mother' countries are different to those who simply switch nationality completely. Examples of other foreign players representing different national football teams were in fact often provided by other fans. For instance, Fan 12 asked:

May 2009 07:57pm
12: Where would it end? We would end up like Ireland under Charlton ... a joke.
[Male, English, Tottenham Hotspur FC, aged 49]

Holmes and Storey (2004: 89) have previously written about how in recent decades the Republic of Ireland national football team 'has included a significant number of players born outside Ireland'. These authors go on to conclude that 'the factors influencing players' decisions exist on a spectrum ranging from primarily cultural affinity at one end to primarily career-related on the other' (Holmes and Storey, 2004: 101). An example from the past is Mick McCarthy being the captain of the Irish national team, despite being English (Gibbons, 2010).

Fans were also divided as to whether Almunia – a person from another European nation gaining naturalisation as a British citizen – could be considered to be the same as or whether he is entirely different to a person with mixed heritage. Others were keen to indicate that Almunia would only choose to play for England because he did not get chosen to represent Spain and others seemed to disagree with this (apart from most Arsenal fans), for instance:

May 1 2009 06:43pm
29: I don't think I'd have a problem with it if it weren't for the fact that he'd obviously much rather play for Spain if he could. [Male, English, Blackburn Rovers FC, aged 21]

August 31 2009 02:33am
47: If Spain wanted him he'd never even consider playing for England, so why should we consider picking him? In principle I've got no problem [with] someone moving to England to settle, gaining nationality and deciding they want to represent the country. But Almunia is just a mercenary in this situation; you shouldn't be able to shop around to see what country you play for if your real one doesn't want you. Players should have to choose a country at age 21 out of the ones they qualify for and only be able to change that in exceptional circumstances. [Male, English, Queens Park Rangers FC, aged 24]

Almunia was often compared with Owen Hargreaves who had chosen to play for England due to his English parentage, despite having Canadian citizenship and the fact that his footballing skills were honed in the German Bundesliga rather than the EPL. Some fans suggested the Almunia case was no different to that regarding Hargreaves, for example:

May 1 2009 07:45pm
60: I don't like the idea but it's no different from Owen Hargreaves really. [Male, English, West Ham United FC, aged 45]

May 5 2009 03:44pm
6: I don't think it's a prerequisite to be English through and through. Owen Hargreaves' link to England is fairly tenuous when you consider he grew up in Canada, worked in Germany etc. At least Almunia lives and works in the country he could potentially be playing for. Hargreaves had six teams to choose from, LOL! You can't say he picked England because he felt deeply English! [Female, English, Leeds United FC, aged 24]

Whereas others disagreed and felt the Almunia and Hargreaves cases were totally different:

May 1 2009 07:53pm
47: Hargreaves qualified for several (through family) and chose England from the offset. Almunia qualified for Spain but they didn't want him, now he wants to play for someone else … [Male, English, Queens Park Rangers FC, aged 24]

May 1 2009 09:50pm
18: Hargreaves has ties to England … Owen Hargreaves. Manuel Almunia. See the difference? (Smiley face emoticon). [Male, English, Juventus FC, aged 28]

May 5 2009 03:49pm
60: (Hargreaves) chose what's best for him but he had a selection opportunity through blood ties, what ties does Almunia have? [Male, English, West Ham United FC, aged 45]

September 12 2009 05:33pm
34: Hargreaves and Almunia are different cases imo.[19] Both of Hargreaves' parents are English but they immigrated (*sic*) to Canada. That's very different to gaining citizenship for living here long enough. [Male, English, Manchester United FC, aged 30]

Almunia's case was compared with that of the Spanish player Nacho Novo who was also eligible for British citizenship through playing in the Scottish Premier League (SPL) for eight years in October 2008. Novo considered playing for the Scottish national team as he had not been picked by Spain but had played for Galicia who are a national team not formally recognised by FIFA (Crolley and Hand, 2006). In response to this, there was a supposed 'gentlemen's agreement' between the UK FAs that they would not pick 'foreign' players for their national

---

19 'imo' is an abbreviation for the phrase 'in my opinion'.

teams. This was an issue raised by forum members and could well be the reason why a player without English heritage has never been picked for the national team. However, it was difficult to find any firm evidence that this agreement had actually been made and this is an area ripe for further research.

Conclusion

Overall, findings presented in the current chapter highlighted the multiple ways in which the construct of English national identity is debated by English fans via their everyday discussions on football-related issues. Quite often the debates went beyond football to reveal how English national identity is best described as 'multi-layered' and in a 'state of flux' at the current stage of societal development characterised by advanced global (and European) interconnections, of which the Internet forum itself is an example. The prospect of fielding a GB football team for the London 2012 Olympics and the Almunia case best illustrated the contested nature of what constitutes Englishness and how fragile this national construct is at the beginning of the twenty-first century.

The Team GB issue seemed to unearth simultaneous attachments to England, Britain and specific English localities. Most English fans recognised the difference between the constructs of English and British, whereas some still seemed to amalgamate them, either intentionally or inadvertently. In a similar fashion to what was observed in pubs during World Cup 2006 (Chapter 4), 'wilful nostalgia' (cf. Maguire, 2011b; Giulianotti and Robertson, 2009) for British achievements was still visible in fans' views regarding the GB football team for 2012. A number of fans actively tried to establish an Englishness which was separate from Britishness by resisting the assimilation of England into Britain. This 'Little Englander' (cf. Maguire, 2011a) response and discussions regarding the north-south divide within England provided further examples of the ways in which English football fans often cling on to older layers of identification in response to global and European integrative forces. Whilst Elias (1991) has been criticised by Fletcher (1997) for not attending to the intricacies of the divisions that exist within England (particularly the so called north-south divide) it is clear that the concept of changes in the we-I balance applies equally well here as it did in the observations made during World Cup 2006 (Gibbons, 2010; Gibbons and Lusted, 2007).

The Almunia case highlighted some interesting divisions amongst the views of English fans on English national identity and the national football team. Whereas some fans argued that 'blood' or birthplace should determine whether a player should be permitted to represent England by playing for the national football team, other fans argued that British citizenship gained through naturalisation was a sufficient criterion. There were also fans who stressed that talent should be the determining factor in selecting national teams regardless of actual nationality, as is the case in English club football. Discussions on the Almunia case seemed to reinforce previous research regarding 'foreign' players in other national teams only gaining 'notional' acceptance by fans (cf. Holmes and Storey, 2004; 2011; Millward, 2007). Whilst Maguire's (2011a) 'Little Englander' thesis was again clearly evident amongst fans' reactions to the Almunia case, there were also other fans who seemed to accept the diminishing of contrasts that had occurred as a result of global flows such as European integration and the resultant increase in the number of possibilities / varieties this offered.

Giulianotti and Robertson (2009: 107) summarise that 'as labour markets have globalized, more complex differences arise in relation to the imported player, his club, its supporters, its home nation, and his national team'. This was certainly what has happened with regards to the Almunia case. Giulianotti and Robertson (2009: 109) go on to stress how dual citizenship, naturalisation or even completely switching nationality 'already occurs in many other labour markets' outside football, but how football governing bodies are attempting to challenge this homogenising process. They highlight how UEFA and FIFA have already attempted to counter this possibility (or certainly limit it) by restricting the number of non-nationals at clubs through championing the '6+5' rule whereby only five non-national players would be allowed to start fixtures (this is reminiscent of the case prior to the Bosman ruling in 1995/6). Giulianotti and Robertson (2009: 110) note that FIFA regulations had previously allowed uncapped players to change national allegiance after living in their new nation for only two years. However, to tighten regulations, the 2008 FIFA Congress voted to raise the term to five years.

As was alluded to earlier in this chapter, these findings could also be partially explained by Giulianotti and Robertson's (2009: 58) reconfiguration of Billig's (1995) concept of 'banal nationalism' into understanding how international football creates opportunities for 'exceptional nationalism'. This contradicts the more routinely experienced 'banal cosmopolitanism' that characterises contemporary social life according to these authors. However, as evidence for this assertion, Giulianotti and Robertson (2009: 58) fail to go beyond citing the fact that national flags become 'suddenly ubiquitous' during international tournaments, whereas the evidence provided in the current chapter and Chapter 4 suggests the 'national' identity articulated by English fans is more multidimensional in nature than the ubiquitous display of the St George's Cross suggests. These findings provide an effective example of what Elias (1991) termed 'changes in the we-I balance'. English national identity currently seems to be undergoing a state of flux and observations of fan behaviour during World Cup 2006 and debates amongst football fans, illustrate the multi-faceted nature of this national construct.

Chapter 6

The Club versus Country Debate in English Football and the Diverse Use of the St George's Cross

Introduction

In this chapter, further findings from more 'everyday' or 'banal' (Billig, 1995) interactions between fans within the online community investigated are used to argue that the significance of club / locality-based attachments as well as the diverse use of the St George's Cross, both highlight the challenges posed to English national identity by the globalisation and Europeanisation of elite-level English club football. It is concluded that this can be explained using Elias's (2000) 'diminishing contrasts, increasing varieties' whilst also directly challenging some of the 'myths' discussed in Chapter 1 regarding the reasons underlying the increased ubiquity of the St George's Cross at English football matches.

As in Chapter 5, the current chapter is divided into two main sections where evidence on two further themes from the online participant observation study is discussed under various sub-headings. In the first section, the variety of ways in which club football appeared to regularly dominate interactions amongst English fans (even in discussions concerning international football matches and competitions) are discussed in relation to previous literature. English clubs were also often used to reaffirm and preserve local identities in the face of advancing globalisation processes that are significantly altering the links between football and national identity. In the second section, the ways in which fans specifically debated their feelings towards the use of the St George's Cross flag are discussed in relation to previous literature. Findings revealed how this 'invented tradition' (Hobsbawm, 1983) was being used in multi-faceted ways by both English and non-English fans.

Club and Locality-based Attachments

From the time the author spent as a member of the online community it became clear to see that discussions relating to club football took priority over those about international football for the vast majority of English fans. Most fans (although not all) had blatant references to the English clubs they supported incorporated in their on-screen avatars (graphical representations of forum members). Whilst real examples cannot be displayed in order to maintain the anonymity of the forum members, it must suffice to explain that each post a fan made was accompanied by their avatar. Fan's avatars included various indications of their identities which tended to revolve around their club rather than their country.

Some of the most deliberate cases of avatars displaying club-based affiliations were to have a club's full name, epithet or abbreviation incorporated into a fan's screen name, for instance 'LFC Dave'. Many fans would also then have a picture of a specific club player or club badge underneath this and they might also either include a larger picture of a player or club badge as a signature line underneath the actual posted message, part of a song / chant sang by fans at games quoted, or even a scoreboard depicting a momentous score line against a rival club. As avatars would appear for every post a fan made, forum members were in little doubt about what clubs their peers supported. These were also updated constantly to reflect what was happening at the time in terms of players being transferred between clubs, club kits or logos changing, fans singing or chanting new songs on the 'terraces' and so on.

Club over Country?

Another clear indication that club concerns were dominant within the online community was that they were even mentioned in discussion threads about international matches as they occurred, or within other threads relating to the England national team. This was evidence to support King's (2003) 'rejection of England' thesis. The 'club over country' debate is briefly discussed by Giulianotti and Robertson (2009: 107–10) who, among some other examples from around the world, draw upon the 'Rooney-Ronaldo' incident discussed in Chapter 4 of the current book. However, the diversity of ways in which English fans' concerns relating to club football tend to dominate those to do with international football on a more banal everyday basis, is something that previous studies have not sought to understand using empirical research until now.

Even during England's 'friendly' match against their main rivals Germany on 19 November 2008, English fans were often primarily concerned about showing the most overt support for English players who played for the clubs they supported. This took precedence over discussions of specific incidents that were occurring as the match was taking place. Club rivalries were also never far from surfacing during this game, for instance, when England and Chelsea Captain, John Terry, arguably the lynchpin of the England team's defence, appeared to be injured, fan 63 posted:

> November 19 2008 10:30pm
> 63: Terry was limping (three smiley face emoticons). [Male, English, Arsenal FC, aged 23]

And a Chelsea fan retorted:

November 19 2008 10:39pm
11: Iron man will recover ... so don't get your hopes up. [Male, English, Chelsea FC, aged 28]

Similarly, in the thread relating to the England vs. Slovakia friendly match on Saturday 28 March 2009, the superiority of the club game emerged again in various guises. Fan 40 voiced his views on international football in the following way:

March 23 2009 12:28am
40: 4pm, what a shite time for friendly. Why not kick off after the 3 o clock domestic games have finished? International football pisses me off. [Male, English, Port Vale FC, aged 23]

Other English fans demonstrated club rather than country related concerns for particular players. In the following example, fan 61 implies that some players were attempting to drop out of international duty due to supposed injuries so that they would be fit to represent their clubs:

March 24 2009 07:59pm
61: Funny how when Internationals roll around, key players for both Club and Nation get mysterious injuries. [Male, English, FC Barcelona, aged 23]

Even during the match it was apparent that club concerns were at the forefront of fans' minds:

March 28 2009 06:51pm
60: Oh fuck me (Ashley) Cole down injured this is a disaster for West Ham. [Male, English, West Ham United FC, aged 45]

March 28 2009 07:14pm
60: Rooney is going to have to play 90 mins tonight as well as on Wednesday. Fergie will be doing his nut.

March 28 2009 08:01pm
73: Nice to see the 500th England goal at Wembley go to a Chelsea lad [John Terry]. [Male, English, Chelsea FC, aged 24]

Only a few days later, club concerns emerged again in the thread relating to England's next match against Ukraine on Wednesday 1 April 2009, even though this was a crucial World Cup Qualifier. For example, when one fan took exception to others discussing club related issues, another was quick to state that club issues override country ones. This example started with an Aston Villa fan being upset at one of his club's key players (Gabriel Agbonlahor, nicknamed 'Gabby') being called up to play in the World Cup Qualifier:

> March 31 2009 10:06pm
> 16: Can't believe Gabby is in ... hope he doesn't play. [Male, English, Aston Villa FC, aged 27]
>
> April 1 2009 07:53am
> 60: Why? [Male, English, West Ham United, aged 45]
>
> April 1 2009 10:11am
> 51: Because he's been shit for quite a while and playing adding more games to his legs isn't going to help him find his form for Villa and stop them free-falling. [Male, English, Sporting Clube de Portugal FC, aged 35]
>
> April 1 2009 10:19am
> 60: Tough shit sorry but it's a national game and a world cup qualifier, fucks me off people moaning we have just lost Cole for the season. I'm not happy about it but it happens. He's needed, been called up, and has to play, fuck Villa they don't matter at the moment getting to the world cup does.
>
> April 1 2009 11:13am
> 19: Club over country though, that's why people get annoyed when players pick up injuries in pointless friendlies towards the business end of the season. [Male, English, Arsenal FC, aged 21]

The viewpoint expressed by fan 60 here that international football should override club football when it comes to World Cup qualification is very similar to that expressed by the fan observed during World Cup 2006 who stated that club-related rivalries did not matter when the English national team were competing (see Chapter 4 and Gibbons and Lusted, 2007: 303). Fan 19's opposing viewpoint is illustrative of one of the unintended consequences of the global expansion of EPL football: the weakening of feelings of national solidarity around the English national team. Both responses can be explained by Elias's (2000) notion of 'diminishing contrasts, increasing varieties' because the seemingly homogenising forces of globalisation have led to heterogeneous responses on the part of fans of the same nationality.

In a discussion thread about England submitting a bid to host the 2018 World Cup, both English and 'global' fans or 'satellite supporters'[1] were discussing the possible opportunities that might result from England winning the World Cup bid

---

1 'Global fans' or 'satellite supporters' are terms used to describe fans from other countries that actively support English clubs (Kerr and Emery, 2011; Rookwood and Chan, 2011).

in terms of the expansion of Manchester United's stadium at Old Trafford, rather than anything about English national pride:

> January 28 2009 03:32am
> 10: Hope England get it. Then the FA and the government will fork out for an Old Trafford expansion (smiling clapping emoticon). [Male, Norwegian, Manchester United FC, aged 27]

> January 29 2009 04:10pm
> 40: I don't think Old Trafford has any more room to be expanded. The South Stand is the only stand that is 'too small' and there are issues with residents over sunlight and what not if another tier is added. [Male, English, Port Vale FC, aged 23]

> January 29 2009 04:28pm
> 30: There was talk last year of submitting plans to extend Old Trafford to a 96,000 seater, don't know how far the plans went though. [Male, English, Manchester United, aged 51]

> January 29 2009 04:33pm
> 10: It's possible but will be very expensive, the rail track and station will have to be built into the south stand, and a residential area has to be bought out and demolished. Estimated cost to expand the south stand to match the west and east stand is £150m.

These findings provide support for Kerr and Emery's (2011) claims that satellite supporters can express intense loyalty for, and in-depth knowledge of, English EPL clubs. Such examples further indicate how EPL football is involved in the diminishing of contrasts between fans of different nationalities and how the 'established' group of English fans of EPL clubs is broadening, with the aid of these kinds of global Internet discussion forums, to incorporate non-English fans who were previously considered 'outsiders' by this group (Elias, 2000; Elias and Scotson, 1994).

In addition, quite often, although not always, the club over country viewpoint was linked to the importance of locality over nation and the north-south divide pertaining to support for the English national team, or even in relation to the very idea of there being an all-encompassing sense of 'Englishness'. The very concept of English national identity was itself being both challenged and diversified. In a discussion thread the author started about use of the St George's Cross by English fans, a Newcastle United supporter clearly expressed how both his club and locality were more important to him than anything to do with England in the following extract:

June 22 2008 07:01pm
20: I don't feel particularly strong *(sic)* about a team that not only play in a shit, corporate bowl but play in a city that is fucking miles away from where I live. It'd be easier for me to watch Scotland than England. And it kind of puts me off the international scene a bit. I'd much rather go and watch Newcastle over England, every day of the week. I feel more passionate about being a Geordie than being English, when you live up here you feel quite cut off from the rest of the country and it sort of makes you sway towards Newcastle over England when it comes to football. [Male, English, Newcastle United FC, aged 32]

In response to this, similar sentiments were expressed by a Mancunian Manchester United supporter who echoes King's (2000; 2003) evidence regarding the rejection of England:

June 22 2008 11:23pm
8: I feel passionately about United, and Manchester, and I don't about England ... I am certainly infinitely closer to those emotions with my team and my city than with my country. [Male, English, Manchester United FC, aged 29]

The author then asked Fan 8 the following:

June 23 2008 06:23pm
1: So is that the case with things in life other than football too – I mean, if pushed, would you say you have a stronger affinity with Manchester than England/Britain?

To which Fan 8 responded:

June 23 2008 06:53pm
8: Certainly. Moving away from sport, I love my city, I love the streets, the architecture, the history. Part of it is my football team as well; that's a huge part of my identity, and I would suggest, thousands of others. I get the tram into the city centre in the sunshine or the rain and it's beautiful. I come home on the train after some time away and it pulls into the station and I love it. I don't get that from being elsewhere in England – it's not my home, it's just other bits of the same country, bits that don't really mean much to me.

Whilst one might expect this of a Manchester United supporter following King's (2000; 2002) research and that of others since (cf. Giulianotti and Robertson, 2009; Millward, 2011), it was interesting to note that this was not only apparent for fans of leading EPL clubs, but also some fans of clubs situated lower in the English professional league system. These fans have not formed the focus of much previous research because they have hitherto been considered 'outsiders' to the impacts of global forces experienced by more 'established' groups of EPL fans

(Gibbons and Lusted, 2007; Mainwaring and Clark, 2012). One illustration of this can be observed in the following response after the author asked a Leeds United fan a similar question related to club versus country support:

> June 23 2008 08:25pm
> 26: Leeds without a doubt. I don't feel I can relate to any of the English players. With Leeds, I watch them week in week out, so you feel like you know them better, and therefore are more involved with them. Plus, I'm more likely to see Leeds players walking around town than any England player. And even if I did see an England player I wouldn't feel comfortable to approach them, because they seem so far away from me. [Male, English, Leeds United FC, aged 26]

The author then probed further by asking:

> June 23 2008 08:29pm
> 1: So if the England team contained some Leeds players, would you feel differently? Outside of football, would you say that you have a stronger affinity with Leeds over the English nation?

To which he replied with the following, which seemed to suggest his affinity with his club was stronger than that to his nation, despite his claim that both were of equal importance to him:

> June 24 2008 12:13pm
> 26: Possibly, but I would only be interested in the Leeds players rather than the England team. I suppose an example of this is when N Ireland played England, and Healy scored the winner.[2] With him playing for Leeds I was delighted that he scored, and actually cheered the goal! Outside of football, I'd say the affinity is pretty much even. I'm proud to come from Leeds, I'm also proud to be English. I don't think I favour one more than the other.

This simultaneous expression of local and national identifications further highlights the multi-layered and situational nature of English national identity that football fandom draws out. It was also of interest to note that fans were already highly aware of the club versus country debate, as suggested by Rookwood and Millward (2011) in relation to their study of Liverpool fans. Some evidence of this can be observed by the fact that Fan 9 started a discussion thread by introducing a fan poll asking members whether they would prefer their club or England to win a major competition. Of the 22 fans that responded to the poll, 15 (68%) answered 'Your club team' whereas only 7 (32%) answered 'England'. In his initial post,

---

2   David Healy is a Northern Irish international (striker) who played for Leeds United between 2004 and 2007.

Fan 9 explained how the debate arose, his own view on the issue, and that he was interested to find out what other English fans felt:

> September 5 2008 10:49am
> 9: We've all read the extracts from Jamie Carragher's autobiography about how he wasn't that bothered when England lost and that he valued a Liverpool win more than an England one and it started off a debate in my office about what you'd rather see: England win the world cup or your club win the league or cup. For me it's a no brainer, I'd much rather see England lift the world cup than see Brum win something, it's something I have longed for all my life as an England football fan. However I'm sure there will be differing opinions on here. What do you reckon?[3] [Male, English, Birmingham City FC, aged 24]

Further debate ensued between this English fan and others. It became apparent that there were different reasons underlying fans' preferences for either club or country. A number of fans explained they had stated 'club' as their answer because they disagreed with how many England players seemed to display a lack of passion when playing for their country:

> September 5 2008 10:57am
> 50: At this moment in time I would put club above country every time … . However, if the England set up got to a point where it was run as it should be and we actually had players that showed some pride in playing for their country then my opinion might change, but as it is at the moment I really couldn't give a toss how England fare. [Male, English, Manchester United FC, aged 53]

Fan 18 agreed that the lack of passion the players seemed to have in playing for their country was the main reason for his antipathy towards the English national team:

> September 5 2008 11:04am
> 18: Club I guess, I have more civic than national pride as well, although that may be because of dual heritage, it means I become passive in some situations. At the moment England are pretty much an embarrassment but it isn't the results or ability that makes you lose pride in their performance it is the application. I have more pride in La Nazionale but then as (fan 50) points out when you have a team that can challenge to a level and you see the work ethic there and the team at least trying to pull in the same direction then you can't have any complaints. If they are good enough then bonus but if they are not at that time then you can't argue. [Male, English, Juventus FC, aged 28]

---

3 Jamie Carragher is a 'home-grown' Liverpool FC defender who famously retired from international football in order to concentrate on being fit to play for his club. 'Brum' is a nickname used to refer to the city of Birmingham or Birmingham City FC.

A Leeds United fan encompassed the feelings of many English fans in the following post which met with agreement from a number of others contributing to the thread:

> September 5 2008 12:04pm
> 26: The closest thing I can describe my feelings for England and club are like mothers and girlfriends (smiley face emoticon). England = Mother – You love them but only cos you have to! They annoy the hell out of you, and do things that just don't follow logic. Club = Girlfriend – You choose them, or they choose you. They bring the highest highs and the lowest lows. And at the moment, England don't even feel like a mother, more like a mother-in-law. [Male, English, Leeds United FC, aged 26]

Thus it became apparent that the England national team's lack of success coupled with the growing global significance of EPL football were key factors leading many English fans towards a preference for club over country. However, there was also evidence of further divisions among these fans regarding feelings towards their club and the national team that require elaboration.

Differences and Similarities Between Fans of Large and Small Clubs

When it came to the club versus country debate there were a number of differences and similarities between the views of fans of large clubs and those of smaller or lower level clubs. Some of this evidence reinforced that provided by King (2000; 2003) and also Rookwood and Millward (2011: 41) who found that at Liverpool 'many local supporters have demonstrated their sense of local identity by chanting 'We're not English, We are Scouse' and rejecting multiple forms of Englishness'. However, in the current study counter-evidence seemed stronger in some instances, highlighting the simultaneity of feelings of sameness and difference amongst English fans.

Starting with the supportive evidence, the following extracts are taken from a debate that gradually emerged between a Notts County fan and a Liverpool fan about feelings towards the England national team.[4] This kind of debate is evidence to suggest some English fans of more successful EPL clubs, such as Liverpool, regard the England national team as serving the interests of fans of lower level clubs who very rarely get the opportunity to experience competition against any non-English opposition:

> May 5 2009 11:11pm
> 87: That is exactly the reason I don't see myself as English. It is for the lesser teams to support England in my view like your own, lol. [Female, English, Liverpool FC, aged 35]

---

4   At this time Notts County played in 'League Two' of the English Football League which is the fourth tier of English professional football. At the time of writing they play in the third tier 'League One'.

> May 5 2009 11:18pm
> 14: You mean the oldest league club in the world? Be quiet, little club, if you want to talk history, we clearly have more of it than you. You are only a cast off team for our rejects, such as Finnan and Pennant. Jog on, with a pen in your hand. [Male, English, Notts County FC, aged 22]
>
> May 5 2009 11:26pm
> 87: (Rolling around on the floor laughing emoticon) That's funny that. You mean any player that has any ounce of talent wants to leave you for a team like us. Lmao.[5] You are speaking to a fan of the most successful English club in history. So write that on your St George's flag.

Yet, examples of counter-evidence could also be found that went against King's (2003) 'rejection of England' thesis and Rookwood and Millward's (2011) supporting evidence. The following extracts are from two different English Manchester United fans who felt that they had a stronger affinity to England than to Manchester United:

> September 5 2008 10:54am
> 30: Country for me, I was only 7 when England won the World Cup, and I'd love to see them win it again in my lifetime, but it's easy for me to say that, because my club has won loads of trophies, I suppose someone who follows a team that won f**k all would rather see their club side win something first. [Male, English, Manchester United FC, aged 51]
>
> September 5 2008 11:01am
> 7: England win the world cup. That was always the ultimate prize for me even before we won the Premier League in 93 and Champions League in 99. [Male, English, Manchester United FC, aged 31]

Thus these fans suggest that Manchester United's continual success in both domestic and European competitions and the England national team's relative lack of success might have contributed to a desire for the national team to win something. Later on in this thread a Birmingham City fan suggested that his club's lack of success was actually the reason that pushed him towards wanting to see England win more than his club:

> September 5 2008 02:21pm
> 9: The only success I have ever known in my lifetime with Birmingham is winning the Johnston's paint trophy (Autowindscreens shield at the time) and the old division two title. But it's still my ultimate footballing dream to see England win the World Cup. It would be a truly memorable experience to be

---

5 'Lmoa' is an abbreviation for the phrase 'laugh my arse off'.

part of and would last longer in history than any club success ever could. [Male, English, Birmingham City FC, aged 24]

These findings suggest that the relationship between club and country is perhaps more complex than previous authors have suggested. This is probably due to the fact that the views of fans of lower level, smaller and less successful English clubs have not often been considered in much previous academic research (Clark, 2006; Gibbons and Lusted, 2007; Mainwaring and Clark, 2012). On a number of other occasions fans in this online community were suggesting that English club football dominated and held more meaning than the English national team because the latter play irregularly and/or have been largely unsuccessful in the recent past. The following fan suggested why Sheffield Wednesday's success was more meaningful to him than that of the England national team:

September 5 2008 02:25pm
53: Club success would feel far better, smaller group of people, more time money energy and emotion invested by everyone involved, and not everyone can get involved in celebrations. [Male, English, Sheffield Wednesday FC, aged 38]

Much later in the thread relating to the England versus Ukraine match, after the team had only narrowly won the world cup qualifier 2–1 in a game they were expected to win convincingly, a Liverpool fan voiced his frustration with the national team's performance:

April 2 2009 12:11am
70: Absolutely shocking and boring game. Our nation is shit as a football team and need to sort it out if we are ever going to get close to a major trophy anytime soon. [Male, English, Liverpool FC, aged 24]

The same fan had relayed similar sentiments in England's friendly fixture against Slovakia only the week before:

March 23 2009 12:37am
70: I don't really care for this game. I don't want to watch my national side play poorly, again, and without any passion, again.

In other threads there were further examples of this lack of faith in the England team due to their poor performances. When the author asked fan 6 why she no longer followed England and had become more devoted to Leeds United, the following conversation unfolded:

April 14 2009 04:35pm
6: I don't think I have always felt like this. When football was more of a casual thing for me I supported England as well, in the sense that I would follow their

games, keep up to date with news etc. But as I began to devote more time to my domestic club, I realised England wasn't really in keeping with my beliefs. [Female, English, Leeds United FC, aged 24]

April 16 2009 01:32pm
1: What's the difference when it comes to your domestic club though? Why are you more passionate about them do you suppose?

April 16 2009 01:38pm
6: I don't know. I guess it could simply be down to the fact that I supported them first … . Football was not for me until I began to support Leeds, then I felt more of a connection to the whole thing. After Leeds, when I had a better understanding of the game, I started to watch other clubs as well as international games but it always felt secondary and with England, it never felt like they were my team. I have also felt for sometime that England don't really represent England – the values … feel wrong for me. The adulation of the divas, the favouritism, the crazy PR … it just doesn't feel right. I know that football is just an industry now, but I think it's personified with the England team.

April 16 2009 02:21pm
1: Do the problems that exist with the England team just reflect the commercialisation/globalisation of the English Premier League?

April 16 2009 02:27pm
6: To an extent, yes. But I think it's also because international games drift in and out of your life, there is no constant there.

April 17 2009 05:05pm
1: So if Leeds didn't play regularly and England did, would you follow England more than Leeds?

April 20 2009 12:51am
6: No. I mean … Man United play regularly but I don't want to support them. England are just some other team.

In this case, club was chosen above country primarily because the English national team felt distant from the more regular engagement this fan felt with her local club. The irregularity with which the national team compete, against the regularity of club football appeared to be one key aspect, but there was also a sense that the England national team no longer represented the English nation or at least this fan as an individual within it. The national sense of belonging or meaning seems to have been lost by the England team solely comprising EPL players and therefore not representing the majority of English clubs at lower levels. Such a finding provides more complex evidence to support Abell et al.'s (2007) contention that feelings of English national sentiment and support for the England national team do not always go hand in hand. However, it also highlights the diversity of possibilities for identification that have been enhanced by the seemingly homogenising processes of globalisation and European integration: diminishing contrasts, increasing varieties (Elias, 2000).

Authenticity Based on Locality

Research on non-English fans of EPL clubs is still lacking (Kerr and Emery, 2011; Rookwood and Chan, 2011), despite the fact that 211 countries around the world now broadcast EPL games (Millward, 2011). There are many EPL supporters' clubs situated all over the world, with some dating back as far as the late 1950s (cf. Armstrong and Mitchell, 2008). This is evidence that the EPL has become an aspect of global culture that is projected as a homogenous entity across the globe in the kind of Marxist fashion envisaged by Wallerstein (2000, cited in Giulianotti and Robertson, 2009: 40). The responses of English fans to this global homogeneity were interesting to observe in the findings of the online participant observation study.

Rivalries between clubs tended to inform the majority of discussion topics within the online community and English fans were continually testing one another (and non-English fans) to assess how 'authentic' their support for their club was. This usually revolved around proximity of home or place of birth to the club ground suggesting that clubs were still regarded as important in reaffirming and preserving local identities amongst English fans despite the obvious globalisation of EPL football. Much of this 'authenticity testing' revolved around Manchester United and their fan base being largely from outside Manchester and even outside England. Non-English or 'foreign' fans of English clubs were often targeted by their English counterparts for being 'inauthentic' and the core aspect of this was related to locality. At times, this acted as a kind of anti-globalisation movement seeking to 'promote, reinvigorate and/or establish local organizations' (Maguire, 2011c: 1013). It was evidence of the 'established' group of English fans attempting to protect their local identities in the face of what they regarded as challenges from non-English 'outsiders' (Elias and Scotson, 1994).

The first example of the authenticity of Manchester United fans being questioned was noted in a discussion thread about the use of the St George's Cross flag, when one fan wrote:

June 22 2008 11:12pm
18: Why would a Man Utd fan from Surrey feel affection to Manchester United from a perspective of pride? There is no civic pride there. [Male, English, Juventus FC, aged 28]

Related to this, a whole thread was created by Fan 36 titled 'This proves all man utd fans are fake'. The following list of percentages of supporters from the localities of where EPL clubs were situated (originally alleged to be from a national newspaper) was posted by Fan 36, himself an Arsenal fan:

> September 28 2008 07:40pm
> 36: The Daily Star have published a list of where Premier League supporters come from relative to the club they support
>
> Hull City 88%
> Stoke City 85%
> Wigan Athletic 80%
> Newcastle United 77%
> Middlesbrough 76%
> Aston Villa 73%
> Fulham 73%
> Sunderland 67%
> West Brom 67%
> West Ham 66%
> Blackburn 65%
> Man City 64%
> Portsmouth 63%
> Bolton 57%
> Everton 55%
> Arsenal 53%
> Chelsea 49%
> Liverpool 22%
> Man Utd 20%
>
> Fucking plastic mancs 20% (four rolling around on the floor laughing emoticons). [Male, English, Arsenal FC, aged 25]

In response another Arsenal fan said:

> September 28 2008 07:41pm
> 37: no surprise is it, the top 4 are the bottom 4. [Male, English, Arsenal FC, aged 30]

And a Tottenham Hotspur fan retorted:

> September 28 2008 07:44pm
> 12: From a plastic gooner nice one (smiley emoticon).[6] [Male, English, Tottenham Hotspur FC, aged 49]

---

6   The term 'gooner' refers to a supporter of Arsenal FC who are nicknamed 'The Gunners'.

A Norwegian Manchester United fan also responded with a very interesting point in defence of his club's large contingent of non-English fans:

> September 28 07:45pm
> 27: And why do you believe this is like this? Could success = foreign fans perhaps? [Male, Norwegian, Manchester United FC, aged 36]

This was quickly followed up by support for Fan 12's comment:

> September 28 2008 07:47pm
> 27: If I were him I would never speak of plastic fans ... Look at yourself kiddo (Thumbs up emoticon).

There were no direct responses to this, which indicates other English fans were either in agreement or could not find evidence that foreign fans were undesirable for EPL clubs. Either way, such evidence supports Kerr and Emery's (2011) findings on the growing authenticity of 'satellite supporters' of EPL clubs. The following posts were almost entirely from English fans who were arguing about the authenticity of their fandom and this was largely based on their attendance at matches as well as their localities. Fan 36 begins by replying to Fan 12 calling him 'plastic':

> September 28 2009 08:06pm
> 36: Last game you went to watch was last season (laughing emoticon). [Male, English, Arsenal FC, aged 25]

In an attempt to further shame the Manchester United fans, the forum founder, an Arsenal fan, stated:

> September 28 2008 08:50pm
> 3: Another 20% of that outside Manc land and the rest not in this country, lol.
> [Male, English, Arsenal FC, aged 53]

This kind of comment was surprising coming from an Arsenal fan because his own club's squad were not only fourth from bottom in the list posted, but at the time almost entirely consisted of non-English players and owe much of their recent success to a French manager (Arsène Wenger). In response an English Liverpool fan (39) pointed out that the top EPL clubs are now global brands:

> September 28 2008 09:28pm
> 39: To be honest I'm not that arsed. All I'm saying is Liverpool (as in the city not the surrounding sprawl) has a population of half a million. So to say a large number of fans are from outside is pretty obvious. The larger 'brands' as in the top 4 (inc. the Mancs – smiley face emoticon) are bound to have a massive

global following due to the way they've been marketed over the years. If we were back in the 1950s all wearing flat caps and eating dripping then you might have a point. But as we all know the power of the £ changed the whole thing forever. [Male, English, Liverpool FC, aged 36]

Following this, Fan 39, referring to the *Daily Star* statistics, added:

September 28 2008 09:31
39: ... the stats are as usual a load of bollocks anyway – what do they class as a fan? I'm sure certain members will say I'm not a fan because I only get to go to a few games and mainly watch the games on TV. Even though I've supported Liverpool for most of my life (which in fact would be the same for most ... members).

To this, fan 35, a Newcastle fan, responded:

September 28 2008 09:32pm
35: Surely the surveys were took (*sic*) outside each football ground? So a fan is someone who attends the games? Surely if your (*sic*) in your home city which would be classed as local, and you support and pay to see your local team you're a local fan. [Male, English, Newcastle United FC, aged 22]

Later in the thread when a Birmingham City fan (9) referred to Arsenal, Liverpool, Chelsea and Manchester United as the 'Sky Four' (referring to their reliance on money form the satellite television channel 'Sky'), fan 39 repeated that this was no surprise considering the commercialisation of such clubs:

September 29 2008 10:19am
39: Makes me laugh all of this. Of course the big clubs will have more fans that aren't local! They have MORE fans so therefore more will be from non-local locations. All 4 have fantastic marketing departments in order to make more money – that's what it's about now. I agree it shouldn't be, but like I say it's not 1960 any more people! That's why we have arguably (and completely according to Sky) the best league on the planet! [Male, English, Liverpool FC, aged 36]

The global expansion of EPL clubs was further evidenced by Fan 12 here:

September 29 2008 10:34am
12: On the same subject, an old mate of mine and his Mrs went to Malta the other week and he found there was (*sic*) 3 Spurs supporters clubs on the Island, so him (*sic*) and his Mrs and me are now members of the biggest ... and I know we have at least 2 clubs in the North of Ireland ... and we have a big following in Norway and there's one in Berwick ... so football as (fan 39) has just said has

moved on for the worse imo but every club will have support from all 4 corners of the globe. [Male, English, Tottenham Hotspur FC, aged 49]

This can be supported by research conducted by Armstrong and Mitchell (2008) who engaged in an ethnographic study of Maltese fans in which they noted the ubiquity of EPL football on the island. Fan 30, a Manchester United fan, raised the following point in an attempt to steer the focus away from his club:

September 29 2008 03:25pm
30: Boring, heard it all before, several times on this forum. If United were bottom of the league, no one would give a shit where the supporters come from. [Male, English, Manchester United FC, aged 51]

These examples were an illustration of how globalisation is best understood as what Elias (2000) termed a 'double-bind' between homogenising and heterogenising processes whereby global culture can create local resistance (cf. Maguire, 2005).

Still on the topic of the feelings of English fans towards Manchester United, fan 3 began a thread titled: 'So who will in fact be cheering on the mancs?' This related to the 2009 Champions League Final between Manchester United and Barcelona. A large proportion of English fans posted that they would rather see Barcelona win despite the fact that Manchester United are an English club. As mentioned, the antipathy towards Manchester United has been covered in detail by Mellor (2004), but these findings highlight the extent to which the club is no longer even regarded as being English. Instead, many fans regarded the club as *the* symbol of the globalisation of English club football and ironically decided to support the Catalan club instead. Thus, English national identity was considered to be not at all significant to these fans in this context. Their collective hatred of Manchester United led to more dispersed acts of identification as a kind of anti-globalisation movement similar to that discussed by Maguire (cf. 2011c) in other sporting contexts using Elias's (2000) concept of diminishing contrasts, increasing varieties.

The Diverse Use of the St George's Cross

There were some clear examples across various discussion threads showing how the St George's Cross flag had been used by English fans to represent their national identity. For instance, soon after becoming a member of the online community the author started a discussion thread titled: 'Football and Flags, Are the English unique?' and in the initial post he asked: 'Why do English fans tend to personalise the St George's Cross with club team names / localities so much more than fans of other nations seem to? Do fans of other national teams even do this?' Some familiar examples of overt support for the English national team were found early on, for example:

June 18 2008 05:32pm
3: Because we're proud and want to show the rest what support is about, puts fear into others (smiley emoticon). [Male, English, Arsenal FC, aged 53]

Whilst such an example demonstrated how national identification was still present among some English fans, there were a number of others who felt ambivalent towards the England team and even the English nation:

June 23 2008 07:04pm
7: Do you not feel an affinity to England in a cultural sense? [Male, English, Manchester United FC, aged 31]

June 23 2008 07:05pm
8: What do you mean by a cultural sense? I do the same things as other English people do, I suppose. [Male, English, Manchester United FC, aged 29]

June 23 2008 07:15pm
7: Language, traditions, music, food, pastimes. Stuff that we associate with the English and not say the French or elsewhere.

June 23 2008 07:18pm
8: I probably share most of those things with other English people but I wouldn't say I feel an affinity with other people that do. Me having something in common with other people from England doesn't manifest itself into a sense of national pride or anything like that, for me.

This supports Abell et al.'s (2007) contention that fans can display immense involvement in their support for the England national team, without having any deeper underlying emotional attachment to Englishness. The erosion of feelings of national identification is also one of the varied possibilities related to the impacts of globalisation and one that is certainly what Elias (2000; 1991) would have regarded as evidence of a further civilising spurt. Both Elias's (2000) 'diminishing contrasts, increasing varieties' and Robertson's (1992) 'glocalisation' can be used to suggest this is one among many potential heterogeneous responses to the homogenising aspects of global culture.

Further examples of heterogeneity were apparent in the varied uses of and meanings attached to the St George's Cross. There was some debate over whether fans of smaller / lower level English clubs tended to use the St George's Cross flag to write their club names/localities on more than fans of EPL clubs. This was something observed during World Cup 2006 but as yet has lacked further research (see Chapter 4 and Gibbons and Lusted, 2007). This topic primarily emerged in two threads about the use of the flag by English fans, both of which were originally started by the author and proved popular (with 99 and 68 posts respectively). The following examples are from the first thread:

June 19 2008 09:28am
24: I think it's also to show that you are representing your club on England duty 'a badge of honour'. I do tend to notice that it is mainly northern teams though and usually from the lower leagues. [Male, English, Arsenal FC, aged 41]

June 19 2008 09:53am
12: Never see a lot of Liverpool at England games for some reason (confused emoticon). [Male, English, Tottenham Hotspur FC, aged 49]

June 19 2008 01:57pm
8: This is going to sound patronising, but I think it's true – it's usually fans of smaller clubs that attach themselves to England; in my experience of speaking to people, fans of lower league clubs put country before club more than fans of established top flight clubs. You won't see many United and Liverpool on England flags at England games. There is some antipathy towards England from some fans of these clubs as well. [Male, English, Manchester United FC, aged 29]

The final comment from a Manchester United fan again reinforces King's (2000; 2003) 'rejection of England' thesis. The author decided to make the following post in an attempt to spark further debate on the issue:

June 19 2008 03:00pm
1: That's probably because they're so successful in their own right and actually play and win more international fixtures than England!

June 19 2008 03:19pm
8: I agree. On the flipside, England offers an alternative to fans who rarely challenge for things. Once every 2 years – usually – England are in the latter stages of a tournament, and when that's not the case they are usually playing for qualification into something. It's a fast-track to (relative) success. That combined with the enjoyment some people find in the country coming together (even if they're happy to discount this feeling every week England aren't playing) and supporting one team I think contributes to the composition of match-going England supporters.

In response to an earlier post by fan 20 (a Newcastle United supporter who stated that he had a stronger affinity with his club and locality than with England and the national team), fan 8 wrote:

June 22 2008 11:23pm
8: I agree. If people want to take England flags to our games (which I don't think I've seen to be fair aside from the very occasional one with a United badge in the middle) then fine, but what is it doing there? You wouldn't take a City or Liverpool flag would you? To me it's a different team. A United match is not

a place to celebrate your nationality or another team, it's a place to celebrate your team. I feel passionately about United, and Manchester, and I don't about England. I am not sure I am 'proud' of Manchester or United in particular – as I said earlier, I can only take pride in something I do or have done. But I am certainly infinitely closer to those emotions with my team and my city than with my country.

The second discussion topic started by the author about the use of the St George's Cross also indicated that fans of smaller/ lower level clubs were those who tended to personalise the flag. A Notts County fan reinforced this and it is interesting to note the differences between the views of this fan of a lower league club and those of a Manchester United supporter (such as fan 8) on the use and meaning of the St George's Cross:

April 16 2009 01:23pm
14: We have an England flag with 1862 on it, not only can we take it to away games, we can take it to England games as well to show the club has some representation there. [Male, English, Notts County FC, aged 22]

April 16 2009 01:35pm
1: Who is it you want to portray this message to more – foreigners or other English people?

April 16 2008 01:37pm
14: English people. I doubt many foreigners know who Notts County are anyway (laughing emoticon). I always look out for Notts flags at England games. I can normally spot at least 2 or 3.

April 16 2009 02:09pm
1: So is it nothing at all to do with showing the rest of the world that Notts County exist?

April 16 2009 02:21pm
14: The rest of the world? No, I couldn't give a shit.

Clearly, the global positioning of fan 14's lower league club and locality was not as important to him as it seemed to be for some other fans of top-level EPL clubs. This again illustrates the purely national context within which fans of non-EPL clubs base their cultural identities. In this case the club and the locality are smaller integration units that are being clung onto tightly as 'anchors of meaning' amidst the rapid advances of global culture (cf. Maguire, 2011b).

It was also of interest to note some peculiarities about fans' reasons for personalising St George's Cross flags which highlighted the diverse uses of the flag and the shifting nature of identity formations (Elias, 1991). It seemed as though the St George's Cross was considered to be a symbol of globalisation which had prompted examples of both emulation of English fan practices amongst fans of other national teams and clubs, as well as examples of resistance to such practices (Maguire, 2011c). The majority of English fans who used the flag seemed to only take it to away games, rather than home ones, and some did not take them to games at all. Fan 9 contended that the only reason English people notice the St George's Cross being personalised with club names, emblems and localities is simply because of familiarity with it:

> June 19 10:12am
> 9: I wouldn't say we do it more, it's just more noticeable to us. First off, if we see a St George's flag, we are attracted to it, then if we see a team or place name we know, we have a connection there. We wouldn't have that connection with another country's flag or teams so I guess we just notice our own more. [Male, English, Birmingham City FC, aged 24]

Whilst this fan suggests the St George's Cross can be used to symbolise the English nation and specific local formations of identity simultaneously, fan 14 could not explain why he used the St George's Cross rather than any other flag for displaying his club-based attachments:

> October 8 2008 03:22pm
> 14: It's a St George Cross. I take it away as I don't really want to at home as A: Don't want the hassle of finding a place to put it and B: There's already lots of others there. [Male, English, Notts County FC, aged 22]
>
> October 8 2008 03:28pm
> 1: I see. So why the St George rather than your club's flag?
>
> October 10 2008 11:41am
> 14: No idea. I have a club flag in my room.

Further to this ambivalence to the cultural significance of the 'English' national flag, some non-English fans highlighted that the only reason the St George's Cross was personalised by fans was due to its white background and minimal design. This meant it had space to write things on, unlike the Union flag for instance. In a thread where the author asked fans why they personalised their St George's Cross flag, the following responses arose:

> June 18 2008 06:31pm
> 22: It's perfect for it. I mean our flag has little empty space to put the letter in each corner such as 'M C F C'. So, often you see people here modifying Saint George to team colours and doing it. [Male, American, DC United FC, aged 26]

This American fan then displayed a number of pictures of fans at Major League Soccer (MLS) games using the St George's Cross to display their club team names. The conversation then continued:

> June 18 2008 02:45pm
> 1: Nice one (fan 22). It's strange that the St George is the choice of flag for this, don't you think?

> June 19 2008 02:51pm
> 22: Not really, you have to understand there are many Anglophiles in the States. Many people look to England as the model and emulate it. The English league and national team are very popular in the States.

> June 19 2008 02:55pm
> 1: So for some Anglophiles in the States, do you think it's a way of showing off their English connections?

> June 19 2008 03:00pm
> 22: For some, maybe. Others may have zero connection and just admire English people and their culture. Anglophiles can range from 'I like England' to 'The English people are highest example of humanity which we are all measured by'. Our connection is in part our history, our language and current relationship. Some people just like the English, some like the Italians, have to ask them to know why. Otherwise, it is because the design is perfect for modification. I've never seen a modified American flag at a club match.

Examples of emulation within Europe were also acknowledged. A Spanish fan showed a picture of Spanish Ultras using both the Union flag and the St George's Cross, adding the following:

> June 21 2008 03:26pm
> 25: I can't recall a Spanish flag with a team name on it, although sometimes a player's name or short message is written on the large yellow horizontal band. However, English and British symbols are sometimes used by ultras … probably inspired by their English counterparts. [Male, Spanish, Real Madrid CF., aged 20]

An English-Italian fan also highlighted that the St George's Cross has been used by Italian fans, before explaining why:

> June 19 2008 02:43pm
> 18: Also several Italian sides carry the St George's cross as a club emblem (Milan, Inter, Genoa) and they often have flags with the club name or slogan on the horizontal section. [Male, English, Juventus FC, aged 28]

June19 2008 02:49pm
1: Any idea why they choose the St George flag for this?

June 21 2008 04:01pm
18: They are symbols of those cities, nothing to do with England. St George isn't just associated with England, as I'm sure you know.

A further explanation was also provided in a separate thread about the England national team kit:

March 5 2009 12:31pm
60: Isn't St George the Patron Saint of Milan? [Male, English, West Ham United FC, aged 45]

March 5 2009 10:57am
18: Yes and probably another 50 towns and cities, also the country of Georgia, the clue is in the flag and the name. He is also England's Patron Saint. [Male, English, Juventus FC, aged 28]

March 17 2009 09:17pm
72: In the case of the city of Milan, the cross is actually that of St Ambrose who is the city's main patron saint and was bishop of Milan in the 4th century (Smiley face emoticon). [Male, American, AC Milan FC, aged 27]

March 18 2009 10:55am
18: Ok Ambrosiana, smart arse (smiley face emoticon). The flag itself is still the St George cross, but like most of the holy Christian symbols Ambrose was represented with the red cross on white background.

Overall, the evidence provided in this final theme suggested that the uses of the St George's Cross were diverse in that the primary purpose of displaying the flag was to display club or locality-based affiliations above or in combination with national ones. Use of this supposedly 'English' national symbol often had little to do with representing a specifically English national identity at all. This confirmed the observations made during World Cup 2006 (Chapter 4) and is also evidence to support Elias's (2000) understanding of globalisation and Europeanisation processes as multidimensional.

Moreover, this evidence challenges the assumptions which were made by such authors as Crolley and Hand (2006), King (2006), Kumar (2003) and Weight (2002) that the rise in the appearance of the St George's Cross at English football since Euro 96 somehow signals a rise in an English national consciousness amongst football fans, let alone the wider English population (see Chapter 1).

Conclusion

Some of the unintended consequences of the rapid globalisation of EPL football (alluded to in Chapter 3) are clear to behold in the findings presented in this chapter. The dominance of discussions about English club football was clear. Club-related rivalries were considered much more important than national ones, yet on many occasions, football clubs were used as 'shields' to preserve aspects of local identities and fans were considered more 'authentic' if they had some kind of local attachment to the club they supported. This point divided rather than united English fans and the global significance of EPL football was simultaneously evident in the loyalties expressed by non-English fans of these clubs. In addition, the use of the St George's Cross was found to be diverse. Wide-ranging examples were revealed which demonstrated how this seemingly 'English' symbol of national distinctiveness was itself used as a blank canvas on which to display local English or English club-based affiliations; a flag of convenience unrelated to Englishness at all; or even, a flag used to reinforce non-English local or national identities.

These findings can be best explained using Elias's (2000) notion of diminishing contrasts, increasing varieties. Whilst Maguire (cf. 1994; 1999; 2011a; 2011b; 2011c) has been most prominent in applying this concept to a variety of sporting contexts, it has not been applied to help directly explain the impact of global and European forces on the complex relationship between English national identity and football fan culture using empirical evidence from the opinions of fans themselves until now. Findings highlighted how the simultaneity of the diminishing of contrasts between fans of different nationalities brought about by the global reach of EPL football and the Internet forum itself, as well as the increasing varieties of local/club-based cultural identities that have proliferated as a result of this 'commingling of cultures', occur in a banal fashion within online interactions (Billig, 1995; Elias, 2000; Maguire, 1999; 2011a). This can also be related to what Giulianotti and Robertson (2009: 59) have regarded as 'virtually rooted cosmopolitanism' whereby new collectives are created that go 'beyond old 'national' forms of solidarity' and are instead based on 'preferences for particular world players, managers, clubs, and playing styles'. This creation of 'transnational' identifications seemingly goes beyond the national, but these authors are careful to note that football is still a very powerful reminder of national boundaries and provides opportunities for 'exceptional nationalism' also.

Whilst the homogenising processes of globalisation and Europeanisation appear to have decreased the contrasts between 'local' English fans and 'global' fans of English clubs by enabling them to interact with one another within online communities, it can also be argued that the views of English fans on club versus country issues have simultaneously diversified. As was found in the pub-based observations study (Chapter 4), the St George flag and the national team were not only being rejected by some fans – particularly by many (but not all) fans of the most successful EPL clubs – but this symbol of England was also being used to display local layers of identification.

Chapter 7
Conclusion: Diminishing Contrasts, Increasing Varieties in English Football

Introduction

According to King (2002: 210–11), sociologists of football have a responsibility to ensure that the

> analysis of football would no longer be sociology's poor cousin but would be a central element in setting sociology on its feet by ensuring the discipline's close contact with the individuals whom it putatively seeks to understand. Sociology would then no longer be guilty of mere ivory-tower abstractions but would be capable of the 'deep' understanding of contemporary social processes which it professes to seek.

As in many other areas of the sociology of football that were criticised by Giulianotti (1999) and King (2002), one of the key barriers that has prevented the relationship between English national identity and football fan culture from being fully understood and appreciated is that previous studies in this area have lacked theoretical sophistication and empirical rigour. The distinctive contribution of this book has been to demonstrate how football fan culture illustrates a number of broader sociological debates relating to contemporary English national identity formation. The book has argued that English football should be placed in the context of theoretical debates concerning the broader topics of nationalism and globalisation. Fans' actions and opinions have been used as evidence to illustrate the continued fragility of contemporary English national identity in the early twenty-first century.

Empirically, this book has contributed new evidence that challenges the idea that the rise in the use of the St George's Cross by English football fans signifies a rise in a specifically 'English' rather than 'British' national identity. This assumption was found to be a myth that does not accurately reflect the complexity of reality. Theoretically, the book has provided a sound justification for utilising an Eliasian approach to study the relationship between Englishness and football fan culture. Elias's (1991; 2000) concepts of 'changes in the we-I balance' and 'diminishing contrasts, increasing varieties' were used to demonstrate that this relationship is more multi-faceted than previous research has contended. It has been argued that the Eliasian approach should no longer be ignored in the sociological study of football fandom. The overly negative attitude to Elias and figurational sociologists championed by the football sociologist Giulianotti has actually hindered the theoretical sophistication and empirical rigour deemed fundamental to moving the sociology of football into the mainstream.

Within this concluding chapter, a synopsis of the key findings presented and discussed in the previous three chapters (4–6) is provided. Following this, the main limitations of the research are considered and some alternative theoretical explanations for the findings are suggested. Suggestions for future research in this area are also provided and final conclusions are drawn.

Synopsis of Evidence

As was discussed in Chapter 1, academics have previously *assumed* that the post-Euro 96 rise in the use of the St George's Cross by English football fans equalled an increase in a specifically English national consciousness. The findings presented in this book suggest that this assumption is a 'myth' based upon little evidence. Elias (1978: 52) called upon sociologists to be '*destroyers of myths*' through collecting evidence to reflect human interdependent actions in the context of the multiple figurations they form with as much accuracy as possible. Exploration of the actions and opinions of English football fans themselves indicated that the relationship between English national identity and football fan culture is multi-faceted. The visible rise in the appearance of the St George's Cross around the English national team and domestic club football since Euro 96 appears to mask many important contradictions inherent in how English national identity is routinely displayed and debated by football fans.

The actions and opinions of English football fans provide effective illustrations to demonstrate how English national identity is currently undergoing a period of flux characterised both by civilising and decivilising spurts (Elias, 2000). For Elias (1978), broad societal units (figurations) such as nations cannot be studied directly because they are simply too large and complex. He said that it is simply

> impossible ... to deal adequately with the problem of people's social bonds, especially their emotional ones, if only relatively impersonal interdependencies are taken in to account. In the realm of sociological theory a fuller picture can be gained only by including personal interdependencies, and above all emotional bonds between people, as agents which knit society together (Elias, 1978: 137).

Elias (1978) suggested sociologists should study large complex figurations like nations indirectly by examining specific elements of the interdependencies that make them up. English football fans represent one such figuration within which there are many 'interdependent networks' (Elias, 1978; 2000). The findings presented in this research study are used to suggest that English football fans provide a suitable microcosm through which to observe the complexities of contemporary English national identity.

Whilst many English football fans *seem* to have aligned themselves to a more specific form of Englishness due to the decline of the British Empire and in the face of European integration and devolution processes by choosing to fly the 'English' St George's Cross, underlying this superficial mask of collective identification, their emotional attachments or 'we-images' are still often based upon those associated with the 'British' state as well as specific 'local' identities within England. In addition, due to the fragility of Englishness, the successive failures of the national team and the hegemony of the globalised EPL, English clubs, rather than the national team, have come to form the central element of identification for most English fans.

The findings from both research studies pointed towards 'English'; 'British'; and, 'local' attachments being deemed essential components of expressions of Englishness by English fans, especially around the national team. In addition, the power of EPL club football and the England national team's lack of success were found to present significant challenges to the very existence of any coherent or commonly shared notion of English national identity amongst English fans. Local and often interrelated club-based attachments were being enhanced by both of these challenges often at the expense of attachments to the English nation.

The pub-based study (Chapter 4) was descriptive in essence and highlighted *what* was happening, in terms of the ways in which fans in pubs had come to display and articulate Englishness themselves whilst watching the national team's progress in the 2006 World Cup on television. Furthermore, the online participant observation study (Chapters 5-6) revealed, in greater depth, the extent of the complexities underlying the relationship between English national identity and football fan culture by drawing upon current debates from a specific figuration of fans that interacted within an online community. Through discussions about football-related issues, conceptions of what Englishness is and should be based upon in the first decade of the twenty-first century were observed. The online participant observation study in particular, generated opinions from English football fans themselves on the topic of English national identity and this was something absent from previous studies in this area.

Like with all research endeavours, it is important to reflect upon the research process undertaken in order to provide suggestions for future research in this area. Whilst a justification for the 'new' settings used in the research for this book have been provided in Chapter 3 (and the methodologies for each study are detailed in the Appendix), there are reflections on some specific aspects of the research process that require further explanation here in the interest of guiding future work and to place the present work in sharper perspective. In what follows some critical reflections are offered on both *empirical* and *theoretical* aspects of the research that informs this book.

Empirical Reflections

The best words to describe the research process taken are 'diverse' and 'developmental'. The 'triangulated' approach to data collection was taken in order to gain different views on the same issue (Moore, 2000). Both research studies were designed to collect data from different but indirectly related figurations. Each research study was designed to build upon that which preceded it in terms of moving further towards understanding the complexities underlying the relationship between English national identity and football fan culture. However, each of the studies conducted had limitations.

Perhaps the main limitation of the pub-based observation study (Chapter 4) was that the sample of venues visited was only seven in total, all of which were situated within two counties in the north-west of England. This has no doubt negatively impacted upon the external validity or generalisability of the findings to other areas of the country where different manifestations of Englishness might have been observed. Whilst the sample of pubs used was admittedly one of convenience – as was the case in Weed's (2006) 'pub ethnography' – a larger randomly chosen selection of venues throughout England would have made the findings more representative. However, it is important to recognise that the pub-based observations did not on their own form the main component of the research conducted in the current book. When combined with the findings from the fourteen-month online participant observation study (Chapters 5–6), it is clear that the varied displays of Englishness encountered do not seem abnormal.

External validity was also a limitation of the online participant observation study. Initially, a number of online surveys were conducted with fans within specific football forums during World Cup 2006, Euro 2008 and the summer of 2009 in order to collect data on the opinions of football fans regarding English national identity (see Gibbons, 2011). Whilst the three online surveys together generated responses from 1355 English fans (a much more representative sample than the 93 who contributed to the online participant observation), the data obtained from these surveys did not provide the same detailed, rich insights as those obtained from the online participant observation study. As such, and due to lack of space, the decision was made not to include the online survey data in this book. The findings generated from the online surveys also suggested multi-faceted expressions of Englishness were apparent in the views expressed by English football fans (Gibbons, 2011). Therefore, these findings reinforce those from the online participant observation study.

A key concern with using data from online communities is whether those who use them are representative of other fans (Gibbons and Dixon, 2010). Indeed, there is research to suggest the web is not accessible to all (see Chapter 3). Further comparisons of data with non-Internet samples would help demonstrate the similarity or difference of the target audience between online and offline results. Such a methodology was implemented by Liptrot (2007) in an online survey of fans of 'punk-rock' music. Palmer and Thompson (2007) analysed online communities as part of (and to complement) ethnographic fieldwork when studying a group of South Australian Rules football supporters known as 'The Grog Squad'. The researchers used the website 'rocketrooster.com' and the online supporters' forum known as 'The Roost' to follow reactions to the build-up and subsequent post-mortem of matches. They concluded that the Internet 'provided an important complement to the face to face field work, and, in turn it provided a crucial mechanism through which the 'Groggies' maintained their particular cultural identity' (Palmer and Thompson, 2007: 191).

Furthermore, these authors made reference to proposed distinctions between 'direct' (such as attending live games) and 'indirect' (such as following sport via mass media) forms of fandom as cited by Wann et al. (2001). They argued that in this particular case, the hypothesised and stereotypical chat room 'nerds or geeks' lacking the capacity for meaningful social interaction was simply a myth. For 'the Groggies' no distinction between direct and indirect consumption existed: 'The fact that the Groggies also have ongoing, real time contact sits in opposition to other studies of fans for which the Internet is their principal form of communication' (Palmer and Thompson, 2007: 197). In addition, B. Wilson (2007) and Harvey et al. (2014) allude to a number of sport-related transnational movements that have used the Internet as their primary source of interaction. These have included anti-sweatshop movements and anti-Olympic movements (among others).

As discussed in Chapter 3, online interactions are now being recognised by academics who study English fans as important sources of data regarding the maintenance of local, national and European identities. Millward's (2011) *The Global Football League: Transnational Networks, Social Movements and Sport in the New Media Age*, clearly highlights the significance of this area for more fully understanding the practices of different figurations of English fans. 'New' figurations of football fans exist that are yet to be adequately researched using social scientific methods and sociological theory. The diversity of ways in which English fans interact using new media technologies are still lacking theoretically-guided empirical research. The 'online' versus 'offline' false dichotomy persists due to current typologies of fandom which privilege some forms of fandom above others (cf. Crawford, 2004; Dixon, 2013; Gibbons and Dixon, 2010).

Currently, empirical research assessing the views of fans of smaller/lower league or even non-league English clubs is seriously lacking (cf. Clark, 2006; Gibbons and Lusted, 2007; Gibbons and Nuttall, 2012; Mainwaring and Clark, 2012). The vast majority of research on English fandom is related to fans of the elite clubs of the EPL. This is problematic considering the views of such fans may not be representative of the majority of the English football fan base. Whilst the findings presented in this book have helped to highlight this considerable lacuna, studies that are more specifically focused on gathering the views of fans of smaller or lower-level clubs are still required. This is particularly important if claims made about English national identity are to be considered representative of all English fans.

Added to this, the views of fans of other sports need to be compared with those of football fans in order to identify whether the relationship between English national identity and football fan culture is distinct. Malcolm (2009) has suggested that English football and cricket fans may have a number of similarities and differences in terms of their views on the supposed rise of Englishness in recent times. The problem is that Malcolm has not asked cricket fans themselves about these issues and as such evidence remains purely observational or based largely on media sources – similar to most research on football and Englishness to date. Do diverse displays and articulations of identity underlie the ubiquitous displays of the St George's Cross in other sports too? Further research is required in order to determine this.

As mentioned in Chapter 1, a specific type of Englishness was under exploration in this book – that of male, white, working class football fans. It must therefore be recognised that the research conducted is only partially representative of English fans. Whilst issues of class, ethnicity and gender were mentioned to varying degrees in relation to the composition of the samples of fans under research, in hindsight a more thorough and nuanced analysis of the 'intersectionality' of class, ethnicity, gender and national identity would have been beneficial to explore in further detail. Recent research has recognised the importance of aligning class and ethnicity in the study of English identity (cf. Condor and Fenton, 2012). Future research should explore these layers of identity in more detail.

Theoretical Reflections

Elias's (1991) 'changes in the we-I Balance' as well as Elias's (2000) 'diminishing contrasts and increasing varieties' were found to be of particular relevance for explaining the significance of the findings obtained. Elias (1991) argued that there has been a very-long unplanned trend-line in the development of human society towards integration into larger and more diverse networks of interdependent people organised into more and more interlocking layers. This is clearly observable in the long-term unplanned movements in the size and complexity of figurations into which human beings have been socialised throughout history.

Whilst Elias (2000) has previously been criticised for showing a preference for civilising processes (van Krieken, 1998), in seeking to highlight the importance of his simultaneous recognition of *decivilising* processes, Mennell (1990) gave a number of examples of de-civilised spurts throughout history. Among other aspects, decivilising processes are 'marked by ... shorter chains of social interdependence' according to Mennell (1990: 205). Elias's (1991) concept of the 'drag-effect' is a particularly good example of the possibilities for reversals in the direction of the civilising process – a process that is still widely misunderstood by many sociologists who suggest it simply follows a linear incremental trajectory.

Elias (1991) recognised that people in contemporary European nation-states have developed multi-layered identities comprising: local; regional; national; supra-national; and, global aspects. It is these overlapping affiliations that form the flexible and complex network of the 'habitus' of a person. Thus, instead of viewing a person's identity as fixed and immovable, it is perhaps more appropriate to view it as a process that may be subject to change. Individuals living in twenty-first century Europe have come to develop a very strong and deeply internalised 'national' layer to their habitus (Elias, 1991; 1996), yet underlying this they simultaneously maintain other layers that may be of many different vintages and have the potential to conflict with one another – for example, local with national and national with supranational (Mennell, 1994). Elias (1991) termed the potential conflict between newer and older planes of affiliation, where people cling to smaller and older we-groups in the face of new larger amalgamations, the 'drag-effect', but he expected that integration into larger and more complex integration planes (such as 'Europe') would gradually increase over time. Elias (1991) observed that this has been the case thus far throughout the course of human societal development where there has been what he referred to as many 'changes in the we–I balance'.

At the time Elias (1991) was writing, in the late twentieth century, the European community consisted of only twelve member states (Chryssochoou, 2001). The European Union (EU) now consists of 28 member states and this is clear evidence that centripetal forces are still advancing and 'Europe' is expanding on the 'political' level, although not so yet at the 'emotional' level (Guibernau, 2011; Roche, 2010). Elias (1991) succinctly explained how individuals living in nation-states within Western Europe at the latter end of the twentieth century were in a 'double-bind'. Whilst they were being moved towards increasing assimilation into a 'united' Europe politically via virtue of various agreements between the ruling elites of leading Western European nations, at the same time the personality or 'we-image' of individual European citizens was still firmly rooted in their national contexts. Hobsbawm's (1983) idea of how 'invented traditions' such as flags and anthems were created by ruling elites to instil emotional attachments to nations; Anderson's (1991) understanding of how nations became 'imagined communities' in the minds of individuals; and, Billig's (1995) notion of how the national ideology is maintained on an 'everyday' basis via 'banal nationalism', all highlighted the significance of the nation to citizens living in many nation-states in late twentieth-century Europe.

Despite the strength of nationalism, Elias (1991) suggested that the European political unit had already taken over from the nation-state as the principal survival unit for Western Europeans in the late twentieth century and that this was evidence that Western European society as a whole was undergoing a civilising spurt. Yet, as always with the civilising process, Elias was careful to note that it is *not* simply a uni-linear process. Elias recognised that Western European nations were in a transitional phase as the identities of the vast majority of European citizens, aside from some elites, were still clearly dragging along the 'baggage' of nationalism. This 'drag-effect' was therefore emotionally holding European citizens back from further integration into a united Europe which has thus far failed to instil anything like as deep a 'we' feeling as 'nationalism' has (Elias, 1991; 1996).

Although he fails to mention the work of Elias (1991), Guibernau (2011: 303), has argued that the EU has still, at the beginning of the second decade of the twenty-first century, only succeeded in generating a 'non-emotional identity' amongst the vast majority of European citizens largely because it has thus far been 'a top-down project designed and carried out by selected intellectuals and political leaders after 1945'. Guibernau (2011: 311) states that 'Europe shares a history of internal confrontation and war that is more conducive to enmity and distrust than to collaboration', a point which Elias (1991; 1996; 2000) often made when explaining how the European civilising process did not always follow a linear trajectory and necessarily involved various de-civilising spurts. According to Guibernau (2011: 312),

> the nation retains the emotional attachment of its citizens and when it becomes alien to them or too wide and distant, individuals turn to regional, ethnic, local and other forms of identity tying them to more sizeable communities than the EU.

This leads Guibernau (2011: 314) to conclude that at the beginning of the twenty-first century, 'national identity remains much more powerful than the still incipient 'non-emotional' European identity'.

Even though he was writing in the penultimate decade of the twentieth century, Elias's (1991) 'drag-effect' can be used to help explain the late twentieth/early twenty-first century rise or resurgence in a specifically 'English' national consciousness which a number of scholars have commented upon (see Chapter 1). Drawing upon Elias's work, it is apparent that Englishness is currently multi-layered and has been in a continual state of flux due to the following interrelated processes which began to gather momentum in the latter half of the twentieth century: the increasing decline of the British Empire and associated decline of the British economy after the Second World War; movements by Britain into the larger European integration unit especially since the 1970s; and, most recently, devolution of the 'Celtic' nations of the UK since the late 1990s. Although British is the official nation-state unit for the English (as it is for the Scots, Welsh and Northern Irish) and is a larger integration unit, it seems that English (a smaller unit with a longer history) is itself being re-articulated in light of the political fragmentation of Britain.

Such a figurational or Eliasian theoretical framework has in recent years been unpopular amongst the majority of scholars who have engaged in sociological studies of football fans. By criticising the figurational approach so heavily, one of the most prominent sociologists of football, Giulianotti, appears to have actually hindered progress in overcoming the lack of theoretical sophistication he charged researchers of football with over a decade ago. The use of Eliasian ideas, just like those of other social thinkers, is surely something that should be encouraged if true theoretical diversity is desired.

As was detailed in Chapter 2, Elias's distinctive approach to sociology has often been criticised both from within the sociology of sport (cf. Giulianotti, 2004) and from the sociological mainstream (cf. van Krieken, 1998). However, the limitations of the figurational approach are not a justifiable reason for researchers to avoid using Eliasian theory considering no theory can claim complete immunity from criticism (Inglis and Thorpe, 2012). Recently, in a special issue of the journal *Sport in Society*, Maguire (cf. 2011d) has demonstrated the diversity of sports-related topics that his own research conducted over the last two decades has sought to address primarily drawing upon Eliasian concepts. Maguire (2011d: 856) states that there 'is much more work to be done if we are to capture the diminishing contrasts and increasing varieties that characterise global sport and civilising processes'.

As was also noted in Chapter 2, and has been mentioned at various points throughout this book, the main limitation of using an Eliasian framework to guide this research is that Elias himself did not fully discuss the intricacies of English national identity (Fletcher, 1997). Fletcher (1997: 105–6) criticised Elias for neglecting the intricacies of the relationships between the 'nations' within the UK and the English north-south divide in particular. Whilst this is a fair criticism because it is a void within Elias's work, in the current book Elias's (1991) 'changes in the we–I balance' and his (2000) 'diminishing contrasts, increasing varieties' have been used to make sense of the English reliance upon both Britain and specific English regional / local identities. Thus, it is hoped that the current book can be regarded as an example of how Eliasian ideas can be used to study aspects of Englishness and specific figurations that Elias himself did not cover in his own work.

It was also noted in Chapter 2 that Elias's general sociological approach has similarities with those of Bourdieu as well as Giddens. Delanty and O'Mahony (2002: 47) effectively summarise that

> Bourdieu, Elias and Giddens ... have in their different ways laid the foundations of a non-dualist conception of agency and structure. In these theories, agency has a certain autonomy and social structures are conceived of in a way that does not undermine the autonomy of the social actor.

Whereas Giddens's work is much more theoretical than empirical (Inglis and Thorpe, 2012), Elias and Bourdieu both maintain empirical-theoretical approaches to sociology (de Jong, 2001; Paulle, van Heerikhuizen and Emirbayer, 2012). Perhaps the key similarity between Bourdieu and Elias related to the research undertaken in this book is the fact both conceived of 'habitus' as central for understanding how individuals internalise aspects of societal structures through socialisation into particular groups that comprise society. These groups are termed 'figurations' by Elias and 'fields' by Bourdieu (Paulle et al., 2012). Indeed, de Jong (2001: 65) states that both theorists 'hated the popular usage of analytically separating individuals from social collectivities'. Although Bourdieu did not entirely agree with Elias's overriding focus on historical continuity, both shared an emphasis on relational thinking regarding the concept of power or 'capital' that pervades all human relationships (Paulle et al., 2012). Dixon (2012; 2013) has recently used Bourdieu's 'theory of practice' to help explain the process through which individuals become football fans through acts of consumption. The importance of what Elias (1991; 1996) terms the 'national habitus' to understanding 'the origins of football fandom practice' (Dixon, 2012: 336) would be an interesting avenue for future research drawing upon both Elias and Bourdieu.

Furthermore, Giddens and Bourdieu are both regarded as theorists of 'structuration' in different ways (Inglis and Thorpe, 2012). Giddens's work is arguably influenced by Elias's 'processual image of social reality' given that Elias and Giddens were colleagues at the University of Leicester in the 1960s (Inglis and Thorpe, 2012: 163). Giddens's (1984) 'structuration theory' highlights how social actors and the structures they form both impact one another. According to Horne and Jary (2004: 131), Giddens's 'duality of structure' refers to how 'the structural properties of social systems are both the *medium* and *outcome* of the practices they organise'. A limitation of the current book is that all of the similarities between each of these three theorists have not been thoroughly explored. Further research should seek to understand how all three theorists could be used in combination with one another. Indeed, as Dixon (2013: 33) summarises in relation to the study of football fandom practice,

> theoretical approaches that share a desire to understand how individual action is organised within mundane activities, whilst simultaneously recognising structural features that are reproduced through individual action, have much to offer.

Whilst Elias's (1991; 2000) concepts of 'changes in the we-I balance' and 'diminishing contrasts, increasing varieties' have been the principal ideas used to explain the actions and opinions of fans presented in this book, alternative explanations are possible. For instance, various globalisation theories have been used by authors such as Giulianotti and Robertson (2009), King (2003) and Millward (2011) to help explain the impacts of globalisation and Europeanisation on English football fans, particularly those of EPL clubs. Perhaps most relevant of these is Robertson's (1995) concept of 'glocalisation' whereby 'local and global realities interact and co-evolve through a series of mutual engagements and in response to various human actions' (Kennedy, 2010: 47). The concept of 'glocalisation', particularly what Giulianotti and Robertson (2009: 45) refer to as the 'duality of glocality', has clear similarities to Elias's (2000) 'diminishing contrasts, increasing varieties' in terms of being able to explain the diversity of ways in which football fans have displayed and articulated layers of Englishness around the national football team. These can be regarded as heterogeneous responses to the homogenising forces of globalisation and Europeanisation. Yet, other than Maguire (cf. 2011a), thus far sociologists of football have not drawn upon these clearly very useful Eliasian concepts.

It is worth pointing out that Giddens's (cf.1990) later work is specifically focused on globalisation, regarding it as a phenomenon that is 'multi-dimensional', just as Elias (2000) and Robertson (1992) have contended. Giddens (2009: 147 *emphasis in original*) proposes that through advancing globalisation processes, 'we are faced with a move towards a new *individualism*, in which people have actively to construct their own identities'. Here Giddens points towards the fact that globalisation operates on both an external and internal basis for individuals – it is something that individuals are impacted by and have little control over, but it is also a process that individuals can respond to in their own ways.

This inherently processual approach to the impacts of global forces has clear parallels with Elias's (1991; 2000) concepts of 'changes in the we–I balance' and 'diminishing contrasts, increasing varieties' as well as to Robertson's (1992; 1995) notion of 'glocalisation'. Elias (1991; 2000) contended that an aspect of the civilising process involves nation-states giving way to global homogenising forces – particularly at a political and economic level – as has been the case throughout history where smaller integration units have gradually been superseded by larger ones, such as in the case of the growth of the European Union since 1945 (Guibernau, 2011). Yet Elias (1991) also used the term 'drag-effect' to highlight how individuals within Europe still hold strong feelings for their national or even local layers of identification in the face of global and European forces. The result is older and newer layers of identity have interacted to form new or more diverse expressions. This is similar to what Giddens (2009: 147) states is 'part of an ongoing process of creating and re-creating our self-identities' or what Robertson referred to as processes of 'glocalisation' whereby the 'interpenetration of the 'local' and the 'global' can produce new forms of specifically 'local' culture, while at other times distinctive new combinations of local and global can be created' (Inglis and Thorpe, 2012: 279).

Thus both Robertson's (1992; 1995) 'glocalisation' and Giddens's (1990; 2009) approach to global processes, or what he refers to as 'late modernity', could be used as alternative explanations for understanding the ways in which contemporary English national identity is currently undergoing a state of flux – something that has been shown in this book via looking at the diverse conceptions of English national identity expressed by English football fans in specific contexts. Whilst Robertson's 'glocalisation' thesis has been used to inform aspects of Maguire's (cf. 1999; 2011a; 2011b; 2011c; 2011d) work which seeks to extend Elias's (2000) notion of 'diminishing contrasts, increasing varieties' in relation to many different global sport-related cultures, the work of Giddens remains largely under-utilised in the sociology of sport according to Horne and Jary (2004), and in relation to football fandom specifically according to Dixon (2011). Future research would benefit from exploring the various parallels between Giddens and Elias in relation to the impact of globalisation upon the relationship between English national identity and football fan culture.

Concluding Remarks

The research findings presented in this book suggest that 'British' and 'local' attachments were still clearly evident under the mask of the overt display of the seemingly coherent 'English' banner of the St George's Cross. This illustrates the 'drag-effect' Elias (1991) envisaged whereby individuals respond to their incorporation into larger units of organisation (in this case Europe) through reverting to smaller and / or older or deeper layers of their identities which in the English case are state and locality based. Both 'British' and 'local' layers of identification were being held onto by English fans in the face of global and European processes of integration. Underlying the ubiquitous display of the St George's Cross were also examples of the priority afforded to English club football which itself has become a symbol of the impact of globalisation and European integration, rather than evidence of an emotional attachment to England.

In writing about the centripetal forces that were gradually increasing in Western Europe (and globally) since the Middle Ages, Elias (2000) suggested that the comingling of separate cultures over history had created certain homogenising processes stemming from the West. Thus Elias argued that the barriers between cultures had gradually, over centuries, been diminishing due to increases in webs of interdependence between different figurations of people throughout Europe and globally. European integration and wider globalisation processes are large social processes that are not necessarily new, but have gathered significant momentum over the latter half of the twentieth century. However, Elias also recognised that such homogenising processes had simultaneously led to the creation of new heterogeneous varieties, as elements of one culture would be combined with those of another.

Applying this Eliasian concept to the long-term development of many modern sports that had originated in England, yet had become global entities, Maguire (1999: 213) suggested 'in the late twentieth century we are witnessing the globalization of sports and the increasing diversification of sports cultures'. Increasing globalisation and European integration processes that have impacted upon elite level English club football appear on the surface to be homogenising processes, but they actually often stimulate the articulation of heterogeneous identifications on the part of English football fans. Whilst the likes of King (2003), Levermore and Millward (2007) and Millward (2006; 2011) have shown that this is the case for EPL club fans, findings from the two studies presented in this book indicated that similar articulations of heterogeneity were visible around the English national team during World Cup 2006 and by fans of clubs who compete at lower levels of English football. However, it is important to point out that these are not articulations of new layers of identity. According to Maguire and Burrows (2005: 142), sport is

> an arena in which processes of personal identity testing and formation are conducted. Different sports represent individuals, communities, regions and nations. A key feature of the sports process is that it is used by different groups – established, emergent and outsider groups – to represent, maintain and/or challenge identities. Sports have performed this role since they became important national practices in the 1880s.

The observations made of fan behaviour during World Cup 2006 (Chapter 4) indicated that the display of English national sentiment was not necessarily the sole or even the intended purpose of this practice. It seemed that the flag was rather being used as a kind of blank canvas or flag of convenience by many English fans who used it as a space to display their local- and/or club-based attachments which were considered more relevant.

The online participant observation study revealed that there was also evidence to suggest that non-English fans used the supposedly 'English' national symbol of the St George's Cross to represent various layers of their identities (Chapter 6). There were also fans that could not explain why they engaged in this practice and were simply emulating others. Added to this, in the conversations fans were having in the online community analysed it became apparent that the English national team's lack of success since 1966 explained why more and more English fans were turning to their English clubs, particularly larger EPL clubs, as they not only play more regularly than the national team but also win competitions against foreign opposition much more often.

Adding even further complexity to this, there were discussions about what English national identity is and should be based upon. This came to the fore through discussions about the prospect of there being a British football team at the London 2012 Olympics and the possibility that Arsenal's Spanish goalkeeper, Manuel Almunia, could play for the English national team through naturalisation as a British citizen (Chapter 5). Both of these issues highlighted the real differences between 'England as the nation' and 'Britain as the state', and more importantly, the reliance of Englishness on Britain and the difficulties in separating one from the other. Furthermore, even though these two issues were clearly focused on English national identity, concerns regarding English club football were never far from the surface. For instance, some English Arsenal fans had concerns about whether playing for England would put too much pressure on Almunia which might negatively impact on his performances for the club. Other Arsenal fans were simply keen to have one of their club's players in the England team and cared little about the fact he was not actually English. There was other clear evidence that club football was considered far more important than international football and this was even apparent when the English national team were competing.

Such findings are examples of Elias's (2000) notion of 'diminishing contrasts, increasing varieties' because they are evidence that the globalisation and Europeanisation of English football has led to the growth of the EPL, a league consisting of more foreign than English players (Jackson, 2010), and one within which the top teams regularly compete against foreign opposition to the extent that it makes the national team's fixtures seem irregular or even 'exceptional' (Giulianotti and Robertson, 2009). Since the 1995 Bosman ruling, English clubs have been permitted to field teams comprising entirely non-English Europeans in pan-European competitions. The only remaining 'English' things about such clubs are the fact that they are situated in English towns and cities, yet these local identities have themselves become 'disembedded' from their national contexts (cf. Giulianotti and Robertson, 2004; 2009; King, 2003; Millward, 2011).

Overall, the findings presented in this book suggest that the increased display of the St George's Cross by English football fans does *not* illustrate the emergence of a unified English national consciousness. English national identity is itself a highly contested and fragile concept. Empirical evidence was required in order to clarify the complex nature of the relationship between English national identity and football fan culture. Elias remains largely under-used within the sociology of English football fandom and it is hoped that the current research has demonstrated the utility of some of Elias' (1991; 2000) ideas.

The relationship between English national identity and football fan culture has been, and continues to be, constantly challenged by European integration and globalisation processes. Whilst devolution has forced the English to come up with a national identity they can call their own, prompting the re-invention of the St George's Cross as an indicator of English national distinctiveness, the national community that is imagined is clearly not one homogenous group and is often based on 'British' and 'local', rather than, or in addition to, specifically 'English' attachments. The England national team's lack of success and the dominance of EPL club football, present key challenges to the very existence of a relationship between English national identity and football fans, particularly in relation to their feelings towards the national team. The very idea of having an English national team to represent English people has recently been challenged by both the Almunia case and the requirement for 'Team GB' to field a football team for the London 2012 Olympics.

Whilst (at the time of writing) a player without any ties to England has never represented the English national team, the diminishing of contrasts made possible by the globalisation of EPL football continues to make this situation more and more likely in future as English football diversifies and loses its association with national identity. The continued existence of separate national teams for each of the four nations within the UK is still in question following the 2012 Olympics. Even though some players in the GB football team as well as members of the BOA wanted a 'united' team in future (Toney, 2012; Winter, 2012), the fact that only English and Welsh players were picked to play with no representatives from Scotland and Northern Ireland makes the possibility of a future team unlikely (Daily Mail, 2012). The decision of the English FA to not allow members of the Euro 2012 England national team to play for GB in the Olympics is another example of division rather than unification between the UK football associations. Had the GB football team been as successful as Team GB were in other sporting events at this Olympics, then having a united football team in future Games, and even in the World Cup and European Championships, may have been something supported by many football fans.

In order to build on the research presented in this book, which took place prior to the London 2012 Olympics, a further study is required to assess whether the short existence of the GB football team, the success of Team GB in other sports and the success of the whole event, have united or divided people within the separate nations of the UK or indeed whether the memory of the Games did anything for Britishness in the long term. Both opportunities for integration and division are made possible via the medium of sport and this has been demonstrated in the current book via the use of studies on specific figurations of fans. If the direction of Elias's (2000) civilising process is to continue the way it has done in the past then centripetal forces will eventually win over centrifugal ones. English football fandom is an important aspect of this process and should not be ignored.

Appendix:
Research Strategy

Methodology for Pub-based Observation Study

Observations of how English fans displayed national identity during the 2006 World Cup were undertaken in a sample of seven English public houses, nightclubs and bars (referred to here under the umbrella term 'pubs'). The goal was to discover what national 'we' group ideal/image was being displayed or articulated by fans themselves in relation to the national team (Elias and Scotson, 1994; Elias, 1991; 1996).

May (2001: 173) defines participant observation as 'engaging in a social scene, experiencing it and seeking to understand and explain it. The researcher is the medium through which this takes place'. This was the case in the pub-based study. Observations were conducted in pubs that were showing each of the England team's matches 'live' on television during the 2006 World Cup Finals. The objective was primarily to observe and experience the ways in which fans showed support for the England national team during the tournament. The seven different venues the author attended were situated around Lancashire and Cumbria (counties in the north west of England). These venues generally comprised young (mostly 18–40), white (90%), males (70%). However, as a general rule, the larger the venue, the greater the number of women and the more equal the ratio of women to men. Moreover, the smaller the venue, the less racially diverse (and more 'white') the audience.[1] This is similar to what was experienced by Weed (2006) in his 'pub ethnography'.

The attraction of the pub as a venue for women to watch 'live' football may be higher than the attraction of the stadium. Although there is little further evidence to substantiate this assertion, based upon a review of research on the demographics of sports spectators, Crawford (2004: 57) summarised that, 'though women may be attending certain sports in higher proportions, they are still predominantly attending male sports, and often remain marginalized within sport fan communities'. There is also evidence from Jones (2008) suggesting women made up 15–20% of football crowds who attended EPL matches in 2006. More recently, Pope (2012) has suggested this figure has not risen much with female fans making up around 19% of crowds attending EPL games in 2012. Elsewhere Pope (2011: 471) has also highlighted that 'women's experiences have been largely invisibilized' in football fan research and she suggests there are a number of 'wider gendered problems … that underlie much research on male and female

---

1 All of this information was recorded in the author's field notes.

fans'. Although not the main focus of this book, it nonetheless raises important questions regarding the inter-sectionality of gender, English national identity and football fan culture that requires more in-depth investigation in future.

The setting chosen for the pub-based study during World Cup 2006 was different for each England match and the author went to each venue an hour before kick-off to catch the 'build up' and obtain a position where fans could be observed and a television showing the match was still also in view so that fans' reactions could be placed in the context of what was occurring on the screen. As is made clear in Chapter 4, reactions of fans were one of the key ways in which aspects of national identity were apparent. As per the pub ethnography conducted by Weed (2006), field notes were taken during and after each match out of view of participants, usually in toilet cubicles during the matches and in the author's car outside the venue directly after the final whistle. This approach to recording data almost as it happened was taken in order to minimise the impact of the researcher on the setting of the fieldwork, to maximise clarity and to avoid specific details being lost from memory. Field notes were later transcribed on the day of or the day after each match had taken place. The researcher remained alcohol-free in order to ensure clarity in recording events accurately. The flexibility of the method of observation was therefore very important. May (2001:159) defines fieldwork as

> a continual process of reflection and alteration of the focus of observations in accordance with analytic developments. It permits researchers to witness people's actions in different settings and routinely ask themselves a myriad of questions concerning motivations, beliefs and actions.

Similar to Weed (2006), the author is a young, white male who is familiar with going to pubs with the intention of watching 'live' sport. Thus the author was confident that he 'fitted in' and would be easily accepted by 'a pub football audience' (Weed, 2006: 80). Although the author was a participant in the research setting through being an England fan himself and regularly watching matches on television in a pub setting, he did not interview other fans or record his own conversations with them, but listened to conversations/remarks and observed behaviour whilst continually reflecting on their significance. Therefore the type of observation conducted is perhaps best described as 'unobtrusive (nonreactive) observation, conducted with people who are unaware of being studied' (Angrosino, 2005: 732). Moreover, if using the membership roles developed by Adler and Adler (1987, cited in Angrosino, 2005: 733), the author can be regarded as a 'peripheral member researcher' – a researcher who believes they can develop a desirable insider's perspective *without* participating in those activities that constitute the core of group membership.

Furthermore, whilst the method of observation was ethnographic in nature, the methodological approach taken cannot be regarded as ethnography in itself. Although the researcher immersed himself in an aspect of the everyday life of the participants (i.e., the pub), the same group of people were not observed for every match and for an extended period of time. It is this lack of engagement with the same group over a long period of time that defines ethnography (Silk, 2005). That said, many researchers use the term 'ethnography' interchangeably when discussing methods such as observation (cf. May, 2001), and according to Silk (2005: 70), given the

> broadness of the term ethnography, there is perhaps a danger in attributing the term ethnographic to research in sports studies – nearly all qualitative work could actually fit under such a label.

Use of this research method was designed to highlight the diversity of ways in which fans chose to express their national identity in relation to the England national team during World Cup 2006. However, the opinions of fans themselves were still required in order to more fully understand what was observed.

Methodology for Online Participant Observation Study

The vast majority of football clubs have created fan discussion forums on their websites, as have many governing bodies and associations related to football. There is also a plethora of more 'unofficial' sites, many of which are not formally linked to any club, governing body or association (cf. Kennedy and Kennedy, 2010). The online fan community within which the participant observation study that underpins Chapters 5 and 6 was conducted could be regarded in this way and was chosen specifically because of its independence from any single club, governing body or association. The online community is an independent website created, maintained and for the use of football fans from all over the globe. The site was established in 2007 and remains active at the time of writing with well over 1,000 members, a figure that continues to grow.

In total, 93 members of the online community contributed to the 29 discussion threads that were used as data in this study. Table A.1 provides a summary of the demographics of the members who contributed. Whilst most of the sample was English (62%) and it was their comments that provided the vast majority of the data on the relationship between English national identity and football fan culture, fans of other nationalities also contributed with some comments that were utilised as comparative data. The majority of this figuration of fans were male (92%) and the age range was large. The Premier League (2010) claimed that 19% of those who attended Premier League fixtures during the 2008/9 season were female, although there is not much evidence available on the attendances of lower-level clubs. As mentioned in relation to the pub audience, further research is also required to assess the demographics of football fans that utilise online discussion forums.

Table A.1 Nationality, gender and age of online participant observation participants

Characteristic	Composition of Sample
English	62%
Non-English	38%
Males	92%
Females	8%
Mean Age	30 years
Age Range	18–69 years

Sveningsson (2009: 72) contends that, 'when studying online environments, it may often be too difficult to obtain informed consent'. Specifically focusing on participant observations within chat rooms/discussion forums, she goes on to explain that because members 'log-on' and 'log-off' rapidly, the window of opportunity for informing and gaining consent is minimal. Also, she highlights that if a researcher were to post a message asking for consent every time a new member logged on, other members might get annoyed and the rapport the researcher was attempting to establish could be seriously under threat meaning the opportunity to obtain rich data could be compromised. Sveningsson also states that even if researchers took the time to write and send private messages to all potential participants, there would be very little time left on the part of the researcher to observe online interactions —the very point of conducting the research in the first place.

Many of Sveningsson's concerns are closely aligned with the guidelines provided by 'The Association of Internet Researchers' (AoIR).[2] Although the AoIR ethics working group recommend that it is sometimes acceptable to collect data online *without* informed consent, providing the material is *not sensitive* and the *online environment is public*, Sveningsson (2009: 73) urges that 'the variables of public/private and sensitive/not sensitive are not as unambiguous as they may seem at first glance' and therefore require further consideration in Internet-based research, particularly that which is ethnographic in nature.

Sveningsson suggests that 'public' and 'private' online environments cannot be simply dichotomised. Rather than simply conceiving of such online spaces as

---

2   The AoIR ethics working group's final report can be found at: http://aoir.org/reports/ethics.pdf (Accessed Nov. 2010). This information is cited in Sveningsson (2009: 73), but the author also learnt of this resource when he attended a one-day workshop event titled 'An Introduction to Online Research Methods', which took place at the ESRC Regional Training Centre, University of Cardiff, on 13 February 2008. This formed part of the TRI-ORM (Training Researchers in Online Research Methods) project that was undertaken between May 2007 and May 2009 as part of the ESRC Research Development Initiative.

either public or private, instead Sveningsson (2009: 75) argues that it is more accurate to consider where specific domains might exist along the following four-point continuum: first, *public environments*, such as web pages or completely open chat rooms; second, *semi-public environments*, such as most web communities or social network sites; third, *semi-private environments*, such as companies or organisations intranets; and fourth, *completely private environments*, such as online photo albums or private/invite only sections of chat rooms or web communities. Considering the online fan community used within this study was a 'member-only' discussion forum and in order to become a member fans must first complete a registration form and agree to various terms and conditions of membership, it seems reasonable to class it as second along Sveningsson's continuum. The forum is a 'semi-public' environment because it is 'in principle accessible to anyone, but it first requires membership and registration' (Sveningsson, 2009: 75). The only exception to this is that 'guests' are able to view pages. As such, it is perhaps more accurate to define the online community used in this research as sitting somewhere in-between being a public and a semi-public online environment.

Considering the online community drawn upon in this research is closer to the public end of the spectrum than it is to the private end, it was decided that informed consent was *not* required in the online participant observation study. Instead steps were taken to ensure the participant observation was conducted in an overt fashion through the author initially declaring to the online forum moderators (and later to forum members) that he was an academic researcher interested in the views of fans who interacted on the site. First, this involved emailing the main moderators of the site and detailing the purposes of the research to them. Establishing the 'authenticity' of the researcher is crucial to accessing any research domain and this is no different when accessing online environments (Garcia et al., 2009; Hine, 2000). The forum founder agreed to allow the author access to the online community in order to conduct the research.

According to Sveningsson (2009), another important ethical consideration is whether the content of forum members' posts are sensitive or not. The content of the online community used in this study can be viewed freely by absolutely anyone, it is only if one wants to post that they are required to register. This ensures that anyone who makes an active decision to become a member is acutely aware that anything they post is in the public domain. This makes the possibility of members posting personally sensitive information somewhat unlikely. In addition to this, the content that the researcher was interested in using as data for the current study related to discussions on the topic of English national identity and its links to football fan culture. Such a topic is what Sveningsson (2009: 80) would regard as 'public content' because it relates to 'societal matters' (Englishness and football) rather than any aspects of individuals' private lives. The author was primarily interested in the kinds of public issues that were discussed on the forum that highlighted the diversity of viewpoints that exist in relation to the topic. Therefore, the content of the data gathered within the online participant observation is regarded as ethical both in its nature and scope.

Although initial access to the online community was fairly straightforward, the choice to conduct the online participant observation overtly may have impacted upon the relationships made with the participants and latterly to the content of the findings. According to Garcia et al. (2009: 71), the 'researcher's identity can affect how conspicuous they are in the setting and the likelihood that potential informants will be willing to talk to them'. The alternative to the overt approach taken here would have been to infiltrate the online domain and conduct research covertly. Although this might have generated different data due to members being completely unaware that they were being researched, it is doubtful to have been ethically viable and for this reason the kind of deception it is easy to maintain in anonymous online settings was avoided here (Garcia et al., 2009).

This online participant observation study differed from the 'unobtrusive (nonreactive)' pub-based observation of fans in a number of ways. The main difference was that the author maintained involvement in the online forum over a sustained period and was thus involved in interacting with members of the community often on a daily basis, rather than observing their behaviour alone as he did in the pub-based study. Therefore the type of observation conducted here embodies the most involved of the three ways of conducting observation-based research outlined by Angrosino (2005: 732) who states that it is

> participant observation, grounded in the establishment of considerable rapport between the researcher and the host community and requiring the long-term immersion of the researcher in the everyday life of that community.

Referring back to the membership roles that were discussed earlier in relation to the pub-based observation study, the author was an 'active' member researcher in the online fan community, rather than a 'peripheral' member researcher as he was in the pub-based study. Active member researchers are

> those who become involved with the central activities of the group, sometimes even assuming responsibilities that advance the group without necessarily fully committing themselves to members' values and goals. (Adler and Adler, 1987, cited in Angrosino, 2005: 733)

According to Murthy (2008: 840), 'the role of observer can still sometimes be considered 'passive' in the eyes of ... chat room users if the researcher is not overtly interacting with them'. This was certainly not the case with the online participant observation employed here. The author became a member of the online forum and actively contributed through posting new discussion topics as well as joining in existing discussion threads started by other users on a daily basis. Therefore the author was an 'active' rather than a 'passive' participant in terms of his engagement with the research participants.

Appendix: Research Strategy 167

The author joined the online community on 12 June 2008 and went on to make 204 posts, the final one being 12 September 2009.[3] The online community had three levels of membership: 'Member'; 'Advanced Member'; and, 'Elite Member'. These levels were based upon frequency of posts over time – the more posts the higher the level. It was up to the forum moderators to allocate membership categories and these appeared to be periodically revised. There were also three levels of moderator who had various responsibilities for ensuring the content of all areas of the site were policed effectively: 'Moderator'; 'Super Moderator'; and, 'Root Admin'. Those at the 'Root Admin' level were the first members of the forum, including its founder, and therefore had most responsibility for maintaining the integrity of the site, for example banning members who made offensive posts. Other than this, a 'Guest' was someone who was just visiting the site without becoming a member and had restrictions placed on the forum areas they could access and contribute to.

Having already secured permission to join the forum for research purposes from the founder via email, steps were taken to ensure members were explicitly aware of the author's presence and intentions. The author's initial post was made within the 'New Signings' area of the forum where new members were directed to in order to introduce themselves. When the author initially introduced himself in this area he used the following information in order to establish his authenticity as a legitimate academic researcher:

> June 12 2008 11:06am
> 1: Hi, I'm an academic researching various aspects of football fandom through asking fans their views and opinions of current issues (particularly in the English Game). **Moderators — I have requested permission from (fan 3) in admin to post on this forum.**
>
> Any information you give me will be anonymous and used solely for academic conference proceedings, journal articles, books and for teaching purposes. I will never ask for or record any information that might lead to forum members being identified (such as names, email addresses or IP addresses).
>
> I look forward to talking to you about your views and opinions.
> (Fan 1)

This initial post was well received by forum members, a number of whom seemed genuinely interested in the research. This acted as a kind of 'rubberstamp' so that other fans felt they could trust the author. This proved important in the author establishing 'rapport' with some key forum members (or 'gatekeepers'), an essential requirement of any ethnographic research study (O'Reilly, 2009). Some

---

3 Some fans' responses to questions the author asked before 12 September 2009 were collected after this date and have been included in some of the extracts presented in Chapters 5 and 6.

of the first interactions the author had with other forum members arose in relation to this initial post. For instance:

> June 12 2008 11:09am
> 3: Hello mate good luck and welcome to the forums. [Male, English, Arsenal FC, aged 53]
>
> June 12 2008 11:30am
> 1: Many thanks (fan 3)!
>
> June 12 2008 11:23am
> 4: I'm sure you will get a lot of replies from this footie mad lot. [Female, English, West Ham United FC, aged 60]
>
> June 12 2008 11:31am
> 1: I hope so! Cheers for your support!
>
> June 12 2008 03:57pm
> 9: I'd be interested in knowing your findings once you have finished your research. [Male, English, Birmingham City FC, aged 24]
>
> June 12 2008 05:31pm
> 1: Cheers (fan 9). I'll let you know the main findings as and when (thumbs up emoticon).

Within this initial discussion thread and others, there were examples to highlight the author gaining rapport and acceptance amongst forum members. This usually revolved around explaining what the research was about, for instance:

> June 12 2008 02:52pm
> 6: Welcome! … . Hope the research goes well. What exactly is it for? [Female, English, Leeds United FC, aged 24]
>
> June 2008 03:49pm
> 1: Cheers (fan 6)! It's for an academic research project I am conducting on the opinions of football fans on key issues within English football at the moment. Therefore it's partly to do with finding out the significance of football in the lives of fans today but also to do with the link between English national identity and football. The thing is that academics often make assumptions on what fans think without actually asking them! Basically I want to change that by asking fans themselves. Your help is very much appreciated.

> June 24 12:08pm
> 7: Generally is it the concept of nationalism that you are interested in? [Male, English, Manchester United FC, aged 31]
>
> June 24 2008 04:38pm
> 1: Yes, that's what I'm interested in specifically as well as the significance of football in people's lives.

Another fan in this thread wanted to ask about the author's football-related credentials and this had the impact of initiating further rapport. For example:

> June 24 2008 04:54pm
> 13: Out of interest, do you support any teams. Where abouts are you from? [Male, English, Leeds United FC, aged 25]
>
> June 24 2008 05:01pm
> 1: Well I loosely follow Gillingham FC because I'm originally from Kent. However ... I saw a few Liverpool games when I was young and now tend to follow them too. I live in Teesside at the moment so have seen a few Boro games as well.
>
> June 24 2008 05:09pm
> 13: (Smiley face emoticon) We relegated the gills last season (Smiley face emoticon).
>
> June 25 2008 05:01pm
> 1: Thanks for reminding me of that! (Angry, then smiley emoticons).
>
> June 24 2008 05:17pm
> 11: Hope you're proud of yourselves ... poor Gillingham ... (emoticon with shades). [Male, English, Chelsea FC, aged 28]

This rapport building was also evident in later threads, for example:

> December 4 2008 04:50pm
> 7: Have you come to any conclusions regarding your research yet (fan 1)? [Male, English, Manchester United FC, aged 31]
>
> December 5 2008 12:26pm
> 1: It's still ongoing I'm afraid ... . On this forum there seems to be a real mix of opinion on English identity and football though! Sorry for being a bit vague at the moment. I'll go into my findings in more depth when I've got some more evidence.

> February 25 2009 06:16pm
> 63: (Fan 1) you should post more with polls and stuff (thumbs up emoticon). [Male, English, Arsenal FC, aged 23]
>
> March 4 2009 04:55pm
> 1: Ok ... I will do (Cheers emoticon).
>
> March 5 2009 06:56pm
> 63: nice one (Thumbs up emoticon).

Despite the above demonstrations of rapport and acceptance being built between the author and other forum members, there were also instances where the author felt as if he was being kept out of conversations deliberately. In three of the 29 threads the author made posts that were completely ignored. At the time this was frustrating and almost as if the more 'established' members were purposefully ignoring the author because they considered him an 'outsider' to the group (Elias and Scotson, 1994). However, the author gradually came to realise that he was simply asking fans far too many questions rather than discussing football-related issues with them. There seemed to be a fine line between asking questions as part of a conversation and asking general questions for anyone to answer. The latter seemed to glean far fewer responses and upon realising this, the author was careful to only ask general questions when he began new discussion threads.

Towards the end of the first twelve months of being an active member of the forum other members actually started to overtly make fun of the fact that the author asked 'too many' questions:

> May 5 2009 04:45pm
> 18: So you finally give an answer rather than asking a question! [Male, English, Juventus FC, aged 28]
>
> May 5 2009 04:51pm
> 6: I was stumped by it, so I just left the thread (smiley face emoticon). [Female, English, Leeds United FC, aged 24]
>
> May 6 2009 12:12pm
> 1: Perhaps I will ask less questions from now on! (Embarrassed emoticon).

Now that the procedures involved in the research conducted in this book have been detailed, the Eliasian methodological framework that guided data collection and analysis in both research studies requires further explanation.

Data Collection and Analysis

The sources of data obtained from these studies consisted of field notes from pub-based observations and transcripts from discussions with and between fans in the online community. Both forms of qualitative data were 'coded' using the same method of analysis. This qualitative coding approach is termed 'qualitative discourse analysis'. Maguire and Poulton (1999) conducted such an analysis on English newspaper coverage of the Euro 96 football competition and focused upon the portrayal of English national identity whilst relying upon Elias's (1991) notion of 'changes in the we-I balance'; Elias and Scotson's (1994) theory of 'established/outsider relations'; and Elias's (1996) 'national identity codes'. The concepts of 'invented traditions' (Hobsbawm, 1983) and 'imagined communities' (Anderson, 1991) were also drawn upon by these authors. An issue with Maguire and Poulton's analytical framework, which the current book sought to develop in relation to its utility for studying the relationship between English national identity and football fan culture, is that these authors did not refer to any non-sport related literature on the 'problems' with English national identity. This literature has been reviewed in Chapter 2 in relation to Elias's (1991) notion of 'changes in the we-I balance' and Elias's concept of 'diminishing contrasts, increasing varieties'. This combination of subject-specific literature and sociological theory was used for guiding the analysis of the data.

Practically, the qualitative discourse analysis used was similar to that suggested by Miles and Huberman (1994: 56), who state that the

> challenge is to be explicitly mindful of the purposes of your study and of the conceptual lenses you are training on it – while allowing yourself to be open and reeducated by things you didn't know about or expect to find ... you will have to accompany each wave of data collection with a corresponding exercise in condensation and analysis. This step is where coding and other forms of ongoing, iterative action come in.

'Codes', also referred to by Miles and Huberman (1994: 56) as 'tags or labels for assigning units of meaning', were developed using a 'semi-inductive' coding technique. The term 'semi-inductive' best describes the specific technique used because although categories were not predetermined and arose from the data itself, the author used his understanding of Eliasian theoretical concepts and his knowledge of the main 'problems' or 'anxieties' associated with Englishness to inform the data collection and analysis. This means that the coding approach used partially resembled the 'grounded' approach originally developed by Glaser and Strauss (1967). Analysis of the data began by manually developing a list of initial codes based upon an interpretation of the meanings the author extracted from the data under analysis. In each of the two studies the analysis involved extracts from field notes and online discussions being assigned an initial theme before being grouped into codes with similar extracts.

This initial coding process used for each data set resulted in a long list of provisional codes and so it was essential to re-read the data a number of times in order to reduce the amount of codes into fewer but more comprehensive qualitative categories that were distinct enough from one another to be classed as separate codes, but still related to the overall research objectives. This is congruent with the suggestions made by Gratton and Jones (2010: 240, emphasis in original) that 'codes'

> should be *valid*, that is they should accurately reflect what is being researched, they should be *mutually exclusive*, in that codes should be distinct, with no overlap, and they should be *exhaustive*, that is all relevant data should fit into a code.

In Chapters 4–6 dominant codes are indicated by headings (in bold font) and sub-codes appear as italicised sub-headings. Key extracts are used to demonstrate recurrent themes in the data.

Epistemological and Ontological Concerns

During the research process the author was presented with the 'double bind' of 'involvement and detachment' discussed by Elias (1987).[4] That is, the

> problem confronting those who study one or the other aspects of human groups is how to keep their two roles as participant and as inquirer clearly and consistently apart ... to establish the undisputed dominance of the latter (Elias, 1987: 16).

The author has attempted to take the 'detour via detachment' advocated by Elias (1987) through continually reflecting on the methods of data collection and analysis utilised and has strived to be as detached as possible from the topics of English national identity and football fandom without losing sight of the fact that he is inevitably involved in the very processes under exploration. The author has been careful to reflect on that fact that he is himself an English person and a football fan and therefore holds the belief that football is an important means through which English national identity is manifest in everyday life.

This level of involvement, or what some may term 'subjectivity', could be regarded as one of the limitations of the research conducted as it may have led to researcher bias in both data collection and analysis. However, the author's level of involvement in the subject matter also meant that credibility and authenticity of the studies undertaken was high as it motivated the researcher's desire to accurately reflect the significance of the actions and opinions of fans themselves (Gratton and Jones, 2010). This high level of internal validity no doubt compromised the external validity of the research conducted, but this is a problem inherent in all qualitative research where the aim is to gather rich, in-depth data from within

---

4 See the final section of Chapter 2 for a brief critical appraisal of Elias' 'involvement and detachment'.

'natural' or 'real-life' settings (Holliday, 2008; Richards, 2005; Silverman, 2000). It is therefore important to acknowledge that this research involved two case studies of distinct areas in which English national identity was displayed and/ or debated. This means that the findings provide only a partial account of the relationship between English national identity and football fan culture and may not fully reflect the actions and opinions of other samples of fans in different spatial and temporal contexts. Some of the more specific limitations inherent in each of the studies conducted are discussed in further detail in the 'Empirical Reflections' section of Chapter 7.

Bibliography

Abell, J., Condor, S., Lowe, R.D., Gibson, S. and Stevenson, C. (2007) Who ate all the pride? Patriotic sentiment and English football support. *Nations and Nationalism*, 13 (1), 97–116.

Abercrombie, N. and Longhurst, B. (1998) *Audiences*. London, Sage.

Ackroyd, P. (2002) *Albion: The Origins of the English Imagination*. London, Chatto & Windus.

Alabarces, P., Tomlinson, A. and Young, C. (2001) Argentina versus England at the France '98 World Cup: narratives of nation and the mythologizing of the popular. *Media, Culture & Society*, 23 (5), 547–66.

Anderson, B. (1991) *Imagined Communities: Reflections on the Origins and Spread of Nationalism*. London, Verso.

Andrews, D.L. and Ritzer, G. (2007) The grobal in the sporting glocal. *Global Networks*, 7 (2), 135–53.

Angrosino, M.V. (2005) Recontextualizing Observation: Ethnography, pedagogy, and the prospects for a progressive political agenda. In N.K. Denzin and Y.S. Lincoln (eds), *The Sage Handbook of Qualitative Research* (Third Edition). London, Sage, 729–45.

Appadurai, A. (1994) Disjuncture and difference in the global cultural economy. In M. Featherstone (ed.), *Global Culture: Nationalism, Globalization and Modernity*. London, Sage, 295–310.

Appadurai, A. (1996) *Modernity at Large: Cultural Dimensions of Globalization*. London, University of Minnesota Press.

Armstrong, G. and Giulianotti, R. (2001) (eds) *Fear and Loathing in World Football*. Oxford, Berg.

Armstrong, G. and Mitchell, J.P. (2008) *Global and Local Football: Politics and Europeanisation on the Fringes of the EU*. Abingdon, Routledge.

Armstrong, J. (2006) Beer We Go. *Mirror News*, 28 June 2006, available at: http://www.mirror.co.uk/news/top-stories/2006/06/28/beer-we-go-115875-17302491/ (Accessed Apr. 2007).

Aslet, C. (1997) *Anyone for England: A Search for British Identity*. London, Little Brown.

Aughey, A. (2007) *The Politics of Englishness*. Manchester, Manchester University Press.

Auty, C. (2002) Football fan power and the internet: net gains? *Aslib Proceedings*, 54 (5), 273–9.

Back, L., Crabbe, T., and Solomos, J. (2001) *The Changing Face of Football: Racism, Multiculturalism and Identity in the English Game*. Oxford, Berg.

Bairner, A. (2006) The Leicester School and the Study of Football Hooliganism. *Sport in Society*, 9 (4), 583–98.

Barraclough, E.M.C. (1971) *Flags of the World*. London, Frederick Warne & Co.

Bartrum, G. (2004) *British Flags and Emblems*. Scotland, Tuckwell Press.

Baym, N. (1997) Interpreting soap operas and creating community: inside an electronic fan culture. In S. Kiesler (ed.), *Culture of the Internet*. Mahwah, NJ, Lawrence Erlbaum, 103–19.

Baym, N. (2002) Interpersonal life online. In A. Leah and S. Livingstone (eds), *Handbook of New Media: Social shaping and consequences of ICTs*. London, Sage, 62–76.

BBC News (2004) North East votes 'no' to assembly. *BBC News Online article*, Friday 5 November 2004, available at: http://news.bbc.co.uk/1/hi/uk_politics/3984387.stm (Accessed Jan. 2008).

BBC News (2006) Football rights 'hat-trick' for Sky. *BBC News Online article*, Friday 28 April 2006, available at: http://news.bbc.co.uk/1/hi/business/4953846.stm (Accessed Nov. 2010).

BBC News (2009) Born Abroad: An Immigration Map of Britain. *BBC News Online database*, available at: http://news.bbc.co.uk/1/shared/spl/hi/uk/05/born_abroad/around_britain/html/overview.stm (Accessed Feb. 2009).

BBC News (2013) Timeline: Scotland's road to independence referendum. BBC News Online article, Friday 15 March 2013, available at: http://www.bbc.co.uk/news/uk-scotland-scotland-politics-20546497 (Accessed Jul. 2013).

BBC Sport (2000) Italy v England past meetings. *BBC Sport Online article*, Tuesday 14 November 2000, available at: http://news.bbc.co.uk/sport1/hi/football/1022732.stm (Accessed Apr. 2011).

Beck, P. (1999) *Scoring for Britain*. London, Frank Cass.

Bell, D. (2007) Cyberculture. In G. Ritzer (ed.), *Blackwell Encyclopedia of Sociology*. London, Blackwell Reference.

Bennett, A. (2005) *Culture and everyday life*. London, Sage.

Bennett, T. (2005) The media sensorium: cultural technologies, the senses and society. In M. Gillespie (ed.), *Media Audiences*. Maidenhead, Open University Press, 51–96.

Billig, M. (1995) *Banal Nationalism*. London, Sage.

Blake, A. (1999) Chants Would Be a Fine Thing. In M. Perryman (ed.), *The Ingerland Factor: Home Truths from Football*. Edinburgh, Mainstream, 109–18.

Blunkett, D. Rt. Hon MP (2005) A New England: An English Identity within Britain. Speech to the Institute for Public Policy Research (ippr) 14 March 2005, available at: http://www.ippr.org/images/media/files/publication/2011/05/a%20new%20england_1336.pdf (Accessed Jan. 2008).

Body, R. (2001) *England for the English*. London, NEP.

Bond, R., Jeffery, C. and Rosie, M. (2010) The importance of being English: national identity and nationalism in post-devolution England. *Nations and Nationalism*, 16 (3), 462–68.

Bourdieu, P. (1977) *Outline of a Theory of Practice* (originally published in French 1972, trans. Richard Nice). Cambridge, Cambridge University Press.

Bourdieu, P. (1984) *Distinction: A Social Critique of the Judgement of Taste* (originally published in French 1979, trans. Richard Nice). London, Routledge & Kegan Paul.

Bowker, B.M. (1976) *England rugby: a history of the national side, 1871–1976.* London, Cassell.

Boyle, R. and Haynes, R. (2004) *Football in the New Media Age.* London, Routledge.

Boyle, R. and Monteiro, C. (2005) 'A Small Country with a Big Ambition': Representations of Portugal and England in Euro 2004 British and Portuguese Newspaper Coverage. *European Journal of Communication*, 20 (2), 223–44.

Bradshaw, P. (2010) The Great Escape binds England footballers to failure. *Guardian. co.uk Film Blog*, 28 June 2010, available at: http://www.guardian.co.uk/film/filmblog/2010/jun/28/england-great-escape-world-cup (Accessed Apr. 2011).

Bragg, B. (2007) *The Progressive Patriot: A search for belonging.* London, Black Swan.

Brown, A. (2007) 'Not For Sale'? The destruction and Reformation of football communities in the Glazer takeover of Manchester United. *Soccer and Society*, 8 (4), 614–35.

Bryant, C.G.A. (2003) These Englands, or where does devolution leave the English? *Nations and Nationalism*, 9 (3), 393–412.

Bryant, C.G.A. (2006) *The Nations of Britain.* Oxford, Oxford University Press.

Bryson, L. and McCartney, C. (1994) *Clashing Symbols: A report on the use of flags, national anthems and other national symbols in Northern Ireland.* Belfast, Institute of Irish Studies.

Burdsey, D. (2006) 'If I ever play football, Dad, can I play for England or India?' British Asians, sport and diasporic national identities. *Sociology*, 40 (1), 11–28.

Burdsey, D. (2007) *British Asians and Football: Culture, Identity, Exclusion.* London, Routledge.

Burdsey, D. (2011) (ed.), *Race, Ethnicity and Football: Persisting Debates and Emergent Issues.* Abingdon, Routledge.

Burdsey, D. and Chappell, R. (2001) "And if you know your history": An examination of the formation of football clubs in Scotland and their role in the construction of social identity. *The Sports Historian*, 21 (1), 94–106.

Burdsey, D. and Randhawa, K. (2012) How can professional football clubs create welcoming and inclusive stadia for British Asian fans? *Journal of Policy Research in Tourism, Leisure and Events*, 4 (1), 105–11.

Byrne, B. (2007) England – whose England? Narratives of nostalgia, emptiness and evasion in imaginations of national identity. *The Sociological Review*, 55 (3), 509–30.

Carrington, B. (1998) Football's coming home but whose home? And do we want it? Nation, football and the politics of exclusion. In A. Brown (ed.), *Fanatics! Power, Identity and Fandom in Football.* London, Routledge, 101–23.

Carrington, B. (1999) Too many St. George Crosses to bear. In M. Perryman (ed.), *The Ingerland Factor: Home Truths from Football*. Edinburgh, Mainstream, 71–86.

Cashmore, E. and Cleland, J. (2012) Fans, homophobia and masculinities in association football: Evidence of a more inclusive environment. *British Journal of Sociology*, 63, 370–387.

Castells, M. (1996) *The Informational City*. Oxford, Blackwell.

Chen, S. and Wright, T. (2000) (eds), *The English Question*. London, Fabian Society.

Chisari, F. (2000) 'Definitely not Cricket': The Times and the Football World Cup 1930–1970. *The Sports Historian*, 20 (1), 44–69.

Chisari, F. (2005) 'The Cursed Cup': Italian responses to the 1985 Heysel Disaster. In P. Darby, M. Johnes and G. Mellor (eds), *Soccer and Disaster: International Perspectives*. London, Routledge, 77–94.

Chryssochoou, D.N. (2001) *Theorizing European Integration*. London, Sage.

Clark, T. (2006) "I'm Scunthorpe 'til I Die": Constructing and (Re)Negotiating Identity Through the Terrace Chant'. *Soccer and Society*, 7 (4), 494–507.

Cleland, J. (2010) From passive to active: The changing relationship between football clubs and football supporters. *Soccer and Society*, 11, 537–52.

Cleland, J. (2013) Discussing homosexuality on association football fan message boards: A changing cultural context. *International Review for the Sociology of Sport*. Epub ahead of print 18 February 2013. DOI: 10.1177/1012690213475437.

Colley, L. (1996) *Britons: Forging the Nation: 1707–1837*. London, Vintage.

Collins, T. (2006) History, Theory and the 'Civilizing Process'. *Sport in History*, 25 (2), 289–306.

Colls, R. (2002) *Identity of England*. Oxford, Oxford University Press.

Condor, S. and Fenton, S. (2012) Thinking across domains: Class, nation and racism in England and Britain. *Ethnicities*, 12 (4), 385–93.

Conway, R. (2012) London 2012: Home nations should back Team GB – Fifa official. *BBC Sport Online*, available at: http://www.bbc.co.uk/sport/0/football/17254225 (Accessed Mar. 2012).

Corbett, D.P., Holt, Y. and Russell, F. (2002) (eds), *The Geographies of Englishness: Landscape and the National Past 1880–1940*. London, Yale University Press.

Coyle, J. (2002) International Football. In R. Cox, D. Russell and W. Vamplew (eds), *Encyclopedia of British Football*. London, Frank Cass, 185–8.

Crabbe, T. (2003) 'The Public Gets what the Public Wants': England Football Fans, 'Truth' Claims and Mediated Realities. *International Review for the Sociology of Sport*, 38 (4), 413–25.

Craven, N. (2005) Don't mention the war! *The Daily Mail Newspaper Online*, available at: http://www.dailymail.co.uk/news/article-371234/Dont-mention-war.html (Accessed Apr. 2011).

Crawford, G. (2001) Characteristics of a British ice hockey audience – major findings of the 1998 and 1999 Manchester Storm Ice Hockey Club supporter surveys. *International Review for the Sociology of Sport*, 36 (1), 78–81.

Crawford, G. (2002) Cultural tourists and cultural trends: commercialization and the Coming of The Storm. *Culture, Sport, Society*, 5 (1), 21–38.

Crawford, G. (2003) The career of the sport supporter: the case of the Manchester Storm. *Sociology*, 37 (2), 219–37.

Crawford, G. (2004) *Consuming Sport: fans, sport and culture.* London, Routledge.

Critcher, C. (1994) England and the World Cup: World Cup Willies, English football and the myth of 1966. In J. Sugden and A. Tomlinson (eds), *Hosts and Champions: Soccer cultures, national identities and the USA World Cup*. Aldershot, Arena, 77–92.

Crolley, L. and Hand, D. (2002) *Football, Europe and the Press*. London, Routledge.

Crolley, L. and Hand, D. (2006) *Football and European Identity: Historical Narratives through the Press*. London, Routledge.

Cronin, M. (2002) Irish Football. In R. Cox, D. Russell and W. Vamplew (eds), *Encyclopedia of British Football*. London, Frank Cass, 188–90.

Cull, N.J. (2002) Great Escapes: 'Englishness' and the prisoner of war genre. *Film History*, 14 (3/4), 282–95.

Curia (2011) Court of Justice of the European Union Press Release No 102/11, Luxembourg, 4 October 2011, available at: http://curia.europa.eu/jcms/upload/docs/application/pdf/2011-10/cp110102en.pdf (Accessed Nov. 2011).

Curnow, S. (2006) Devolution for Cornwall. *BBC Action Network*, available at: http://www.bbc.co.uk/dna/actionnetwork/A9474889 (Accessed Jan. 2008).

Curry, G., Dunning, E. and Sheard, K. (2006) Sociological Versus Empiricist History: Some Comments on Tony Collins's 'History, Theory and the "Civilizing Process". *Sport in History*, 26 (1), 110–23.

Curtice, J. (2009) Is there an English backlash? Reactions to devolution. In A. Park, J. Curtice, K. Thomson, M. Phillips and E. Clery (eds), *British Social Attitudes: the 25th Report*. London, Sage, 1–23.

Curtice, J. and Heath, A. (2000) Is the English Lion about to roar? National identity after devolution. In R. Jowell, J. Curtice, A. Park, K. Thomson, L. Jarvis, C. Bromley and N. Stratford (eds), *British Social Attitudes 17th Report: Focussing on Diversity*. London, Sage, 155–74.

Daily Mail (2012) Pearce names Team GB squad with Bellamy and Giggs fronting strong Welsh contingent. *Mail Online*, 3 July 2012, available at: http://www.dailymail.co.uk/sport/olympics/article-2167672/London-2012-Olympics-Team-GB-mens-football-squad-revealed.html (Accessed Nov. 2012).

Dart, J. (2009) Blogging the 2006 FIFA World Cup finals. *Sociology of Sport Journal*, 26, 107–26.

Davey, K. (1999) *English Imaginaries: Six Studies in Anglo-British Modernity*. London, Lawrence & Wishart.

Davey, K. (2001) No Longer 'Ourselves Alone' in Northern Ireland. In D. Morley and K. Roberts (eds), *British Cultural Studies*. Oxford, Oxford University Press, 79–95.

De Jong, M. (2001) Elias and Bourdieu: the cultural sociology of two structuralists in denial. *International Journal of Contemporary Sociology*, 38 (1), 64–86.

Delanty, G. (2006) Nationalism and Cosmopolitanism: The Paradox of Modernity. In G. Delanty and K. Kumar (eds), *The Sage Handbook of Nations and Nationalism*. London, Sage, 357–68.

Delanty, G. and Kumar, K. (2006) (eds), *The Sage Handbook of Nations and Nationalism*. London, Sage.

Delanty, G. and O'Mahony, P. (2002) *Nationalism and Social Theory*. London, Sage.

Dixon, K. (2011) A 'third way' for football fandom research: Anthony Giddens and Structuration Theory. *Soccer and Society*, 12 (2), 279–98.

Dixon, K. (2012) Learning the game: Football fandom culture and the origins of practice. *International Review for the Sociology of Sport*, 48 (3), 334–48.

Dixon, K. (2013) *Consuming Football in Late Modern Life*. Surrey, Ashgate.

Dixon, K. (2013) The football fan and the pub: an enduring relationship. *International Review for the Sociology of Sport*. EPub ahead of print, 18 November 2013. DOI:10.1177/1012690213501500.

Dunne, S. (2009) The Politics of Figurational Sociology. *The Sociological Review*, 57 (1), 28–57.

Dunning, E. (1999) *Sport Matters: Sociological Studies of Sport, Violence and Civilization*. London, Routledge.

Dunning, E., Murphy, P., Waddington, I., and Astrinakis, A.E. (2002) (eds), *Fighting Fans: football hooliganism as a world phenomenon*. Dublin, University College Dublin Press.

Dunning, E., Murphy, P. and Williams, J. (1988) *The Roots of Football Hooliganism: A Historical and Sociological Study*. London, Routledge & Kegan Paul.

Duke, V. and Crolley, L. (1996) *Football, Nationality and the State*. London, Addison Wesley Longman.

Easthope, A. (1999) *Englishness and National Culture*. London, Routledge.

Edensor, T. (2002) *National Identity, Popular Culture and Everyday Life*, Oxford, Berg.

Edensor, T. and Millington, S. (2008) 'This is Our City': branding football and local embeddedness. *Global Networks*, 8 (2), 172–93.

Edmunds, J. and Turner, B.S. (2001) The re-invention of England? Women and 'cosmopolitan' Englishness. *Ethnicities*, 1, 83–108.

Elias, N. (1971) The Genesis of Sport as a Sociological Problem. In E. Dunning (ed.), *The Sociology of Sport: A Selection of Readings*. London, Frank Cass, 88–115.

Elias, N. (1978) *What is Sociology?* London, Hutchinson.

Elias, N. (1986) Introduction. In N. Elias and E. Dunning (eds), *Quest for Excitement: Sport and Leisure in the Civilising Process*. Oxford, Basil Blackwell, 19–62.

Elias, N. (1987) *Involvement and Detachment*. Oxford, Basil Blackwell.

Elias, N. (1991) *The Society of Individuals*. Oxford, Basil Blackwell.

Elias, N. (1996) *The Germans*. Cambridge, Polity Press.

Elias, N. (2000) *The Civilizing Process: Sociogenetic and Psychogenetic Investigations* (Revised Edition). Oxford, Basil Blackwell.

Elias, N. (2008a) Public opinion in Britain. In R. Kilminster and S. Mennell (eds), *Essays II: On Civilizing Processes, State Formation and National Identity* (The Collected Works of Norbert Elias, Volume 15). Dublin, University College Dublin Press, 215–29.

Elias, N. (2008b) National peculiarities of British public opinion. In R. Kilminster and S. Mennell (eds), *Essays II: On Civilizing Processes, State Formation and National Identity* (The Collected Works of Norbert Elias, Volume 15). Dublin, University College Dublin Press, 230–55.

Elias, N. (2012) *On the Process of Civilisation: Sociogenetic and Psychogenetic Investigations* (The Collected Works of Norbert Elias, Volume 3). Dublin, University College Dublin Press.

Elias, N. and Dunning, E. (1986) The Quest for Excitement in Leisure. In N. Elias and E. Dunning (eds), *Quest for Excitement: Sport and Leisure in the Civilising Process*. Oxford, Basil Blackwell, 63–90.

Elias, N. and Scotson, J.L. (1994) *The Established and the Outsiders: A Sociological Inquiry into Community Problems*. London, Frank Cass.

End, C.M. (2001) An examination of NFL fans' computer mediated BIRGing. *Journal of Sport Behavior*, 24 (2), 162–81.

Europa (2013) How the EU works: Countries, *Europa Website*, available at: http://europa.eu/about-eu/countries/index_en.htm (Accessed Jul. 2013).

Ewen, N. (2012) Team GB, or No Team GB, That is The Question: Olympic Football and the Post-War Crisis of Britishness. *Sport in History*, 32 (2), 302–24.

Fisch, O. (2003) 'The Great Escape' – the Film. *BBC h2g2 Edited Guide Entry*, 17 April 2003, available at: http://www.bbc.co.uk/dna/h2g2/A978104 (Accessed Feb. 2009).

Fletcher, J. (1997) *Violence & Civilization: An introduction to the work of Norbert Elias*. Cambridge, Polity Press.

Foucault, M. (1974) *The Order of Things: an Archaeology of the Human Sciences*. London, Routledge.

Frith, D. (2007) *Australia Versus England: A Pictorial History of Every Test Match Since 1877* (12th edn). Melbourne, Viking.

Garcia, A.C., Standlee, A.I., Bechkoff, J. and Cui, Y. (2009) Ethnographic Approaches to the Internet and Computer-Mediated Communication. *Journal of Contemporary Ethnography*, 38 (1), 52–84.

Garland, J. (2004) The Same Old Story? Englishness, the Tabloid Press and the 2002 Football World Cup. *Leisure Studies*, 23 (1), 79–92.

Garland, J. and Rowe, M. (1999) War Minus the Shooting? : Jingoism, the English Press, and Euro 96. *Journal of Sport and Social Issues*, 23 (1), 80–95.

Garland, J. and Rowe, M. (2001) *Racism and Anti-Racism in Football*. Basingstoke, Palgrave.

Geertz, C. (1994) Primordial and Civic Ties. In J. Hutchinson and A.D. Smith (eds), *Nationalism*. Oxford, Oxford University Press, 29–34.

Geey, D. (2011) Has Mrs Murphy changed the face of football broadcasting? *Synopsis to lecture delivered at The Birkbeck Sport Business Centre, 10*

November 2011, available at: http://www.sportbusinesscentre.com/news/2011-11-04 (Accessed Nov. 2011).

Gellner, E. (1964) *Thought and Change.* London, Weidenfeld and Nicholson.

Gellner, E. (1983) *Nations and Nationalism.* Oxford: Blackwell.

Gibbons, T. (2010) Contrasting representations of Englishness during FIFA World Cup Finals. *Sport in History*, 30 (3), 422–446.

Gibbons, T. (2011) English national identity and the national football team: the view of contemporary English fans. *Soccer & Society*, 12 (6), 865–879.

Gibbons, T. and Dixon, K (2010). Surf's up! A call to take English soccer fan interactions on the Internet more seriously. *Soccer & Society*, 11 (5), 599–613.

Gibbons, T., Dixon, K. and Braye, S. (2008) 'The way it was': an account of soccer violence in the 1980s. *Soccer & Society*, 9 (1), 28–41.

Gibbons, T. and Lusted, J. (2007) Is St George enough? Considering the importance of displaying local identity while supporting the England national soccer team. *Annals of Leisure Research*, 10 (3/4), 291–309.

Gibbons, T. and Nuttall, D. (2012) Using e-surveys to access the views of football fans within online communities. *Sport in Society*, 15, 1228–1241.

Giddens, A. (1984) *The Constitution of Society: Outline of the Theory of Structuration.* Cambridge, Polity Press.

Giddens, A. (1990) *The Consequences of Modernity.* Cambridge, Polity Press.

Giddens, A. (2009) *Sociology* (Sixth Edition). Cambridge, Polity Press.

Giles, J. and Middleton, T. (1995) (eds), *Writing Englishness 1900–1950: An introductory Sourcebook on National Identity.* London, Routledge.

Giulianotti, R. (1999) *Football: a Sociology of the Global Game.* Oxford, Polity Press.

Giulianotti, R. (2002) Supporters, Followers, Fans, and Flâneurs: A Taxonomy of Spectator Identities in Football. *Journal of Sport & Social Issues*, 26 (1), 25–46.

Giulianotti, R. (2004) Civilizing games: Norbert Elias and the sociology of sport. In R. Giulianotti (ed.), *Sport and Modern Social Theorists.* London, Palgrave Macmillan, 145–60.

Giulianotti, R. and Robertson, R. (2004) The globalization of football: a study in the glocalization of the 'serious life'. *British Journal of Sociology*, 55 (4), 545–68.

Giulianotti, R. and Robertson, R. (2009) *Globalization & Football.* London, Sage.

Glanville, B. (2010) *The Story of the World Cup.* London, Faber & Faber.

Glaser, B.G. and Strauss, A.L. (1967) *The Discovery of Grounded Theory: Strategies for Qualitative Research.* Chicago, Aldine.

Gratton, C. and Jones, I. (2010) *Research Methods for Sports Studies* (Second Edition). London, Routledge.

Groom, N. (2006) *The Union Jack: A Biography.* London, Atlantic.

Grundy, S. and Jamieson, L. (2007) European Identities: From Absent-Minded Citizens to Passionate Europeans. *Sociology*, 41 (4), 663–80.

Guibernau, M. (2011) The birth of a united Europe: on why the EU has generated a 'non-emotional' identity. *Nations and Nationalism*, 17 (2), 302–15.

Guttmann, A. (2000) The Development of Modern Sports. In J. Coakley and E. Dunning (eds), *Handbook of Sports Studies*, London, Sage, 248–59.

Hall, S. (1992) The new ethnicities. In J. Donald and A. Rattansi (eds), *Race, Culture and Difference*. London, Sage.

Hamelink, C.J. (2000) *The Ethics of Cyberspace*. London, Sage.

Hamil, S., Michie, J., Oughton, C. and Warby, S. (1998) (eds), *Football in the Digital Age: Whose Game is it Anyway?* London: Mainstream Publishing.

Harvey, J., Horne, J., Safai, P., Darrell, S. and O'Neill, S.C. (2014) *Sport and Social Movements: From Local to Global*. London: Bloomsbury Academic.

Haseler, S. (1996) *The English Tribe: Identity, Nation and Europe*. Basingstoke, Macmillan.

Hastings, A. (1997) *The Construction of Nationhood: Ethnicity, Religion and Nationalism*. Cambridge, Cambridge University Press.

Haugaard, M. (2006) Nationalism and Liberalism. In G. Delanty and K. Kumar (eds), *The SAGE Handbook of Nations and Nationalism*. London, Sage, 345–356.

Hay, R. and Coyle, J. (2002) Scottish Football Association. In R. Cox, D. Russell and W. Vamplew (eds), *Encyclopedia of British Football*. London, Frank Cass, 280–282.

Hay, R. and Joel, T. (2007) Football's World Cup and its Fans – Reflections on National Styles: A Photo Essay on Germany 2006. *Soccer & Society*, 8 (1), 1–32.

Haynes, D. (1996) *England v. Scotland: The Auld Enemy*. Chorley, Sport in Word.

Haythornthwaite, C. (2001) The Internet and Everyday Life. *American Behavioural Scientist*, 45 (3), 363–82.

Hechter, M. (1975) *Internal Colonialism: The Celtic Fringe in British National Development, 1536–1966*. London, Routledge and Kegan Paul.

Heffer, S. (1999) *Nor Shall My Sword: The Reinvention of England*. London, Weidenfeld & Nicolson.

Held, D. (2002) Culture and political community: National, Global and Cosmopolitan. In S. Vertovec and R. Cohen (eds), *Conceiving Cosmopolitanism: Theory, Context and Practice*. Oxford, Oxford University Press, 48–58.

Henry, I.P. (2003) Sport, the Role of the European Union and the Decline of the Nation State? In, B. Houlihan (ed.), *Sport and Society: a student introduction*. London, Sage, 330–44.

Hill, J. (2002) *Sport, Leisure and Culture in Twentieth-Century Britain*. Basingstoke, Palgrave.

Hills, M. (2002) *Fan Cultures*. London, Routledge.

Hills, M. (2007) Fans and Fan Culture. In G. Ritzer (ed.), *Blackwell Encyclopedia of Sociology* (Volume 4). London, Blackwell Reference, 1637–41.

Hine, C. (2000) *Virtual Ethnography*. London, Sage.

Hobsbawm, E. (1983) Introduction: Inventing Traditions. In E. Hobsbawm and T. Ranger (eds), *The Invention of Tradition*. Cambridge, Cambridge University Press.

Hobsbawm, E. (1990) *Nations and Nationalism since 1780*. Cambridge, Cambridge University Press.

Hobsbawm, E. (1995) *Age of Extremes: The Short Twentieth Century, 1914–1991*. London, Abacus.

Holliday, A. (2008) *Doing and Writing Qualitative Research* (Second Edition). London, Sage.

Holmes, M. and Storey, D. (2004) Who are the boys in green? Irish identity and soccer in the Republic of Ireland. In A. Smith and D. Porter (eds), *Sport and National Identity in the Post-War World*. London, Routledge, 88–104.

Holmes, M. and Storey, D. (2011) Transferring national allegiance: cultural affinity or flag of convenience? *Sport in Society*, 14 (2), 253–71.

Holt, R. (1989) *Sport and the British*. Oxford, Clarendon Press.

Horne, J. (2005) *Sport in Consumer Culture*. Basingstoke, Palgrave Macmillan.

Horne, J. and Jary, D. (2004) Anthony Giddens: Structuration Theory, and Sport and Leisure. In R. Giulianotti (ed.), *Sport and Modern Social Theorists*. London, Palgrave Macmillan, 129–44.

Hughson, J., and Poulton, E. (2006) Only genuine fans need apply: an organisational analysis of the English Football Association's response to football supporter stereotypes. *International Journal of Sport Marketing*, 2, 69–82.

Hutchins, B., Rowe, D. and Ruddock, A. (2009) "It's Fantasy Football Made Real": Networked Media Sport, the Internet, and the Hybrid Reality of MyFootballClub. *Sociology of Sport Journal*, 26 (1), 89–106.

Hutchinson, J. (1987). *The Dynamics of Cultural Nationalism: The Gaelic Revival and the Creation of the Irish Nation State*. London, Allen & Unwin.

Hyllegard, R., Mood, D.P. and Morrow, Jr., J.R. (1996) *Interpreting Research in Sport & Exercise Science*. London, McGraw-Hill.

Idessane, K. (2012) London 2012: No Scotland or N Ireland in Olympic football squad. *BBC Sport*, 29 June 2012, available at: http://www.bbc.co.uk/sport/0/olympics/18653453 (Accessed Nov. 2012).

Inglis, D. and Thorpe, C. (2012) *An Invitation to Social Theory*. Cambridge, Polity Press.

Jackson, J. (2010) World Cup 2010: England are 'paying the price of foreign Premier League'. *The Guardian Online*, available at: http://www.guardian.co.uk/football/2010/jul/08/jose-luis-astiazaran-la-liga-england (Accessed May 2012).

Jackson, P. (2011) *The EDL: Britain's "new far right" social movement*. Northampton, University of Northampton/Radical New Media Publications.

James, P. (2006) Theorizing Nation Formation in the Context of Imperialism and Globalism. In G. Delanty and K. Kumar (eds), *The SAGE Handbook of Nations and Nationalism*. London, Sage, 369–81.

Jenkins, H. (1995) "Do you enjoy making the rest of us feel stupid?" alt. tv.twinpeaks, the trickster author and viewer mastery. In D. Lavery (ed.), *Full of Secrets: Critical Approaches to 'Twin Peaks'*. Detroit, Wayne State University Press, 51–69.

Jennings, P. (2011) *The Local: A History of the English Pub* (Second Edition). Gloucestershire, The History Press.

Johnes, M. (2002) Welsh Football Association. In R. Cox, D. Russell and W. Vamplew (eds), *Encyclopedia of British Football*. London, Frank Cass, 322–23.
Johnes, M. (2005) 'Heads in the Sand': Football, Politics and Crowd Disasters in Twentieth-Century Britain. In P. Darby, M. Johnes and G. Mellor (eds), *Soccer and Disaster: International Perspectives*. London, Routledge, 10–27.
Johnes, M. (2008) '*We Hate England! We Hate England?*' National Identity and Anti-Englishness in Welsh Soccer Fan Culture. *Cycnos*, 25 (2), 143–57.
Joinson, A.N. (2005) Internet behaviour and the Design of Virtual Methods. In C. Hine (ed.), *Virtual Methods: Issues in Social Research on the Internet*. Oxford, Berg, 21–34.
Jones, E. (1998) *The English Nation: The Great Myth*. Stroud, Sutton Publishing.
Jones, K.W. (2008) Female Fandom: Identity, Sexism, and Men's Professional Football in England. *Sociology of Sport Journal*, 25 (4), 516–37.
Katz, J.E., Rice, R.E. and Aspden, P. (2001) The Internet, 1995–2000: access, civic involvement and social interaction. *American Behavioral Scientist*, 45 (3), 404–18.
Kedourie, E. (1960) *Nationalism*. London, Hutchinson.
Kelly, J. (2011) What will fans chant at a Team GB football match? *BBC News Magazine*, available at: http://www.bbc.co.uk/news/magazine-13875231 (Accessed Jun. 2011).
Kelly, W. (2004) *Fanning the flames: fans and consumer culture in contemporary Japan*. New York, SUNY press.
Kelso, P. (2012a) David Beckham left out of Team GB football squad for London 2012 Olympics. *The Telegraph*, 28 June 2012, available at: http://www.telegraph.co.uk/sport/olympics/football/9361704/David-Beckham-left-out-of-Team-GB-football-squad-for-London-2012-Olympics.html (Accessed Nov. 2012).
Kelso, P. (2012b) British Olympic Association chief executive Andy Hunt criticises Football Association for lack of support. *The Telegraph*, 14 August 2012, available at: http://www.telegraph.co.uk/sport/olympics/9476068/British-Olympic-Association-chief-executive-Andy-Hunt-criticises-Football-Association-for-lack-of-support.html (Accessed Nov. 2012).
Kennedy, P. (2010) *Local Lives and Global Transformations*. Basingstoke, Palgrave.
Kennedy, P. and Kennedy, D. (2010) 'It's the little details that make up our identity': Everton supporters and their stadium ballot debate. *Soccer & Society*, 11 (5), 553–72.
Kerr, A.K. and Emery, P.R. (2011) Foreign fandom and the Liverpool FC: a cyber-mediated romance. *Soccer & Society*, 12 (6), 880–96.
Kilminster, R. (2004) From distance to detachment: knowledge and self-knowledge in Elias's theory of involvement and detachment. In S. Loyal and S. Quilley (eds), *The Sociology of Norbert Elias*. Cambridge, Cambridge University Press, 25–41.
Kilminster, R. and Mennell, S. (2009) (eds) *Essays I: On the Sociology of Knowledge and on the Sciences* (The Collected Works of Norbert Elias, Volume 14). Dublin, University College Dublin Press.

King, A. (2000) Football fandom and post-national identity in the new Europe. *British Journal of Sociology*, 51(3), 419–42.

King, A. (2002) *The End of the Terraces: The Transformation of English Football in the 1990s* (Revised Edition). London, Leicester University Press.

King, A. (2003) *The European Ritual: Football in the New Europe*. Aldershot, Ashgate.

King, A. (2006) Nationalism and Sport. In G. Delanty and K. Kumar (eds), *The Sage Handbook of Nations and Nationalism*. London, Sage, 249–59.

Kumar, K. (2000) Nation and Empire: English and British national identity in comparative perspective. *Theory and Society*, 29, 575–608.

Kumar, K. (2001) 'Englishness' and English National Identity. In D. Morley and K. Roberts (eds), *British Cultural Studies*. Oxford, Oxford University Press, 41–55.

Kumar, K. (2003) *The Making of English National Identity*. Cambridge, Cambridge University Press.

Kumar, K. (2006a) Empire and English nationalism. *Nations and Nationalism*, 12 (1), 1–13.

Kumar, K. (2006b) English and British National Identity. *History Compass*, 4 (3), 428–47.

Lanfranchi, P. and Taylor, M. (2001) *Moving with the Ball: The Migration of Professional Footballers*. Oxford, Berg.

Langlands, R. (1999) Britishness or Englishness? The historical problem of national identity in Britain. *Nations and Nationalism*, 5, 53–69.

Laviolette, P. (2003) Landscaping Death: Resting Places in Cornish Identity. *Journal of Material Culture*, 8 (2), 215–40.

Lee, H. (2005) Implosion, virtuality, and interaction in an Internet discussion group. *Information, Communication and Society*, 8 (1), 47–63.

Levermore, R. and Millward, P. (2007) Official policies and informal transversal networks: Creating 'pan-European identifications' through sport? *The Sociological Review*, 55 (1), 144–64.

Liptrot, M. (2007) A mixed methods approach to researching subculture. *Unpublished Paper delivered at the 'Work in Progress: Research Spaces, Research Journeys' Interdisciplinary Postgraduate Conference*, Department of Sociology, University of Warwick, 1 December, 2007.

Liston, K. (2011) Sport and Leisure. *The Sociological Review*, 59 (s1), 160–80.

Locken, E. (2009) *The Best England Football Chants Ever*. Interviewbooks.com.

McCrone, D. (2002) Who do you say you are? Making sense of national identities in modern Britain. *Ethnicities*, 2 (3), 301–20.

McCrone, D. (2006) A nation that dares not speak its name? The English question. *Ethnicities*, 6 (2), 267–78.

McMenemy, D., Poulter, A. and O'Loan, S. (2005) A robust methodology for investigating Old Firm related sectarianism online. *International Journal of Web Based Communities*, 1 (4), 488–503.

MacPhee, G. and Poddar, P. (2007) (eds), *Empire and After: Englishness in Postcolonial Perspective*. New York, Bergham Books.

MacRury, I. and Poynter, G. (2010) 'Team GB' and London 2012: The Paradox of National and Global Identities. *The International Journal of the History of Sport*, 27 (16–18), 2958–75.

Maguire, J. (1993) Globalization, Sport and National Identities: The Empires Strike Back? *Society & Leisure*, 16, 293–322.

Maguire, J. (1994) Sport, Identity Politics and Globalization: Diminishing Contrasts, Increasing Varieties. *Sociology of Sport Journal*, 11, 398–427.

Maguire, J. (1999) *Global Sport: Identities, Societies, Civilizations*. Cambridge, Polity.

Maguire, J. (2005) (ed.) *Power and Global Sport: Zones of Prestige, Emulation and Resistance*. London, Routledge.

Maguire, J. (2011a) Globalization, sport and national identities. *Sport in Society*, 14 (7/8), 978–93.

Maguire, J. (2011b) Sport, identity politics, gender and globalization. *Sport in Society*, 14 (7/8), 994–1009.

Maguire, J. (2011c) Power and global sport: zones of prestige, emulation and resistance. *Sport in Society*, 14 (7/8), 1010–26.

Maguire, J. (2011d) Reflections on process sociology and sport: 'walking the line'. *Sport in Society*, 14 (7/8), 852–57.

Maguire, J. and Burrows, M. (2005) 'Not the Germans again': Soccer, identity politics and the media. In J. Maguire (ed.), *Power and Global Sport: Zones of Prestige, Emulation and Resistance*. London, Routledge, 130–42.

Maguire, J. and Pearton, R. (2000) The impact of elite labour migration on the identification, selection and development of European soccer players. *Journal of Sports Sciences*, 18 (9), 759–69.

Maguire, J. and Possamai, C. (2005) 'Back to the valley': local responses to the changing culture of football. In J. Maguire (ed.), *Power and Global Sport: Zones of Prestige, Emulation and Resistance*. London, Routledge, 41–60.

Maguire, J. and Poulton, E. (1999) European Identity Politics in Euro 96: Invented Traditions and National Habitus Codes. *International Review for the Sociology of Sport*, 34 (1) 17–29.

Maguire, J., Poulton, E. and Possamai, C. (1999) Weltkrieg III? : Media Coverage of England Versus Germany in Euro 96. *Journal of Sport and Social Issues*, 23 (4), 439–54.

Mainwaring, E. and Clark, T. (2012) 'We're shit and we know we are': identity, place and ontological security in lower league football in England. *Soccer & Society*, 13 (1), 107–23.

Malcolm, D. (2009) Malign or benign? English national identities and Cricket. *Sport in Society*, 12 (4–5), 613–28.

Mandler, P. (2006) *The English National Character: The History of an Idea from Edmund Burke to Tony Blair*. New Haven, Yale University Press.

Mann, C. and Stewart, F. (2000) *Internet Communication and Qualitative Research: A Handbook for Researching Online*. London, Sage.

Mann, R. (2011) 'It just feels English rather than multicultural': local interpretations of Englishness and non-Englishness. *The Sociological Review*, 59 (1), 109–28.

Manzenreiter, W. and Horne, J. (2004) *Football Goes East: The People's Game in China, Japan and Korea.* London, Routledge.

Markham, A.N. (2005) The methods, politics, and ethics of representation in online ethnography. In N.K. Denzin and Y.S. Lincoln (eds), *The Sage Handbook of Qualitative Research* (Third Edition). London, Sage, 793–820.

Martin, S. (2004) *Football and fascism.* Oxford, Berg.

Marx, K. and Engels, F. (1967) *The Communist Manifesto* (with an introduction and notes by A.J.P. Taylor). London, Penguin.

Matless, D. (1998) *Landscape and Englishness.* London, Reaktion Books.

Maxwell, J.A. (2002) Understanding and Validity in Qualitative Research. In A.M. Huberman and M.B. Miles (eds), *The Qualitative Researcher's Companion.* London, Sage, 37–64.

May, T. (2001) *Social Research: Issues, Methods and Process* (Third Edition). Berkshire, Open University Press.

Mellor, G. (2000) The genesis of Manchester United as a national and international 'super-club' 1958–68. *Soccer & Society,* 1 (2), 151–66.

Mellor, G. (2004) 'We hate the Manchester Club like poison': the Munich disaster and the socio-historical development of Manchester United as a loathed football club. In D.L. Andrews (ed.), *Manchester United: A thematic study.* Abingdon, Routledge.

Menary, S. (2010) *GB United? British Olympic football and the end of the amateur dream.* Brighton, Pitch.

Mennell, S. (1990) Decivilising Processes: theoretical significance and some lines of research. *International Sociology,* 5 (2), 205–23.

Mennell, S. (1992) *Norbert Elias: An Introduction.* Dublin, University College Dublin.

Mennell, S. (1994) The formation of We-Images: A Process Theory. In C. Calhoun (ed.), *Social Theory and the Politics of Identity.* Oxford, Blackwell, 175–97.

Menon, S. (2007) A participation observation analysis of the 'Once and Again' Internet message bulletin boards. *Television and New Media,* 8 (4), 341–74.

Miles, M. and Huberman, A. (1994) *Qualitative Data Analysis.* Thousand Oaks, CA, Sage.

Millward, P. (2006) 'We've all got the bug for Euro-Aways': what fans say about European Football Club Competition. *International Review for the Sociology of Sport,* 41 (3/4), 375–93.

Millward, P. (2007) True Cosmopolitanism or Notional Acceptance of Non-national players in English football: Or, why 'bloody foreigners' get blamed when 'things go wrong'. *Sport in Society,* 10 (4), 601–22.

Millward, P. (2008) The rebirth of the football fanzine: Using E-zines as data source. *Journal of Sport and Social Issues,* 32 (3), 299–310.

Millward, P. (2011) *The Global Football League: Transnational Networks, Social Movements and Sport in the New Media Age.* Basingstoke, Palgrave.

Moore, N. (2000) *How to do Research* (Third Edition). London, Library Association Publishing.

Moorhouse, H.F. (1996) One State, Several Countries: Soccer and Nationality in a 'United Kingdom'. In J.A. Mangan (ed.), *Tribal Identities: Nationalism, Europe, Sport*. London, Frank Cass, 55–74.

Murphy, P., Sheard, K. and Waddington, I. (2000) Figurational Sociology and its Application to Sport. In J. Coakley and E. Dunning (eds), *Handbook of Sports Studies*, London, Sage, 92–105.

Murthy, D. (2008) Digital Ethnography: An examination of the use of new technologies for social research. *Sociology*, 42 (5), 837–55.

Office for National Statistics (2013) Internet Access – Households and Individuals, 2012 Part 2, available at: http://www.ons.gov.uk/ons/rel/rdit2/internet-access---households-and-individuals/2012-part-2/index.html (Accessed July 2013).

O'Neill, M. (2004) Unfinished business: the 'significant others'. In M. O'Neill (ed.), *Devolution and British Politics*. Harlow, Pearson, 333–52.

O'Neill, S. (2006) England's travelling supporters are told: mention the war at your peril. *The Times*, Friday 10 March 2006, 33.

O'Reilly, K. (2009) *Key Concepts in Ethnography*. London, Sage.

Palmer, C. and Thompson, K. (2007) The paradoxes of football spectatorship: on-field and online expressions of social capital among the "Grog Squad". *Sociology of Sport Journal*, 24, 187–205.

Parekh, B. (2008) *A New Politics of Identity: Political Principles for an Independent World*. Basingstoke, Palgrave Macmillan.

Parsons, Talcott. (1949) *The Structure of Social Action*. New York, McGraw-Hill.

Parsons, Tony. (2005) Forget the war? It's far too soon. *The Mirror Newspaper Online*, available at: http://www.mirror.co.uk/news/columnists/parsons/2005/12/12/forget-the-war-it-s-far-too-soon-115875-16474483/ (Accessed Mar. 2011).

Paulle, B., Van Heerikhuizen, B. and Emirbayer, M. (2012) Elias and Bourdieu. *Journal of Classical Sociology*, 12 (1), 69–93.

Paxman, J. (1998) *The English: A Portrait of a People*. London, Michael Joseph.

Payton, P. (2002) *Cornwall's history: an introduction*. Redruth, Tor Mark Press.

Pearson, G. (2012) *An Ethnography of English Football Fans: Cans, Cops and Carnivals*. Manchester, Manchester University Press.

Perryman, M. (2006) *Ingerland: Travels with a Football Nation*. London, Simon and Schuster.

Plenderleith, I. (2008) Tartan trauma, Anglo anguish. *When Saturday Comes*, 251 (January), 10–11.

Polley, M. (2004) Sport and national identity in contemporary England. In Smith, A. and Porter, D. (eds), *Sport and National Identity in the Post-War World*. London, Routledge, 10–30.

Pope, S. (2011) 'Like pulling down Durham Cathederal and building a brothel': Women as 'new consumer' fans. *International Review for the Sociology of Sport*, 46 (4), 471–87.

Pope, S. (2012) "The Love of My Life": The Meaning and Importance of Sport for Female Fans. *Journal of Sport & Social Issues*, 37 (2), 176–95.

Porter, D. (2004) 'Your boys took one hell of a beating!' English football and British decline, c. 1950–80. In A. Smith and D. Porter (eds), *Sport and National Identity in the Post-war World.* London, Routledge, 31–51.

Poulton, E. (2003) New Fans, New Flag, New England? Changing News Values in the English Press Coverage of World Cup 2002. *Football Studies*, 6 (1), 19–36.

Pratley, N. and Taylor, D. (2005) 'Man Utd fans vent anger as US tycoon finally wins takeover battle'. *The Guardian*, Friday 13 May, available at: http://www.guardian.co.uk/business/2005/may/13/football.uknews (Accessed Jan. 2008).

Premier League (2010) The changing face of the Premier League. *Premier League Official Website*, available at: http://www.premierleague.com/page/Headlines/0,,12306~2133074,00.html (Accessed May 2011).

Redhead, S. (1993) (ed.) *The Passion and the Fashion: Football Fandom in the New Europe.* Aldershot, Avebury.

Redhead, S. (1997) *Post-Fandom and the Millennial Blues: The Transformation of Soccer Culture*, London, Routledge.

Rheingold, H. (1993) *The Virtual Community: Homesteading on the Electronic Frontier.* Massachusetts, Addison Wesley.

Rhodes, J. (2011) 'It's not just them, it's whites as well': Whiteness, Class and BNP support. *Sociology*, 45 (1), 102–17.

Richards, L. (2005) *Handling Qualitative Data: A Practical Guide.* London, Sage.

Ridings, C.M. and Gefen, D. (2004) Virtual Community Attraction: Why People Hang Out Online. *Journal of Computer-Mediated Communication*, 10 (1), Article 4, available at: http://jcmc.indiana.edu/vol10/issue1/ridings_gefen.html (Accessed Nov. 2010).

Robertson, R. (1992) *Globalization: Social Theory and Global Culture.* London, Sage.

Robertson, R. (1995) Glocalization: time-space and homogeneity-heterogeneity. In M. Featherstone, M.S. Lash and R. Robertson (eds), *Global Modernities*. London, Sage, 25–44.

Robinson, J.S.R. (2008) Tackling the anxieties of the English: searching for the nation through football. *Soccer & Society*, 9 (2), 215–30.

Roche, M. (2010) *Exploring the Sociology of Europe.* London, Sage.

Rogers, G. and Rookwood, J. (2007) Cardiff City Football Club as a Vehicle to Promote Welsh National Identity. *Journal of Qualitative Research in Sports Studies*, 1 (1), 57–68.

Rookwood, J. and Chan, N. (2011) The 39th game: fan responses to the Premier League's proposal to globalize the English game. *Soccer & Society*, 12 (6), 897–913.

Rookwood, J. and Millward, P. (2011) 'We all dream of a team of Carraghers': comparing 'local' and Texan Liverpool fans' talk. *Sport in Society*, 14 (1), 37–52.

Rosie, M., MacInnes, J., Petersoo, P., Condor, S. and Kennedy, J. (2004) Nation Speaking unto nation? Newspapers and national identity in the devolved UK. *The Sociological Review*, 52 (4), 437–58.

Rowe, D., Ruddock, A. and Hutchins, B. (2010) Cultures of Complaint: Online Fan Message Boards and Networked Digital Media Sport Communities.

Ruddock, A. (2005) Lets Kick Racism out of football – and the lefties too! Responses to Lee Bowyer on a West Ham web site. *Journal of Sport and Social Issues*, 9 (4), 369–85.

Ruddock, A., Hutchins, B. and Rowe, D. (2010) Contradictions in media sport culture: The reinscription of football supporter traditions through online media. *European Journal of Cultural Studies*, 13 (3), 323–39.

Russell, D. (1997) *Football and the English: A Social History of Association Football, 1863–1995*. Preston, Carnegie.

Russell, D. (2004) *Looking North: Northern England and the national imagination*. Manchester, Manchester University Press.

Sandvoss, C. (2003) *A Game of Two Halves: Football, Television and Globalization*. London, Routledge.

Sandvoss, C. (2004) Technological Evolution or Revolution? Sport Online Live Internet Commentary as Postmodern Cultural Form. *Convergence*, 10 (3), 39–54.

Sassen, S. (1991) *The Global City*. Chichester, Princeton University Press.

Schimmel, K.S., Harrington, C.L. and Bielby, D.D. (2007) Keep your fans to yourself: the disjuncture between sports studies' and pop culture studies' perspectives on fandom. *Sport in Society*, 10 (4), 580–600.

Schlesinger, P. (1994) Europeanness: A New Cultural Battlefield? In J. Hutchinson and A.D. Smith (eds), *Nationalism*. Oxford, Oxford University Press, 316–25.

Scott, J. and Marshall, G. (2009) *Oxford Dictionary of Sociology* (Third revised edition). Oxford, Oxford University Press.

Scott, M. (2012) Premier League determined to carry on taking action against pubs who use foreign feeds to show action. *The Telegraph*, Friday 24 February 2012, available at: http://www.telegraph.co.uk/sport/football/competitions/premier-league/9105226/Premier-League-determined-to-carry-on-taking-action-against-pubs-who-use-foreign-feeds-to-show-action.html (Accessed Mar. 2012).

Scraton, P. (1999) *Hillsborough: The Truth*. Edinburgh, Mainstream.

Scruton, R. (2000) *England: An Elergy*. London, Chatto & Windus.

Seymour-Ure, C. (1996) *The British Press and Broadcasting since 1945* (Second Edition). Oxford, Blackwell.

Shilling, C. (2011) Series Editor's Introduction. *The Sociological Review*, 59 (s1), 1–4.

Silk, M.L. (2005) Sporting Ethnography: Philosophy, methodology and reflection. In D.L. Andrews, D.S. Mason and M.L. Silk (eds), *Qualitative Methods in Sports Studies*. Oxford, Berg, 65–103.

Silverman, D. (2000) *Doing Qualitative Research: A Practical Handbook*. London, Sage.

Smith, A.D. (1981) *The Ethnic Revival in the Modern World*. Cambridge, Cambridge University Press.

Smith, A.D. (1996) *Nations and Nationalism in a Global Era*. Cambridge, Polity Press.

Smith, A.D. (1998) *Nationalism and Modernism: A critical survey of recent theories of nations and nationalism*. London, Routledge.

Smith, A.D. (2010) *Nationalism: Theory, Ideology, History* (Second Edition). Cambridge, Polity Press.

Smith, D. (2001) *Norbert Elias & Modern Social Theory*. London, Sage.

Smith, M. and Kollock, P. (1999) *Communities in cyberspace*. London, Routledge.

Stone, C. (2007) The role of football in everyday life. *Soccer and Society*, 8 (2–3), 169–84.

Strutt, J. (1903) *The Sports and Pastimes of the People of England* (New Edition by J. Charles Cox). London, Methuen & Co.

Sveningsson, M. (2009) How do various notions of privacy influence decisions in qualitative Internet research? In A.N. Markham and N.K. Baym (eds), *Internet Inquiry: Conversations about Method*. London, Sage, 69–87.

Taylor, M. (2008) *The Association Game: A History of British Football*. Harlow, Pearson.

Taylor, P., Rt. Hon Lord Justice (1990) *The Hillsborough Stadium Disaster: Final Report*. London, HMSO.

Thomas, J.R. and Nelson, J.K. (2001) *Research Methods in Physical Activity* (Fourth Edition). Leeds, Human Kinetics.

Tomlinson, A. (1991) North and south: the rivalry of the Football League and the Football Association. In J. Williams and S. Wagg (eds) *British Football and Social Change*. Leicester, Leicester University Press, 25–47.

Toney, J. (2012) London 2012: Team GB football teams could be repeated for Rio and beyond. *Sportsbeat*, 21 July 2012, available at: http://www.morethanthegames.co.uk/football/2117726-london-2012-team-gb-football-teams-could-be-repeated-rio-and-beyond (Accessed Nov. 2012).

Trilling, D. (2012) *Bloody Nasty people: the rise of Britain's far right*. London, Verso.

Van Krieken, R. (1998) *Norbert Elias*. London, Routledge.

Van Krieken, R. (2003) Norbert Elias. In A. Elliott and L. Ray (eds), *Key Contemporary Social Theorists*. Oxford, Blackwell, 116–22.

Vincent, J. and Hill, J. (2011) Flying the flag for the En-ger-land: *The Sun's* (re) construction of English identity during the 2010 World Cup. *Journal of Sport & Tourism*, 16 (3), 187–209.

Vincent, J., Kian, E.M., Pedersen, P.M, Kuntz, A. and Hill, J.S. (2010) England expects: English newspapers' narratives about the English football team in the 2006 World Cup. *International Review for the Sociology of Sport*, 45 (2), 199–223.

Wadham-Smith, N. and Clift, N. (2000) (eds), Looking into England. *British Studies Now*, 13, London, British Council.

Wakefield, J. (2010) World wakes up to digital divide, *BBC News*, available at: http://news.bbc.co.uk/1/hi/technology/8568681.stm (Accessed Aug. 2011).

Wallerstein, I. (1974) *The Modern World System: Capitalist Agriculture and the Origins of the European World Economy in the Sixteenth Century*. New York, Academic Press.

Walvin, J. (1986) *Football and the Decline of Britain*. Basingstoke, Macmillan.

Walvin, J. (1994) *The People's Game: The History of Football Revisited.* Edinburgh, Mainstream.

Wann, D.L. and Dolan, T.J. (1994) Attributions of highly identified sports spectators. *The Journal of Social Psychology*, 134 (6), 783–92.

Wann, D.L., Melnick, M.J., Russell, G.W. and Pease, D.G. (2001) *Sports Fans: The Psychology and Social Impact of Spectators.* New York, Routledge.

Webster, P. and Hines, N. (2007) Gordon Brown calls for return of home nations football after Euro 2008 debacle, *Times Online*, available at: www.timesonline.co.uk/tol/sport/football/euro_2008/article2922733.ece (Accessed Nov. 2007).

Weed, M. (2006) The story of an ethnography: The experience of watching the 2002 World Cup in the pub. *Soccer and Society*, 7 (1), 76–95.

Weed, M. (2007). The pub as a virtual football fandom venue: An alternative to 'being there'? *Soccer and Society*, 8 (2/3), 399–414.

Weed, M. (2008) Exploring the sport spectator experience: virtual football spectatorship in the pub. *Soccer & Society*, 9 (2), 189–97.

Weight, R. (2002) *Patriots: National Identity in Britain 1940–2000.* London, MacMillan.

Wellings, B. (2002) Empire-nation: national and imperial discourses in England. *Nations and Nationalism*, 8, 95–109.

Wellman, B., Quan Haase, A., Witte, J. and Hampton, K. (2001) Does the internet increase, decrease or supplement social capital? Social networks, participation, and community commitment. *American Behavioural Scientist*, 45 (3), 436–55.

Willett, J. and Giovanni, A. (2013) The uneven path of UK devolution: top-down vs. bottom-up regionalism in England—Cornwall and the North East compared. *Political Studies*, Epub ahead of print 16 May 2013. DOI: 10.1111/1467-9248.12030.

Williams, J. (1998) The changing face of football: A case for national regulation? In S. Hamil, J. Michie, C. Oughton and S. Warby (eds), *Football in the Digital Age: Whose Game is it Anyway?* London: Mainstream Publishing, 94–106.

Williams, J., Dunning, E. and Murphy, P. (1984) *Hooligans Abroad: the Behaviour and Control of English Fans in Continental Europe.* London, Routledge & Kegan Paul.

Wilson, B. (2007) New media, social movements, and global sport studies: A revolutionary moment and the sociology of sport. *Sociology of Sport Journal*, 24 (2), 457–77.

Wilson, W. (2007) All together now, 'click': MLS soccer fans in cyberspace. *Soccer and Society*, 8 (2/3), 381–98.

Winter, H. (2012) London 2012 Olympics: Team GB players ready for England promotion despite penalty defeat to South Korea. *The Telegraph*, 5 August 2012, available at: http://www.telegraph.co.uk/sport/olympics/football/9453899/London-2012-Olympics-Team-GB-players-ready-for-England-promotion-despite-penalty-defeat-to-South-Korea.html (Accessed Nov. 2012).

Wood, M. (1999) *In Search of England: Journeys into the English Past*. London, Viking.
Wyn Jones, R., Lodge, G., Henderson, A. and Wincott, D. (2012) The Dog that Finally Barked: England as an emerging political community. *Institute for Public Policy Research Report*, available at: http://www.ippr.org/images/media/files/publication/2012/02/dog-that-finally-barked_englishness_Jan2012_8542.pdf (Accessed July 2013).
Wyn Jones, R., Lodge, G., Jeffery, C., Gottfried, G., Scully, R., Henderson, A. and Wincott, D. (2013) England and its Two Unions: The anatomy of a nation and its discontents. *Institute for Public Policy Research Report*, available at: http://www.ippr.org/images/media/files/publication/2013/07/england-twounions_Jul2013_11003.pdf (Accessed July 2013).
Young, R.C. (2008) *The Idea of English Ethnicity*. Oxford, Blackwell.

Index

6 + 5 rule 122

Abell, Jackie 11, 100–101, 134–5, 140
Albrow, Martin 25
Almunia, Manuel 17, 87, 108, 117, 120, 159
    Almunia case 108–22, 160
        ethnic versus civic fan debate 109–12
        naturalisation as a British citizen 108, 110–11, 119, 121–22, 159
        talent versus blood fan debate 112–21
American Revolution 22
Anderson, Benedict
    imagined communities 23–4, 39, 78–9, 153, 171
Appadurai, Arjun 38, 60
    post-national identity 60
Arendt, Hannah 44
Aristotle 21
Aughey, Arthur
    English anxieties 3, 16, 17, 38, 103, 171

Barwick, Brian 75
Bauman, Zygmunt 44
Beckham, David 81
Bellamy, Craig 89
Berstein, Elmer 76
Billig, Michael
    banal nationalism 17, 24, 117, 122, 123, 146, 153
Blunkett, David 80, 81
Bosman ruling 57, 122, 159
Bourdieu, Pierre 21, 44, 46, 49, 50, 155
Bradford fire 52
British/Britain
    British Asians 10, 40–41, 73
    British Industrial Revolution 22
    British Social Attitudes Surveys 41

British Union 'Jack' flag 2–3, 8–10, 25, 78, 95, 105, 143–4
Decline of the British Empire 7, 35–7, 40–42, 148, 154
English reliance upon Britain 3, 35, 75, 155
Brown, Gordon 70
Bryant, Christopher 2, 3, 22, 34, 36, 37, 40, 41
Burdsey, Daniel 10, 41, 72, 73, 81, 103

Capello, Fabio 108, 114–15
Carragher, Jamie 130
Carrington, Ben 4, 7, 8, 9, 102
Casillas, Iker 109, 116
Castells, Manuel 60
Celtic nations and nationalisms of the British Isles 6, 8, 22, 35, 40, 84, 88, 97, 102, 154
Charlton, Jack 119
Churchill, Winston 105
club over country debate 59–60, 117, 124–39, 146
Colley, Linda 3, 4, 22, 34, 40, 42
Collins, Tony 43, 50
Colls, Robert 3, 34, 35, 36, 40
Comte, Auguste 43
Cornwall and Cornish identity 35
Crawford, Garry 15–16, 56, 69, 151, 161
cricket 7, 80, 81, 95, 112, 151
Crolley, Liz 4, 5, 6, 8, 67, 74, 120, 145

Daily Star, The 136, 138
Delanty, Gerard 27, 28, 34, 36, 155
Devolution (UK) 1, 10, 35–9, 40–42, 80, 84, 88, 94, 97, 107, 149, 154, 160
Di Livio, Angelo 76
Duke, Vic 4, 5, 6
Dunning, Eric 13, 43, 50, 52
Durkheim, Emile 43, 45, 50

Elias, Norbert
  centripetal and centrifugal forces 33, 40, 47, 75, 153, 158, 160
  changes in the we-I balance 13, 17, 29, 31, 47, 60, 71, 84, 87, 97, 101, 112, 121–2, 147, 152–7, 171
  Civilising Process, The 28, 46–7, 50, 97, 106, 112, 152–7, 160
  comparisons with Bourdieu 21, 44, 46, 49, 50, 155
  comparisons with Giddens 44, 46, 155–7
  critiques of Elias 42–50
  de-civilising processes 46–7, 148, 152, 154
  detour via detachment 12, 49, 172
  diminishing contrasts, increasing varieties 13, 17, 33, 39–42, 57, 60, 64, 71, 79, 82–5, 111, 122–3, 126–7, 135, 139–40, 146–7, 152, 155–60, 171
  double-bind 48, 139, 153
  drag-effect 30, 38–42, 47, 78–80, 84–5, 97, 105, 108, 117, 152–4, 157
  Elias and Englishness 37–42
  established-outsider relations 31–2, 108, 117, 127–8, 135, 158, 170–71
  false dichotomies 15, 47, 151
  figurational/process sociological approach 9, 13, 19–21, 43–5, 154
  figurations 12, 19–20, 29, 61, 148, 152, 155
  'Fisherman in the Maelstrom' 48
  functional democratisation 32, 39
  game models 19–20
  interdependence 19–20, 25, 29, 31, 43, 45–6, 103, 148, 152, 158
  Involvement and Detachment 29, 45, 47–9, 172
  'Leicester School, The' 13, 50, 156
  multi-layered identities 19, 31, 37, 71, 74, 86–7, 91, 101, 106, 108, 121, 129, 152
  national habitus 19, 21–2, 27–34, 155
  private to public monopolies 29, 32
  Society of Individuals, The 29, 45
  sociological significance of sport 3–4, 13, 19, 50
  sociologist as myth slayer 9, 49, 148
  State formation processes 21, 27–9
  unintended consequences 1, 16, 42, 51, 60, 84, 126, 146
  We-images 29, 31, 38, 79–80, 84, 106, 111, 149, 153
  What is Sociology? 43, 45, 178
  Winston Parva 31
English
  basis for identity crisis 34–7
  Football Association (FA) 6, 56, 88
  National football team 6–8, 11, 12, 17, 56, 59, 63, 69, 71–91, 100, 104, 108–21
  north-south divide 38, 106–8, 121, 127, 155
  rivalry with Germany 56, 74–9, 104–5, 115, 120, 124
Eriksson, Sven-Göran 114
ESPN 55
European integration 1, 10, 11, 26, 31–42, 51, 57, 61, 83–5, 97, 106, 117, 122, 135, 149, 154, 158, 160
  Council of Europe 57
  Court of Justice of the European Union (CJEU) 63
  Declaration on European identity 57
  European Commission 55
  European Economic Community (EEC) 57
  European Union (EU) 26–7, 36–42, 57, 63, 110, 153–4, 157
  Pan European identity 57–61, 110, 154
E-zines (online fanzines) 15, 58, 67, 69, 117

FA Cup 52, 58
Far Right groups
  British National Party (BNP) 4, 8, 37
  English Defence League (EDL) 4, 37, 73
  National Front 8, 37
Fédération Internationale de Football Association (FIFA) 4, 5, 88, 90, 109, 120, 122
  World Cup 2, 4, 7, 88–9, 94, 100, 105, 114–15, 125–6, 130–33, 160
    Brazil (1950) 7, 75
    England (1966) 8, 52, 56, 57, 79, 159

England's 2018 bid 126–7
France (1998) 76–7
Germany (2006) 2, 17, 61, 63, 71–86, 87, 91, 104–5, 121–2, 126, 140, 145, 149–50, 158, 161–3
Italy (1990) 10, 56
Japan and South Korea (2002) 77
Sepp Blatter (FIFA President) 88
South Africa (2010) 109
Uruguay (1930) 7
USA (1994) 57
football
  anti-Britishness among English fans 91–8
  English/British national press coverage 7, 53, 56, 73, 79, 89, 108
  English Premier League (EPL) 53–8, 62–3, 80–83, 113, 131–46, 149, 151–2, 156, 158–61
  Europeanisation of club game 13, 17, 57–61, 79, 85, 117, 123, 145–6, 156, 159
  fandom/fan culture
    authenticity debate and fandom typologies 14–16, 57–61, 67–9, 135–9, 151
    female fans 56, 72, 94, 101, 107, 110–11, 120, 131, 134, 161, 163, 164, 168, 170
    globalisation of the game 11, 13, 17, 51–70, 79, 85, 123–46, 158–60
    hooliganism 1, 12, 50, 52–3, 62, 73
    lower league club fans 11, 54–5, 60–61, 79–85, 128–9, 131–5, 140–42, 151, 158, 163
    Sky television (BskyB) 54–5, 62, 138
  sociologists 1, 14, 147, 154, 156
Fletcher, Jonathan 31, 38, 97, 108, 121, 155
Foucault, Michel 44, 46
French Revolution 22

G14 clubs 57–8
Gascoigne, Paul 56, 76
Gellner, Ernest 22
Giddens, Anthony 44, 46, 155–7
Giggs, Ryan 89

Giulianotti, Richard 1, 7, 14, 15, 26, 33, 43, 44, 45, 46, 50, 57, 61, 79, 81, 82, 85, 117, 121, 122, 124, 128, 135, 146, 147, 154, 156, 159
  criticisms of Elias and figurational sociology 43–50, 154–5
  exceptional nationalism 117, 122, 146
  Globalization and Football (with Roland Robertson) 33
  taxonomy of football spectator identities 14–15
'God Save The Queen' (British national anthem) 8, 77–8
Glasgow Celtic and Glasgow Rangers 6, 70, 81
globalisation 1, 10, 11, 13, 25–7, 28, 31, 33, 37, 40, 60–61, 79, 83, 85, 103, 117, 123, 126, 134–5, 139–40, 143, 145–7, 156–60
  theories and concepts
    americanisation 26
    cosmopolitanism 25, 57, 61, 117, 122, 146
    creolisation 26
    cultural imperialism 26
    glocalisation 33, 61, 83, 85, 140, 156–7
    grobalisation 26
    homogenisation-heterogenisation debate 26, 33, 40, 64, 79, 82, 84–5, 122, 126, 135, 139–40, 146, 156–60
    hybridisation 26, 33, 64
    transnational corporations (TNCs) 26, 61
    transnationalism 25–6, 33, 57, 60–61, 80–85, 146, 151
    westernisation 26
Great Escape, The 74–8
Grog Squad 150–51
Groom, Nick 2–3, 9, 40
Guardian, The 76
Guibernau, Montserrat 27, 36, 39, 57, 76, 153–4, 157, 180

habitus 19–22, 28, 30–31, 33, 38–9, 42, 152, 155

difference between habitus and identity 21
Hand, David 8, 67, 74, 120, 145
Hargreaves, Owen 119–20
Healy, David 129
Heath, Edward 57
Heylens case 57
Heysel stadium disaster 52
Hillsborough stadium disaster 52–4
Hine, Christine 65, 66, 165
  Virtual Ethnography 65
Hitler, Adolf 24, 32
  nazism 27, 75, 76
  Swastika 24
Hobsbawm, Eric 3, 22–4, 31, 36, 123, 153
  invented traditions 23–4, 31, 97, 123, 153, 171
Holt, Richard 5–7

Ince, Paul 76
Inglis, David 25–6, 44, 154–7
Institute for Public Policy Research (IPPR) 37, 41, 80, 92
  Future of England (FoE) Surveys 41, 92
Internet 2, 14–17, 51, 55, 58, 64–70, 88, 121, 127, 146, 150–51, 163–70
  computer-mediated communication (CMC) 64–5
  cyberspace 64–5
  digital divide 64

Johnes, Martin 5, 52–3, 70

Kedourie, Elie 22
Kilminster, Richard 38, 46–8
King, Anthony 1, 7, 10–11, 52–4, 56, 58–62, 74, 82–3, 85, 110, 117, 124, 128, 131–2, 141, 145, 147, 156, 158–9
  Europeanisation thesis 52–4, 117
  rejection of England thesis 59, 124, 128, 132, 141
  The End of the Terraces 1, 52–7, 62, 147
  The European Ritual 11, 58–60, 83, 110, 156, 158
Kumar, Krishan 3, 9–10, 22, 27, 34, 36, 40, 74, 145

McCarthy, Mick 119
McCrone, David 3, 34, 36
Maguire, Joseph 8, 13, 25, 33, 57, 60, 68, 71–3, 79, 82–3, 85, 88, 94, 97, 101, 106, 108, 111–12, 121–2, 135, 139, 142–3, 146, 154, 156–8, 171
  application of Eliasian concept of diminishing contrasts, increasing varieties 33, 57, 60, 82, 85, 111, 139, 146, 154–5, 157–8
  Euro 96 study (with Emma Poulton) 8, 13, 57, 71, 73, 79, 106
  little Englander thesis 72, 97, 117, 121–2
  wilful nostalgia 79, 106, 121
Major, John 53
Major League Soccer (MLS) 69, 144
Manchester United FC 11, 12, 54, 58–60, 68, 81–3, 98, 100, 102, 103, 107, 120, 125, 127–8, 130, 132, 135, 137–40, 141–2, 169
  Old Trafford 82, 127
Marx, Karl 20, 28, 33, 43–5, 46, 50
  Marxist interpretations of globalisation 26, 28, 33, 135
  Marxist interpretations of nationalism 23
Menary, Steve 7, 88–9
Mennell, Stephen 21, 30–31, 38, 45, 47, 79, 108, 152–3
Millward, Peter 51, 57–8, 60, 64, 67, 69–70, 83, 85, 110, 117, 122, 128, 129, 131–2, 135, 151, 156, 158–9
Mirror, The 75
Moorhouse, H.F. 5, 7, 88, 91
Murdoch, Rupert 55
Murphy (Karen) ruling 63

nationalism 1, 2, 4, 9, 16, 22–42, 43, 59, 60, 73, 93, 117, 122, 146, 147, 153, 169
  ethnic versus civic 22–4
  meanings 2
  modernist approaches 22–4
  post-modernist approaches 25–7
  traditionalist approaches 24–5
no Team GB campaign 88–9
North East England Referendum 35, 37

Index

Northern Ireland 2–3, 5, 17, 24–5, 35–8, 70, 77, 88–96, 100, 107, 160
   Good Friday Agreement 35
   Northern Irish national identity 8, 24–5, 38–9, 88, 98, 102, 129, 154
Novo, Nacho 120

Office for National Statistics 64
Olympic Games
   Beijing (2008) 90, 94–5
   British Olympic Association (BOA) 88
   International Olympic Committee (IOC) 87
   London (1908) 88
   London (2012) 5, 17, 87–108, 121
      background to GB football team 87–90
   Munich (1972) 5, 88
   Rio (2016) 90
online discussion forums
   as a research setting for participant observation study 64–70, 87–146, 150–51
   avatars 123–4
   emoticons 92
   methodology for online participant observation study 163–70

Parson, Talcott 43–6
   The Structure of Social Action 45
Paxman, Jeremy
   The English: A Portrait of a People 3, 34, 42
Pearce, Stuart 89
Pearson, Geoff
   An Ethnography of English Football Fans 11–13, 63
Perryman, Mark
   Ingerland 8, 11–12, 63
Porter, Dilwyn 7, 10, 52, 100
pubs (public houses)
   as a research setting for observation study 62–3, 71–86, 149–50
   English history 62
   methodology for pub-based observation study 161–3

Reina, Pepe 109, 116

Republic of Ireland 2, 22, 108, 112, 119
   Football Association of Ireland (FAI) 5, 88, 160
   national football team 108, 112, 119
Rheingold, Howard
   The Virtual Community 66
   'the WELL' 66
Richards, Micah 89
Robertson, Roland 25–6, 33, 57, 61, 79, 81–2, 85, 106, 117, 121–4, 128, 135, 140, 146, 156–7, 159
Robinson, Jessica 7–8, 10–11, 74, 84, 100
Ronaldo, Cristiano 82, 124
Rooney, Wayne 82, 110, 124–5
Rugby Union 7, 19, 95, 100, 112
Russell, David 3, 52, 54–6, 80, 83

St George's Cross 2–3, 8–9, 10, 17, 56, 71–4, 77, 79, 80–86, 94–5, 101, 105, 115, 122–3, 127, 132, 135, 139–49, 152, 157–60
   diverse use by fans 71–4, 139–46
   myth of rise in English identity 8–9
Salmond, Alex 103
Sassen, Saskia 60
satellite supporters 126–7, 137
Scotland 2–3, 5–8, 35–8, 40–41, 53, 70, 77, 88–9, 91–6, 100–102, 106–7, 128, 160
   national football team 6, 70, 99, 120, 128
   Scottish Football Association (SFA) 5, 88–90, 160
   Scottish independence 8, 36, 103
   Scottish national identity 6, 8, 33, 36, 38–41, 79, 98–102, 154
   Scottish National Party (SNP) 36, 103
Second World War 6–7, 10, 26, 32, 37, 42, 75–7, 84, 104, 154
Setanta 55
Smith, Anthony 2, 22, 23–6, 28, 57
Smith, Dennis 19, 43–5
Social Sciences Citation Index (SSCI) 44
Sociological Review, The 44
sociology of sport 49–50, 68, 70, 154, 157
structure versus agency debate 45–6, 155–6
Sturges, John 76
Sun, The 109

Taylor, Matthew 5–6, 53, 57
Taylor Report 53–4, 62
Ten German Bombers 74–7
Terry, John 124–5
Thatcher, Margaret 52–3, 59
Times, The 70
Torres, Fernando 113

Union of European Football Associations (UEFA) 52, 57, 88, 89, 90, 122
   Champions League 57–8, 132, 139
   European Championships ('Euros') 7, 89, 160
      Austria-Switzerland (2008) 69–70, 90, 108, 150
      England (1996) 8–9, 57, 71–4, 79, 84–5, 106, 145, 148, 170
      Poland-Ukraine (2012) 89–90, 160
United Kingdom of Great Britain and Northern Ireland (UK), definition 2–3

Van Krieken, Robert 42–9, 152, 154

Wacquant, Loic 46, 49
Wales 2–3, 5–7, 35–41, 53, 70, 77, 88–9, 91–2, 94–6, 99, 100, 106–7
   Football Association of Wales (FAW) 5, 88–90
   national football team 81, 99
   Welsh national identity 8, 31, 38–41, 79, 98–102, 106, 154
Wallerstein, Immanuel 26, 135, 190
Weber, Max 22, 43–5, 50
Weed, Mike 16, 62–3, 150, 161–2
Weight, Richard 8, 74, 145
Wenger, Arsène 137
When Saturday Comes 69
Wright, Ian 76

xenophobia 60, 72, 76, 92, 97, 116, 117